New Perspectives on African Literature, 3

Achebe or Soyinka?
A Study in Contrasts

New Perspectives on African Literature

General Editor:
Eldred Jones
Emeritus Professor of English
Fourah Bay College, University of Sierra Leone
Freetown, Sierra Leone

Achebe or Soyinka?
A Study in Contrasts

KOLE OMOTOSO
Professor of English
University of the Western Cape
South Africa

HANS ZELL PUBLISHERS
London • Melbourne • Munich • New Jersey • 1996

British Library Cataloguing in Publication Data
Omotoso, Kole
   Achebe or Soyinka? : Study in Contrasts. – (New Perspectives on African Literature Series ; No. 3)
   I. Title II. Series
   823

   ISBN 0-905450-38-8

Library of Congress Cataloging-in-Publication Data
Omotoso, Kole, 1943–
   Achebe or Soyinka? : a study in contrasts / Kole Omotoso.
   207p. 22cm. – (New perspectives on African literature: no. 3)
   Includes bibliographical references and index.
   ISBN 0-905450-38-8 (alk. paper)
   1. Achebe, Chinua – Criticism and interpretation. 2. Soyinka, Wole – Criticism and interpretation. 3. Nigerian literature (English) – History and criticism. 4. Nigeria – In literature. 5. Africa – In literature. I. Title. II Series.
   PR9387.9.A3Z855 1995
   820.9'9669–dc20   95-510
                                                                            CIP

Published by Hans Zell Publishers, an imprint of Bowker-Saur, a division of Reed Elsevier (UK) Limited, Maypole House, Maypole Road,East Grinstead, West Sussex RH19 1HH, United Kingdom
Tel: +44 (0) 1342 330100 Fax: +44 (0) 1342 330191

Bowker-Saur is a division of REED REFERENCE PUBLISHING.

Picture credits:
Photograph of Chinua Achebe by Paul Freestone. Courtesy of Heinemann Publishers (Oxford) Limited.
Photograph of Wole Soyinka courtesy of Methuen.
Photographs of Igbo and Yoruba masks by Marguerita Omotoso.

Design and Typesetting by VAP Publishing Services, Kidlington, Oxon, England
Printed on acid-free paper
Printed and bound in Great Britain by Antony Rowe Ltd., Chippenham, Wiltshire

This study is dedicated to the following friends and members of my family for being there to lean on when I was falling:
Jerusha Castley, Christine Ayorinde, Eddie Iroh, Hans Zell, Ken Saro-Wiwa, and Maggie, Akirinmola, Pelayo and Yewande.

Contents

Acknowledgements

Thanks are due to many friends, colleagues and comrades for discussing aspects of this study, for procuring material when they were needed and for reading part or the whole book when there was dire need to get some feedback.

Special thanks are due to Brenda Cooper and Alain Ricard for their suggestions after reading through an early draft of the study.

That the study could finally be finished owed much to the help of Ubuntu, Frontline Resource Centre, a group of people with a concept of self-help from which I benefitted immensely. For this I thank Ronald Campher.

I must express my gratitude to Ladipo and Kemi for their continued support.

A project grant from the University of Western Cape Research Faculty made it possible to acquire the latest publications coming out of Nigeria and the United Kingdom. This has made the updating of the bibliography to 1994 possible. For this I am grateful to the University.

I wish to also thank my publisher and my editors for their patience and support.

I offer this study to Opeyemi and her generation of young Africans who seek understanding and are eager to contribute, not as answers to your questions but in the hope that it helps you to reframe your questions.

Statements

"The burden of these chapters is that the attempt to construct an African literature rooted in African traditions has led both to an understating of the diversity of African cultures, and to an attempt to censor the profound entanglement of African intellectuals with the intellectual life of Europe and the Americas."

Kwame Anthony Appiah, In My Father's House[1]

"I'm an Igbo writer, because this is my basic culture; Nigerian, African and a writer... no, black first, then a writer. Each of these identities does call for a certain kind of commitment on my part. I must see what it is to be black – and this means being sufficiently intelligent to know how the world is moving and how black people fare in the world. This is what it means to be black. Or an African – the same: what does Africa mean to the world? When you see an African what does it mean to a white man?"

Chinua Achebe, interview with Kwame Anthony Appiah[2]

"Well, it's obvious that I'm not an Igbo writer! The 'Nigerian' writer is a creature in formation. Obviously we're bound to end up as a hybridization. Well, I'm not a Hausa writer. There is the Hausa culture, the Tiv culture – we have several cultures in Nigeria – so that makes me primarily a Yoruba writer. There's no question at all about it in my mind, I'm primarily a Yoruba writer, just as you have Occitan writers in France, Welsh writers, Scottish literature, within the same political entity. There is Gaelic literature, literature in Welsh, even when it is written in English, like the works of Powys, for instance."

Wole Soyinka, interview with Jane Wilkinson[3]

"...between them they illustrate the whole course of the new literature of English speaking Africa – and, indeed, in many respects those of other parts of the world which have emerged from the colonial experience."[4]

"By 1966 [Achebe] was already being overtly critical of nationalist politics in A Man of the People. However, like so many others, he failed at that time to see what Fanon saw, namely the dangers posed by an untutored national consciousness to a great socio-political movement *like decolonization. One writer who did see the danger was Soyinka, who made it the main theme in the play* A Dance of the Forest, *which he was commissioned to write for the official celebration of Nigeria's independence in 1960."*[5]

Achebe and Soyinka, belonging to the first generation of African writers, write for and about the self-conscious educated elite which influence the intellectual and political ideas of Nigeria and by extension Africa. This elite is very much more in the tradition of the European intellectual class which believed itself alone constituted the nation. Whatever other languages each member of this African educated elite might speak, they have the English language in common and with it they can, within the same points of reference, and through a common education in the language, discuss the issues of the nation. Achebe and Soyinka have always acted and written in terms of purging the educated elite of bad leadership behaviour. Neither of them has been as critical enough of their ethnic elite as they have been of the Nigerian, and of the African elite. Without being outright ethnic chauvinists, they have refused to express the historical fact that the political and the economic rivalries of the three major ethnic nationalities of Nigeria – the Hausa-Fulani, the Igbo and the Yoruba – have been the dynamo of the Nigerian political and social instability.

It has been left to the writers of another generation to insist on bringing the other non-elite members of the nation into the fore in their writing, thus fulfilling the definition of Rousseau and the other radical political thinkers that writers "should express the collective will of all the people living within its borders." Some of these writers are Femi Osofisan, Festus Iyayi and Ken Saro-Wiwa. They bring into their texts the lives of the poor, the minority ethnic nationalities, and the underprivileged. These writers, while being acknowledged inside Nigeria, have not found the same measure of acceptance overseas as the generation of Achebe and Soyinka.

Notes

1. Appiah, Kwame Anthony, *In My Father's House, Africa in the Philosophy of Culture*, London: Methuen, 1992, p. xiii.

2. op. cit. p. 116. There is no indication that this interview has been published independently of Appiah's book. It is to be assumed that the interview was done towards the writing of the book rather than as published interview on its own.

3. Wilkinson, Jane, *Talking with African Writers*, London: James Currey, 1990 and 1992. p. 96.

4.   Gilbert Phelps on Chinua Achebe and Wole Soyinka in *The New Pelican Guide to English Literature* vol 8, *The Present*, edited by Boris Ford, 1983. pp.342–343.

5. Anna Rutherford, "Introduction: The Essential Heterogeneity of Being" in *From Commonwealth to Post-Colonial*, edited by Anna Rutherford, Sydney, Australia and Coventry, Dangaroo Press, 1992.

Introduction

Chinua Achebe or Wole Soyinka ?

Why would anyone wish to make a choice between Chinua Achebe and Wole Soyinka? After all, both of them are Nigerians and both of them share so much between themselves. They attended similar secondary schools, government colleges in Ibadan and Umuahia, the same University College in Ibadan, and both have followed the humanist tradition of Western Europe and North America in calling for the creation in Nigeria of a civil society.

In spite of these similarities, the fact that is most relevant in their lives and in their writings is their ethnic origins: that Chinua Achebe is Igbo and Wole Soyinka is Yoruba. The details of everyday rituals of existence – birth, naming ceremony, food, drink, coming of age, marriage, managing success, growing old and death – are informed by their ethnic national cultures. These in turn inform their work as writers. Moreover, consciously or unconsciously, the rivalries between the Igbo and the Yoruba during the colonial period of the history of Nigeria have dogged the writings and the actions of these two writers.

Choices are being made between them every day, by those who know their work and those who are ignorant of their work. Such choices are made in Nigeria by Nigerians. Outsiders who know the country intimately enough tend to make this choice also.

But foreigners, who know little about Nigeria and come to the writings of Achebe and Soyinka as they come to the works of other writers from Africa, see these writers as African writers.

In the first place, in spite of coming from two competing ethnic nationalities, both Achebe and Soyinka have the same attitude regarding their roles as writers and as citizens of Nigeria. Both of them also share the same attitudes to their ethnic nationalities. They see themselves not simply as individuals within these two ethnic nationalities but also as speakers and griots, Achebe for the Igbos and Soyinka for the Yorubas. They often speak as if there were no alternative options and opinions within their ethnic nationalities, as if within the experiment of the

Nigerian nation building their ethnic nationalities do not constitute problems for all. Unlike writers in Europe and North
America where writing has virtually lost its links with oral traditions of narratives, Achebe and Soyinka are close to their oral
traditions and speak on behalf of and through their cultures.

The central issue, then, is not that a choice has to be made
between them, but that choices are made all the time, consciously and otherwise, by their fellow compatriots. One of the commonest grounds for making a choice between Achebe and
Soyinka is that of their writing styles. It is said that Achebe is
simple and easy to read and understand while Soyinka is difficult to read, obscure and incomprehensible. As far as some
Nigerian critics are concerned, Soyinka is not in fact attempting
to say anything to anyone. Rather, he is out to demonstrate that
he is able to manipulate the English language far better than the
owners of the language, the English in England, and also to
demonstrate his cleverness.

Chinweizu and his colleagues have attempted to make this
case in their now popular "bolekaja" (aggressive and self-right-
eous) criticism in *Toward the Decolonization of African Literature*[1].
D.S. Izevbaye, almost assumes the obscurity of Soyinka's writing when he opens his essay "Language and Meaning in
Soyinka's The Road"[2] with the following sentences:

> Although *The Road* is one of Soyinka's most exciting plays, it is
> also a 'problem' play because not only does it raise the question
> of linguistic communication and apprehension in the theatre it is
> itself about the problem of communication. Because Soyinka
> writes mainly plays, a form which requires direct and instant
> communication with the audience, it is natural to prefer the more
> accessible of the plays to the obscure.[3]

Bernth Lindfors comes out directly in his essay "Beating the
White Man at His Own Game: Nigerian Reactions to the 1986
Nobel Prize in Literature"[4] Lindfors quotes Achebe's comments
on Soyinka's Nobel Prize for Literature, made at the annual
meeting of the Association of Nigerian Authors in December
1986:

> For me what matters is that after the oriki and the celebrations we
> should say to ourselves: One of us has proved that we can beat
> the white man at his own game. That is wonderful for us and for
> the white man. But now we must turn away and play our own
> game.[5]

As Lindfors observes, Achebe does not spell out the nature of
the European and the African game. The implication cannot be
missed though that Soyinka, as far as Achebe is concerned, is
not playing the African game.

In an answer to a question at a public lecture Achebe seems to
spell out what he meant:

> Well, I think he [Soyinka] makes a cult of obscurity, especially in
> his later work, which to my mind is unnecessary and unfortu-
> nate.[6]

Niyi Osundare, an astute and reader-friendly poet as well as a
linguistic specialist[7] has written about what he terms "the critical and stylistic hallmark of Soyinka's writing" which is 'obscurity'.[8]

> Like Ogun his patron god, Soyinka plies the deep jungle of words
> where daemonic sentences confuse the reader and frustrate his
> wanderings, and metaphors take on the baffling proteanness of
> the chameleon.[9]

Before going on to provide the necessary explication of text,
Osundare cites one essay each by Ossie Enekwe[10] and Biodun
Jeyifo.[11] Enekwe, writes Osundare, "cites obscurity of diction as
one of the 'traits pernicious to his [Soyinka's] fiction'".[12]

Biodun Jeyifo details culturally different and complicated cosmology as well as Soyinka's privatisation of language, be it
Yoruba, English or Greek as the source of 'obscurity' in Soyinka.
Osundare then clarifies the lexical as well as the syntactic problems raised by Soyinka's prose.

Two comments are relevant here. One is the existence of an
attitude among educated Nigerians which seems to assume that
knowing a writer as a person ought to mean knowing what the
writer is saying in his writing without having to make an effort.
The same readers, approaching the works of a Japanese or
Chinese writer translated into English or any other language
that they can read, would expect to arm themselves with background information. Somehow, with African writers such a
preparation does not seem to be needed. Such readers are
encouraged by those writers and critics who make a virtue of
simplicity in creative writing. The second comment is that what
ultimately can be explained cannot be said to be obscure.

"'Metal on concrete jars my drink lobes'" is how Soyinka's *The
Interpreters*, his first novel begins. Compared to the beginning of
Achebe's first novel, *Things Fall Apart*: "Okonkwo was well

known in the seven villages of Umuofia." it would seem as if the Nigerian critics were right. But is the case made?

Hardly. There is the wrong assumption by many of these critics that African languages, which the European language of the writer should shadow, are not capable of obscurity because African languages must communicate. But anyone familiar with cultic language would admit that communication is limited to those who know, what in Yoruba is known as "awon awo" (the knowledgeable ones) and was not meant for "awon ogberi" (those of little knowledge). Oral narratives, be they poetic or prosaic, were not always without linguistic dexterity which the mind of the audience must ponder if they are to enjoy and learn from the narratives. In addition to this point is the one which demonstrates, at least in the history of the English language, that other linguistic backgrounds have enriched the English language from the time of Shakespeare onwards. The Irish English writers have been the most striking example. The problem of identity which this aspect of writing in English, and perhaps in other European languages, raise needs to be dealt with in terms of communities of multi-lingual and multi-cultural expression. That choices are to be made on the basis of one writer being European and another being more African is one of those reductionisms that are encountered in discussions of African cultures and mores.[13]

Under the Achebe being 'afro-centric' and Soyinka 'euro-centric' rubrics, Chinua Achebe, we are told, confronts Europe by demonstrating the clash of African culture with European culture and brings out for all to see the debilitating effect of Europe on African lives. Soyinka, we are supposed to believe on the other hand, does not accept that there is anything clashing between African culture and European or any other cultures for that matter. In fact, it is pointed out that in the introduction to *Death and the King's Horseman* he rejects the idea of a culture clash situation in the encounter between the Yoruba and the British colonial officers of the Yoruba historical period of the play. Soyinka's gibe against Negritude, that a tiger need not declare its Tigritude[14] to show that it is a tiger, has also been held against him.

More needs to be known about the ethnic backgrounds of both writers to demonstrate that such conclusions are premature and even superficial.

As far as their attitudes to politics in Nigeria are concerned, Achebe is considered to be conservative while Soyinka is radical. The reality of their political party memberships and alliances contradict such categorisation. Both Achebe and Soyinka were members of the People's Redemption Party during the Second Republic from 1979 to 1983. The party was founded by Aminu Kano, a Hausa-Fulani, the third member of the troika of ethnic nationalities whose rivalries led Nigeria to civil war and near disintegration between 1967 and 1970. When the People's Redemption Party broke into two factions, Chinua Achebe emerged as one of the leaders of the conservative faction while Soyinka went along with the radical faction.

In the civil war between Nigeria and Biafra, both Achebe and Soyinka were on the side of Biafra. Chinua Achebe was a spokesperson for the short-lived Biafran nation while Soyinka was detained by the Nigerian Federal Government without trial, in solitary confinement for most of the period, on the rumoured accusation that he was gun-running for the state of Biafra. Again, the details of their activities and their aims show deep differences. Chinua Achebe worked for the success of the government and people of Biafra, while Soyinka worked for the possibility of a third force throwing out both the government of Federal Nigeria in Lagos and the government of Biafra in Enugu and replacing them with a radical government for a united Nigeria.

As literary critics, Achebe and Soyinka have not always held the same views. Chinua Achebe has provided solutions to many young Nigerian writers wishing to use English to express themselves. Achebe has a vocal following the way Soyinka does not. Achebe's solution to the use of English in expressing African cultural values, his critical attitude to European writers writing about Africa and Africans, and his somewhat unadventurous use of English ("unrelieved good sense", as Soyinka describes it)[15] have had their influence on many writers in Nigeria and perhaps Africa.

Wole Soyinka, on the other hand, began his critical assault on African literature by condemning Negritude with the gibe of Tigritude. He has gone on to propose an African (Yoruba) alternative understanding of what tragic drama can be and in contrast to the European Aristotelian theory of tragic drama. Wole Soyinka has not been as hesitant as Chinua Achebe in commenting on the works of other African writers, including those of Achebe. Chinua Achebe has been more circumspect in commenting on Wole Soyinka's writing and never at length. One of the better known comments that Achebe has made on Soyinka's writing was not on Soyinka himself but on one of the first major African critics of Wole Soyinka, the influential Sierra Leonean critic Eldred Durosimi Jones for claiming that Soyinka was "universal".[16]

Among critics of Nigerian literature, with the possible exception of Chinweizu, few comment on both writers together, most preferring to deal with aspects of their writings separately. For some critics, Achebe is the quintessential African writer, the exemplar to be followed, the one to inspire others. To others Wole Soyinka is 'WS', our own William Shakespeare (a title another Nigerian writer J.P. Clark[17] disputes on the ground that Soyinka's 'W' is similar to Shakespeare's Bill rather than William) while Denise Kacou-Kome has written a book in French entitled *Soyinka et Shakespeare* comparing both playwrights. As individuals, Chinua Achebe is conventional while Wole Soyinka, as the founder member of the now Nigeria university-wide Pyrates Confraternity[18] is, in the motto of the club, a sworn enemy of convention.

While all these various differences and similarities are important to the understanding of the works of these two writers as well as the understanding of their country Nigeria, these details have little influenced the criticism of their works outside of Nigeria. It is as if they become one unrecognisable 'African' the moment they and their works step out of the boundaries of Nigeria. The case which this book makes is that to the extent that critics within or without Nigeria have ignored their differences to that extent have the criticisms been questionable. Perhaps even inadequate. But this book has a more important duty to perform. The most important political problem of the Nigerian since the naming of the country in 1914 has been the creation of a united stable nation-state comprising all the multi-ethnic, multi-lingual and multi-religious populations of the land. Nigeria has struggled with making 'out of many peoples one people'. Both Achebe and Soyinka, like so many other African writers, have stated the primacy of politics in their artistic as well as their personal lives. In what way then have their works, as well as their personal lives, contributed towards the creation in Nigeria of a community of sensibilities? Given the fact that they write *from* their ethnic national cultures, have they written *towards* the creation of a new Nigerian national consciousness?

The works of Achebe and Soyinka are considered against three main agendas: the pan-African agenda, the Nigerian nation-state agenda and the ethnic national agenda. Most critics of African literature have worked within the pan-African agenda of Africans and African writers. Even when it has been necessary to look for the greater details of issues and incidents within the nation-state and the ethnic nationality which have informed the works and opinions of these writers, these critics have been unwilling or perhaps incapable of giving such attention to the works, and preferring instead to take the easy option of seeing these writers purely and mainly as Africans, working within one African culture that is unanimous and comprehensible to all Africans.

An important aspect of the argument of this study is that both the pan-African agenda and the ethnic national agenda have worked against the possibility of achieving the Nigerian nation-state agenda. Many African writers, including Nigerians, have written from both the point of view of the pan-African agenda and the point of view of the ethnic national agenda without consciously working out the contradictions which these two agendas entail especially in terms of the nation-building agenda of the new nation-state. Just as the tactics and talents needed to make a success of the pan-African agenda differ from those needed to make a success of the nation-state agenda differ politically, they also differ artistically. Between these two agendas comes the ethnic national agenda contradicting the national agenda without vindicating the pan-African agenda. Both Achebe and Soyinka are caught in this contradiction.

NOTES

1. Chinweizu, Jemie, Onwuchekwa & Madubuike, Ihechukwu, *Toward the Decolonization of African Literature*, vol.1: *African Fiction and Poetry and their Critics*, Enugu: Fourth Dimension Publishing Co., 1980.
2. in *Critical Perspectives on Wole Soyinka*, ed. James Gibbs, pp. 90–103.
3. op. cit. p. 90.
4. *Black American Literature Forum*, Wole Soyinka Issue, Part I; vol. 22, No. 3, Fall 1988, pp. 475–488.
5. op. cit. p. 487.
6. *In Person: Achebe, Awoonor, and Soyinka at the University of Washington*, ed. Karen L. Morell, p. 50..
7. Niyi Osundare teaches in the English Department of the University of Ibadan. He is one of the most powerful poets of the younger generation. His collections include *Songs of the Marketplace* 1983; *Moonsongs* 1984 and *Village Voices* 1984. *Waiting Laughters* 1990

(for which he won the 1991 Noma Award for Publishing in Africa); *Midlife* 1993. For a few years he maintained and sustained a column in the *Sunday Tribune* devoted to poetry about everyday issues successfully.

8. See "Words of Iron, Sentences of Thunder: Soyinka's Prose Style" in *African Literature Today*, edited by Eldred D. Jones, no. 13, 1983, pp. 24–37. Another paper, read at the University of Ibadan in 1980, entitled "The Poem as a Mytho-Linguistic Event: Study of Wole Soyinka's 'Abiku'" deals with Soyinka's poetry.

9. ibid. p. 24.

10. Ossie Enekwe is a poet, dramatist and essayist. He edits *Okike,* a sustained literary endeavour (though currently dormant), founded by Chinua Achebe. The essay "Wole Soyinka as a Novelist" cited by Niyi Osundare, appears in *Okike,* no. 9, 1975. pp. 72–86.

11. Biodun Jeyifo, who teaches at Cornell University's Department of English is one of the most influential critics to come out of Nigeria in the 70s and the 80s. His publications include *The Yoruba Professional Itinerant Theatre: Oral Documentation,* 1981; and the publication cited here *Soyinka Demythologized: Notes on a Materialist Reading of A Dance of the Forests, The Road and Kongi's Harvest,* University of Ife (now Obafemi Awolowo University) Monographs, 1984.

12. op. cit. p.24

13. See J. Z. Kronenfeld's essay "The 'Communalistic' African and the 'Individualistic' Westerner: Some Comments on Misleading Generalizations in Western Criticism of Soyinka and Achebe", in *Research on Wole Soyinka,* edited by James Gibbs and Bernth Lindfors, pp. 301–325.

14. This gibe has been read as an attack on Negritude, the African literary movement founded by the Senegalese/French poet Leopold Sedar Senghor and the Martinican/French poet Aimé Cesaire.

15. See preface to the second edition of *Girls at War,* 1977.

16. In the essay "Thoughts on the African Novel" in *Morning Yet on Creation Day,* p. 49.

17. John Pepper Clark is one of the major poets and playwrights of Nigeria and belongs to the same generation as Achebe and Soyinka. His publications include *Song of a Goat,* (play), *Casualties* (poetry), *Ozidi Saga,* (traditional drama) and *America, Their America,* (memoir).

18. As a result of recent grave anti-social behaviour of university clubs which claim to descend from the Pyrates, Soyinka has dissociated himself from the organisation.

I

Living on the Seam of Two Worlds:

Childhood and the Cultural Influences on Achebe and Soyinka

The only children who lived in secluded areas in the early years of the creation of the educated elite in Nigeria were the children of teachers and employees of the Church Missionary Society or the Roman Catholic Church – clergymen, pastors and their higher officials such as headmasters and school inspectors. These children saw the world from behind the hibiscus flower fences and the rose gardens of the parsonage or the missionary school compound. Their lives were wrapped up in the power of the written word either through the Bible or the hymnal companion or the publications of the church as well as the teachers' manuals. They had their places of play – the fields and farms left to them after all the other children had gone home to their houses and huts in the towns and villages. Discouraged from playing any games of chance such as Ludo, Snakes and Ladders and any card games, these special children had only books to play with and they were usually competent in reading even before they began their formal education. They were sometimes allowed to kick a tennis ball around on weekdays but on Sundays they could not play games or whistle or play musical instruments since that was the day of the Lord and they were supposed to keep it holy as if they lived in the early biblical times[1] as described in the *Acts of the Apostles*.

> All the believers continued together in close fellowship and shared their belongings with one another. They would sell their property and possessions, and distribute the money among all, according to what each one needed. Day after day they met as a group in the Temple, and they had their meals together in their homes, eating with glad and humble hearts, praising God, and

enjoying the good will of all people. And everyday the Lord
added to their group those who were being saved.[2]

The families of these children constituted the first Christian
communities in the country. When they sang:

> Christian seek not yet repose
> Hear thy guardian angels say
> Thou art in the midst of foes
> Watch and pray

they meant it literally, living as they did in the midst of pagans
and idol–worshippers. Their parents ensured that the children
did not play or in any other way associate with the children of
'these natives' the pagans.

In a Yoruba novel dealing with the lives of the early
Christians of the second half of the nineteenth century *L'Ojo Ojo
'Un* (In the Days of Yore)[3] we read the following on the isolation
of the early Yoruba Christians:

> Kiki onigbagbo ni o ngbe Abule Onigbagbo nitori isesi ati
> ihuwasi awon keferi ati imale ko le papo mo ti won.[4]

> (Only Christians lived in the Believers' Village because the
> behaviour of pagans and Muslims could not mix with their own.)

Later on though this isolation changed and the Christians did
not mind living with other people in the society:

> Awon onigbagbo ti ri i kedere pe nwon ko le nikan wa ni kiki
> awon ara won titi; bi awon nikan ngbe abule won, nwon nilati ni
> ohun pupo ba awon aladugbo won se po fun idagbasoke adugbo
> ati anfani awon papa.[5]

> (The Christians came to realise clearly that they could not live
> secluded for ever; there were things they had to share with their
> neighbours for the development of the community and for their
> own good too.)

On the point of the changes that the missionaries had to accept
in order for the new Yoruba elite to become Christians it is
appropriate to deal with the composition of the early Christians
and to see how they have been depicted in the writings of
Achebe and Soyinka.

The initial and immediate benefactors of the policies pursued
by the missionaries and the colonial authorities were the slaves,
the servants, mothers of twins who were usually forced to kill
their twins among the Igbos; (in contrast, they are considered
special children among the Yorubas and feted and celebrated in
poetry and in special wood carvings) and people of low caste

such as the osu in Igbo society. Professor A.E. Afigbo has written about the inducements used to persuade the Igbo to become Christians. The Igbos and the Yoruba who needed to be persuaded to join the Christians were the members of the old Igbo and Yoruba elite.

> Much more directly the missionaries attracted people to the school and church with material presents and the flaunting of material wealth.[6]

The opportunistic nature of the Yoruba elite in joining the Christians has been documented in many diaries and records of the history of the Protestant Christian Church in Yorubaland.[7] But it may be more useful here to use Delano's novel *L'Ojo Ojo 'Un*, already referred to above. This historical novel deals with the life of a former warrior of Abeokuta done in by the activities of the anti–slave trade campaigners, the missionaries and the British colonial authorities. The narrator is a young girl who grows up and gets married in the new Christian way at the end of the novel; and a large chunk of the novel is devoted to the problem occasioned by the availability of European alcoholic beverages in Southern Nigeria at this time. Here is the narrator announcing the process which started her father on the road to Christianity:

> Baba mi a ma woye bi igba ti nlo; ojo kan l'o pinnu pe on yio di onigbagbo. O pe iya mi, o ni: 'Igbagbo yi to ba won se; se o nri bi igba ti nyipada nisisiyi. Onigbagbo di eni iyi, ola ati ola; nwon mba oyinbo sowo, nwon mba won na; nwon nla, nwon nlu; oba ori ite papa ti ko fi ti oyinbo se nisisiyi fe je iyan re ni isu ni.[8]

> (My father always observed how the times were changing. One day he decided that he wanted to become a Christian. He called my mother and said: 'It is time to join those Christians; you yourself can see how the times are changing. Christians have become respected people, people of wealth and honour. They trade with the white man, and they make money. A king who fails to do the bidding of the white man can lose his throne.')

Balogun, (his military title in Egbaland) realises how people of his ilk had been made powerless by the new power system emerging. Soldiers caught continuing to kidnap and sell children into slavery were punished severely. He goes to the white missionary to ask what he would have to do to become a Christian. When he had talked to his wife, she had advised him to speak to the missionary because she had heard that the Christians had all sorts of strange rules they must live by. The

white missionary told him that he would have to stop worshipping idols, rest on the Sabbath Day and become monogamous.
Initially, these rules annoyed him, most especially the one about
becoming monogamous. He asked what he was supposed to do
with his wives. The missionary told him that, with the exception
of the first one, he must renounce them. What about the children
from these wives? Like their mothers, said the missionary, they
too must be renounced. Balogun left the missionary fuming and
cursing him, calling him homewrecker, a mad person, and other
epithets that the interpreter would not pass on to the white missionary. All the same, little by little, the missionary was allowed
to come to Balogun's house and preach, not to him but to his
wives and children. In the case of T.A. Adebiyi's biography of
Bishop Akinyele, the Bishop's great grandfather had, in 1853,
insisted that the missionary should come and preach to his
wives and daughters, not to him and his sons:

> You may come to my house, but please confine your talks about
> this Jesus to my wives and their daughters only because I don't
> want my sons turned to cowards.[9]

As time went by Balogun gradually became a Christian without
giving up his wives and without having to feel that he was a
lazy man for not working on Sunday. One of the advantages
which Christians enjoyed was access to European medicine
which the Christians saw was more efficacious than the local
medicine and had regular measures.[10]

Sometimes, traditional institutions were invoked in order to
sanctify the change over to Christianity:

> The oracle, *Ifa*, we understood, was consulted in the evening by
> the chiefs. The Babalawo, or master of Ceremonies, (sic) was
> among the more important chiefs. *Ifa's* reply was favourable to
> us. It was to the effect that the messenger who had come to the
> chiefs and their mission should not be refused, for they were cal-
> culated to do the town good.[11]

When one reads about the level of antagonism with which
Achebe portrays the missionaries it would seem as if they had
no welcome at all among the Igbo. Achebe seems to find no
merit in the position which his father and his contemporaries
took to inaugurate the new era which had been particularly beneficial to the weakest members of the community. In fact,
Achebe takes the side of the ruling elite which had done precious little to help the weak among them. He does not see the
survival need of the weak and the poor in seeking salvation in

the arms of the missionaries. The point to be made, then, is that Chinua Achebe is only interested in defending the Igbo traditional elite in both *Things Fall Apart* and *Arrow of God*. Whatever happened to the poor and the weak and the low caste was their problem. Should this conclusion be disputed, we might wish to look at the single opportunity Achebe has to do something for the low caste in one of his novels *No Longer at Ease*. Obi had met Clara in London at a dance organised by the "London branch of the National Council of Nigeria and the Cameroons at St. Pancras Town Hall".[12] They return to Nigeria on the same boat and so got more involved. Although she becomes pregnant, the fact that she is found out to be an *osu* both by the Lagos branch of the Umuofia Progressive Union and by Obi's parents, ends the relationship.

Wole Soyinka, on the other hand, has been kinder to poor and weak characters in his plays, novels and autobiographies. In *The Strong Breed*, where a poor deformed Ifada is being forced to die for the community, the hero, Eman, found it necessary to replace Ifada as the sacrifice for the sins of the community.

In *The Bacchae of Euripedes*, Soyinka brings in the struggle of the slaves to influence the course of the new religion which Dionysos brings:

> SLAVE LEADER: Because the rites bring us nothing! Let those to whom the profits go bear the burden of the old year dying.[13]

One of the most delightful characters in *Isara : A Voyage Around Essay* is Damian who wanders into Isara from nobody knows where and becomes a solid member of the town. His name becomes Demiyen and later still he assumes a nick name – Semuja – the result of a triumphant self-assertion on Damian's part. Generally then, while Achebe seems to have eyes only for the traditional elite, Soyinka represents the weak and the poor while refusing to defend the point of view of the traditional elite.

The harvest festival was the celebration of the bringing in of the harvest and all the members of the church were pressured to come and praise the Lord with the proceeds of their efforts made successful by the help of the only true God. In Chinua Achebe's *Arrow of God* we see how this festival suddenly resolves the dilemma of the people as far as the issue of the first yam was concerned. Overnight, Ezeulu, the high priest, lost his relevance to his community, his place opportunistically taken by the Christians and their church harvest festival.

In Wole Soyinka's *Kongi's Harvest*, the eating of the first yam becomes a ritual of power demonstration and the winner has to be Kongi in this contestation of the old and the new for power.

While the children of the Christians and the educated elite lived in parsonages and school compounds, the other children, the bulk of the children of the schools lived in the town or village where the house of a shoe maker from Ilorin – perhaps small and even run down and in need of roof-mending, or better still replacement by corrugated iron sheets from England – this house or hut stood next to houses with prosperous cocoa or palm produce, or hides and skins, or that of a ground nut farmer. This was the situation before the age of the first housing estates in the country, before the growing bourgeois salaried class from the different arms of the elite decided to abandon the people and live in secluded low density areas with their electricity and pipe borne water, and Kingsway and Leventis Stores. The children from these increasing material distance could be distinguished from the children of the elite by the fact that they went bare–footed to school or else wore white tennis shoes; they would not be able to change their uniforms in the middle of the week and they were likely to wear the same uniform week in and week out.

The year for these children, besides the church festivities, would also include the Moslem and traditional festivals. The calendar of the year's activities included the various religious festivals: Christian, Moslem and traditional. For the Christians there were the Christmas and Easter festivities which had more to do with the Church in Europe, while the Harvest festival took off from the local rituals of planting and harvesting in the society. The Moslem festivities were those of the ending of the month of fasting, the birthday of Prophet Mohammed and the return to Nigeria of Moslem pilgrims from Mecca and Medina. The traditional festivities were those of the various Gods of the community. While the children behind the hibiscus fences and rose gardens would have been prevented from taking part in these festivals of 'pagans' and idol worshippers, the children of the town and villages would be in the thick of them.

From the dry season to the season of rains, thunder and lightning, one traditional God or the other demanded sacrifice and worship and their followers obliged, no matter what the people of the churches and the mosques said against these practices.

Masquerades appeared, danced, pursued people and re–activated the spots and games of the community before returning to the land of the ancestors accompanied with sonorous drums. Those left behind feasted on specially prepared meats and other foods. The children of the village and the town brought reports of these festivals to their schools. Relatives, previously adequately covered by terms such as fathers, mothers, brothers, sisters, became, in the more specific and distancing English language of the educated elite, uncles, aunts, nephews and nieces. These relatives took part in the festivals and brought reports when they visited these parsonages. But the children of the elite were forbidden to partake of what the church called pagan festivals. The children of those who worked in the church were not to mix with sinners who indulged in satanic beliefs and festivals. Naturally, as sensitive children, some of them wanted to find out more about the world outside the parsonage, and they wanted to be in with the world of the other children with whom they were being asked not to associate.

Chinua Achebe was born in Ogidi on November 16, 1930 and brought up in the parsonage of the Church Missionary Society. Wole Soyinka was born on July 13, 1934 and he grew up partly in the parsonage at Ibara in Abeokuta.

Usually, the role of the teacher and that of the pastor might coincide. At other times, the teacher, especially if he happened to be the head teacher of the school, also stood in as pastor of the church which owned the school and lived in the parsonage.

How have Achebe and Soyinka looked at their childhood? Both writers have spoken about their growing up in what might be called the seam of two worlds and the hope their parents had that they would grow up partial to the new world of western education, the Christian religion, and would reject the old world of traditional religions and Islam. This is how Chinua Achebe has written about his childhood:

> On one arm of the cross we sang hymns and read the Bible night and day. On the other my father's brother and his family, *blinded* by *heathenism*, offered food to idols. That was how it was supposed to be anyhow.[14] (emphasis added)

This is not the place in which to deal with the issue of the words in italics in the quote above from Chinua Achebe. This issue is dealt with in the chapter about what these writers have done with the Gods and Goddesses of their ancestors. (Chapter IV) In spite of seeming here to take the side of the Christians against the idol worshippers, Chinua Achebe did not feel torn between the two worlds. Rather,

> The distance [between the two worlds] becomes not a separation but a bringing together like the necessary backward step which a judicious viewer might take in order to see a canvas steadily and fully.[15]

The essay from which this quotation is taken, entitled "Named for Victoria, Queen of England", is surely a recapturing of childhood and growing up, but it is also clear that the quote is not the judgement of a youngster but the justification of an adult. The view expressed here – that the two worlds were compatible and could live side by side – does not square with the general tone of Chinua Achebe's novels and short stories where he insists on the clash of European and African cultures and a position on which a whole species of the African novel has grown.

Wole Soyinka has written lyrically about his childhood and growing up in Abeokuta. Right from the first page of *Ake: The Years of Childhood*, he conflates the personalities of the Christian God with that of the local Oba (King) and the ancestral masquerades:

> On a misty day, the steep rise towards Itoko would join the sky. If God did not actually live there, there was little doubt that he descended first on its crest, then took his one gigantic stride over those babbling markets – which dared to sell on Sundays – into St. Peter's Church, afterwards visiting the parsonage for tea with Canon. There was the small consolation that, in spite of the temptation to arrive on horseback, he never stopped first at the Chief's, who was known to be a pagan; certainly the Chief was never seen in church service except at the anniversaries of the Alake's coronation. Instead God strode straight into St. Peter's for morning service, paused briefly at the afternoon service, but reserved his most formal, exotic presence for the evening service which, in his honour, was always held in the English tongue. The organ took on a dark smoky sonority at evening service, and there was no doubt that the organ was adapting its normal sounds to accompany God's own sepulchral responses, with its timbre of the egungun, to those prayers that were offered to him.[16]

Here is another quote from a later passage in the same book:

> The elder waited, our chaperon smiled and explained. 'They don't know how to prostrate, please do not take offence.' Reactions varied. Some were so overawed by these aliens who

actually had been heard to converse with their parents in the white man's tongue that they quickly denied that they had ever expected such a provincial form of greeting. A smaller number, especially the ancient ones whose skins had acquired the gloss of those dark beaten etu merely drew themselves up higher, snorted and walked away. Later, they would be mollified by the Odemo, the titled head of Isara, to whose ears their complaints might come.[17]

If our two writers saw the distinction between these two seem-ingly contradictory worlds, if they lived rather dangerously on the seam of these two worlds, it was only natural that they would want to investigate how their situation came about.

Chinua Achebe asked questions about these two worlds very early in his literary career. His first novels were conceived as a trilogy of Igbo history. The first would deal with the past, the second with the coming of the white man and the Christian church while the third would deal with the products of the two worlds of Europe and Africa, his generation.

Things Fall Apart became the first part of the trilogy. The next one would have dealt with the generation of his father, the gen-eration which compromised with the white man and his new ways. In spite of the fact that Chinua Achebe has made the most convincing arguments, through his fiction and his essays, for the need of Africans to compromise with the white man, he thought that those responsible for the compromise are traitors to the tra-ditional values and ways of the Igbo. His father a traitor? Unthinkable!

> So with the folk wisdom which enjoins us to thread warily that narrowest of paths between the forbidden homesteads of rash-ness and cowardice I postponed the story of my father, and moved on to write about my own generation.[18]

The resulting novel is *No Longer at Ease*. What was the problem?

> The major problem was this: my father's generation were the very people, after all, who, no matter how sympathetically one wished to look upon their predicament, did open the door to the white man. But could I, even in the faintest, most indirect, most delicate allusiveness, dare to suggest that my father may have been something... of a... traitor? Tufia! And I don't mean this in a sentimental, soft–headed, filial–duty sense at all, but in relation to concrete things I knew about the man. So the only permissible interpretation of my difficulty had to be that I was perhaps not old enough, or simply did not know as much as I should about what happened.[19]

Unlike Chinua Achebe, Wole Soyinka has not only written about his first eleven years of life but also he has written a reconstruction of the life and times of his father as well as his father's friends and contemporaries. Unlike Chinua Achebe, Wole Soyinka does not see his father and his generation as traitors to the culture of the Yoruba. Only an understanding of the Yoruba attitude to the British conquest of Yorubaland can explain this difference between Achebe and Soyinka. The details of this attitude on the part of the Yoruba must be left to a later chapter. Here only a little of the explanation can be given. The Yoruba acceptance of the British conquest did not recognise treachery as an issue in the coming of the white man to Yorubaland. Yoruba compromise with the British conquest came in two stages. There was an initial stage of complete rejection, under the guidance of the Yoruba returnees from Sierra Leone at the end of the slave trade, of anything to do with Yoruba and Islam. Later, towards the end of the nineteenth century and at the beginning of the twentieth century, there was a modification of this position. As a result of this re–definition, the Yoruba began to insist on combining things Yoruba with things British in order to re–create their society anew. Thus, Yoruba school children marched into their classrooms in the mornings singing:

> A o so 'yinbo, Yes!
> A o so 'de wa, Are![20]

It is important to note that the solution to the problem posed by Achebe had been provided for Soyinka by the generation of Yorubas who, as Chinua Achebe puts it, "opened the door to the white man," a generation that was before Soyinka's father's generation.

In the area of traditional Yoruba religions, the compromise was seen in terms of the following words made into song:

> Igbagbo ko ni k'awa ma s'oro
> Awa o s'oro ile wa o![21]

The syncretism implicit in this position is an aspect of modern Yoruba culture and forms a major aspect of Wole Soyinka's writing.[22]

Wole Soyinka's writing about the generation of his father is part of his process of understanding that these men and women contributed in order to achieve the modern life of the white man while attempting to hold on, perhaps even salvage something of value from their existence prior to the coming of the British.

It is clear then that the two writers see the coming of the white man into the worlds of their fathers from two different perspectives. These perspectives originated with their different ethnic national perspectives. The Igbo saw the British coming as an encounter with a strange Difference, an Other, a Contradiction, an Encounter that can only be negative in terms of its effects on Igbo culture and ways of existence if not a destruction of that culture and its ways. The Yoruba, on the other hand, accepted the negative and saw something positive. They would attempt to compromise and accommodate, perhaps 'shop around' among the offerings of both cultures and hope to put together something new out of the encounter with the white man.

Notes

1. F. Ade Ajayi, *Christian Missions in Nigeria 1841 – 1891: The Making of a New Elite*, especially chapter 2 – Civilization Around the Mission House.

2. *Acts of the Apostles*, Chapter 2, verses 44 – 47 in the Good News Bible.

3. See Albert Gérard, *African Language Literatures, An Introduction to the Literary History of Sub–Saharan Africa*, p. 251. This book provides the important information that Oloye I.O. Delano, the author of *L'Ojo Ojo 'Un* had translated R.L. Stevenson's *Robinson Crusoe* into Yoruba in 1933. According to the list of books at the back of *Tal'o pa Omooba?*, by Kola Akinlade, Macmillan Nigeria have also published another translation of "Itan 'Robinson Crusoe' l'ede Yoruba" by M.B. Odedeyi.

4. Delano, *L'Ojo Ojo 'Un*, p. 52

5. ibid. p. 58.

6. E.A. Afigbo, "The Place of the Igbo Language in Our Schools" in F.I. Ogbalu and E.N. Emenanjo (eds.) *Igbo Language and Literature*, p. 81.

7. See for instance H.J. Ellis and James Johnson, *Two Missionary Visits to Ijebu Country 1892*, Ibadan: Daystar Press, 1974 and T.A. Adebiyi, *The Beloved Bishop: a Biography of Bishop A.B. Akinyele*, Ibadan: Daystar Press, 1969. The author of this English language biography had published an earlier biography of the Bishop in Yoruba published by the same publishers.

8. Delano, *L'Ojo Ojo 'Un*, p. 23.

9. Adebiyi, *The Beloved Bishop*, p. 13.

10. Delano, *L'Ojo Ojo 'Un*, p. 60.

11. Ellis and Johnson, *Two Missionary Visits to Ijebu Country 1892*, p. 21.

12. Achebe, *No Longer at Ease*, p. 22.

13. Soyinka,*The Bacchae of Euripedes*, p. 5.

14. *Morning Yet on Creation Day*, p. 68.

15. ibid. p. 68.

16. *Ake – The Years of Childhood*, (Rex Collings ed.), p. 1.

17. ibid. p. 126.

18. Introduction to *The African Trilogy, Things Fall Apart, No Longer at Ease, Arrow of God*, London: Picador in association with Heinemann, 1988. p. x.

19. ibid. p. x.

20. Translation:
   We shall speak English, Yes,
   We'll speak our Tongue, Hurrah!

21. Translation:
   Christianity will not prevent us
   We shall worship also
   The Gods of our Ancestors.

22. See article by P.J. Conradie –"Syncretism in Wole Soyinka's *The Bacchae of Euripedes*", *South African Theatre Journal*, vol. 4, no. 1, May 1990, pp.61–74.

II

The Nigerian Elite, Achebe and Soyinka and the Colonial Experience

If we notice that Chinua Achebe uses proverbs and wise sayings of the Igbo people to buttress their compromise with the infiltration of the white man into their country, while at the same time he personally rejects and condemns that compromise, we begin to see what Wole Soyinka has described as Chinua Achebe's ambiguity. While Achebe understands the need for the Igbo to compromise with a stronger power in order to survive, he is not in support of a generation of Igbo having been the instrument of that compromise. Writing about *Arrow of God*, Soyinka argues that Achebe deliberately chooses issues which place the central character Ezeulu, the high priest of Ulu, in a position where he has to deal with the here and now while his powers lie in the hereafter:

> The six villages, as a result of an unfruitful consultation, would be locked in the old year for two moons longer. The grandeur of this challenge is only mildly tempered by the specious calculating game of numbers upon which it rests – the fact that there are three yams left instead of one. Again we encounter the priest's dogged secularisation, of the profoundly mystical.[1]

This insistence on Soyinka's part that Achebe fails to place the struggle between the white man and the Igbo in the realm of the mystical stems from Soyinka's own praxis especially in *Death and the King's Horseman*. It also comes from Soyinka's Yoruba religious background where religion confers great responsibility on the priest until he betrays that responsibility. To some extent, Soyinka's response to Chinweizu's and his colleagues' charge of obscurity is also predicated on his Yoruba cultural background including the issue of the Yoruba language. Placed at this language and ethnic level there is no guarantee that critics and writer, Chinweizu and his colleagues and Wole Soyinka can communicate, much less understand one another.

In identifying Achebe's own ambiguous attitude to his material, Soyinka locates one of the major points of tension in the works of his fellow Nigerian. Soyinka's own ambiguity resides in another area, the area of the role of the individual and the role of the community especially at the point of creating new communities. Soyinka would expect the hero–king to lead and sacrifice for the community. While Achebe might share this view of the role of the individual in creating new communities, he is so acutely aware of the role of such individuals in history that he cannot do more than record them as facts of history but he does not see himself celebrating them or celebrating their failure as Soyinka does in *Death and the King's Horseman*.

Chinua Achebe's ambiguous stance is in fact derived from his ambiguous relationship with his material – the colonial experience of the Igbo of Nigeria. What the Igbo have made of their colonial experience disgusts Achebe. For this reason, he seems to have been more comfortable writing on the past of the Igbo, the period before their wholesale immersion in the world of the white man. This is how Achebe speaks of the contemporary Igbo leadership in his pamphlet *The Trouble With Nigeria*:

> The bankrupt state of Igbo leadership is best illustrated in the alacrity with which they have jettisoned their traditional republicanism in favour of mushroom kingships. From having no kings in their recent past, the Igbo swung round to set an all–time record of four hundred 'kings' in Imo and four hundred in Anambra [states]! And most of them are traders in their stall by day and monarchs by night; city dwellers five days a week and traditional village rulers on Saturdays and Sundays! They adopt 'traditional' robes from every land, including, I am told, the ceremonial regalia of the Lord Mayor of London. The degree of travesty to which the Igbo man is apparently ready to reduce his institutions in his eagerness 'to get up' can be truly amazing.[2]

Achebe is unique here as perhaps the only Nigerian writer who has been so harsh in his comments on some of his own people. Soyinka has been critical of Yoruba characters in his novels and plays such as *The Interpreters* or in the sketches. Such criticism has been part of his general satirizing of the new westernized class in Nigeria. Soyinka has definitely not written in a purely political pamphleteering manner, mainly to criticise the Yoruba ethos in the Nigerian society. He is also unique for not accepting the totality of their history, past and present. Rather, we can see in Achebe's choice of which characters in his novels and short stories he gives dignity and which characters he chooses to ridicule. In contrast with characters such as Chief Nanga in *A Man of the People* and Obi Okonkwo in *No Longer at Ease* we have the dignified favourites such as Okonkwo in *Things Fall Apart* and Ezeulu in *Arrow of God* who prefer to live and die by the old tenets of the Igbo community. These men are dignified and they are tragic in their downfall.

Yet, still responding to that ambiguous streak in his make–up, Achebe would want to distil something for the present world. In his South Bank lecture 'African Literature as Restoration of Celebration' he says:

> I offer *mbari* to you as one illustration of my pre–colonial inheritance of art as celebration of my reality; of art in its social dimension; of the creative potential in all of us and of the need to exercise this latent energy again and again in artistic expression and communal cooperative enterprises.[3]

Achebe's concern for the pre–colonial history of the Igbo makes him sensitive to the negative depiction of that period of their history and the history of other African peoples. His much publicised antagonism to Joseph Conrad's *Heart of Darkness* and Joyce Cary's *Mister Johnson* stems from this concern for the Igbo past.[4]

Achebe began his writing career by wanting to write of a more dignified and self–aware and self– assured African world using the pre–colonial society of the Igbo. The instrument with which he was going to counter this European campaign of calumny and denigration is the European novel with specific parameters developed within the social history of Europe not the Igbo instrument of response to foreign antagonism. Could a case be made against Europe in a European language and a European art form?

Achebe told Jonathan Cott in an interview in 1980 about the setting for *Things Fall Apart* and *No Longer at Ease*:

> I had the idea of its being more like Thomas Hardy's Wessex – some place in the mind, occurring again and again... and thus in that way creating a geographical solidity for the zone of the mind. There's actually no place called Umuofia, but its customs and its people are clearly those of Ogidi in Eastern Nigeria, where I am from.[5]

By choosing to address the disfigurement of Igbo with, not an Igbo artistic models but European ones, Achebe, like other

African writers and artists with the same mission, places his project in a major difficulty, a difficulty which has occasioned the type of reactions from Europeans and North Americans, reactions which Achebe berates in his article "Colonialist Criticism."[6] While Umuofia might be supposed to represent Ogidi, the home town of Achebe, it is certainly not a complete representation. Because of his rejection of the present of his people, he deliberately ignores aspects of the history of his home town and so Umuofia is not a true literary replica of it. The following is part of that history as narrated by a Nigerian critic, Ada Ugah:

> Ogidi is the headquarters of Idemili Local Government Council of Anambra State... Ogidi is found along old Enugu–Onitsha road. The Church Missionary Society reached Ogidi in 1892... The first paramount ruler, Igwe Amobi was imposed by the white man. After his death in 1925, there was an interregnum for 20 years. The people then drew up a constitution for their ruler before Amobi II ascended the throne in 1944.[7]

Nowhere in the novels, short stories and essays of Achebe do we encounter this aspect of the new development of kingship consequent on the Igbo encounter with the white man and colonialism. Robert Wren[8] gives some useful information here concerning the person who became Igwe Amobi I:

> In *Things Fall Apart*, there are no worse men than the Africans, trained by the missionaries, and hired by the government to communicate with the people.[9]

He goes on to say on the same page, and this is significant,

> Yet Amobi had – in Agbogu's research and my own inquiries – a good reputation.

Chief Ikedi in *Arrow of God* is supposed to be based on Amobi and Achebe gives us the outrage of Winterbottom to His Highness Ikedi the First, Obi of Okperi. The title that Amobi took was even more flamboyant – Igwe which means 'the highest or the sky'. Perhaps the most touchy aspect of Achebe's rejection of what Igbos made of themselves with the help of colonialism is the fact that his parents were members of that generation raised, trained and used by the white man to communicate with the Igbo people. This touchiness has been responsible for Achebe's reluctance to write about that generation and tease out of their compromise their motivation at that time and their hopes for the future. Rather than bother with this difficult assignment, Achebe has satisfied himself with dealing with the period and generation before his parents and the generation after them. While Achebe's work might not be considered complete until he has dealt with the historical experience of his parents in the same way that he *had* to write *Anthills of the Savannah*, there is no doubt that he has succeeded enormously in his chosen duty of vindicating the African past through looking at the Igbo past.

If his concern is to avoid colonialism and all its evil, and to create from what happened before which was good and what happened after which was generally bad, Soyinka's concern has been different. The Yoruba people had seen and accepted the presence of the white man as another episode in their history, but they could not predict the end result of this encounter. All they could hope for was some positive pay–off to the Yoruba country. To this end, Wole Soyinka insists that the colonial encounter is a mere episode, a catalytic episode only. The catalytic effect of the colonial encounter within the Yoruba society becomes the area of his creative inquiry. This acceptance of the colonial episode as inevitable and perhaps not all evil led to Yoruba's involvement in western education. Western education has led to a new class, a new elite in the Yoruba society whose position is not confirmed by traditional institutions such as chieftaincy or by wealth.

The educated elite has been given many names by various historians.[10] The educated elite was a vociferous crowd. They could not be ignored because they had the ears of the white man and not only the colonial administrators alone. They were the ones who were trained to run churches, to teach in the schools and to man the trading merchandising houses belonging to the white man. Anyone who wanted to be part of the future had to take them into consideration. Yet, to the traditional elite and the colonial administrators the educated elite was not someone to be taken seriously. Many of them were treated as figures of fun. Sidi, the village beauty of *The Lion and the Jewel*, describes teacher Lakunle who wishes to 'wed' her, as a parrot of the white man:

> You are dressed like him
> You look like him
> You speak his tongue
> You think like him
> You're just as clumsy in your foreign ways
> You'll do for him![11]

This image of fun is not unlike that of Royalson in *One Man, One Wife*, a novel by another Yoruba writer, Timothy Aluko.[12] But where Achebe does not differentiate between the educated clowns and the serious persons among the educated elite, committed to re–creating their society, Soyinka does. That is not until the publication of *Anthills of the Savannah*, if one ignores the naivety of the school girls in *Girls at War*.

Yet, in spite of such awareness on the part of Soyinka, whenever the new order encounters the old one, it is the old one which wins. Lakunle loses Sidi to the village chief. The final capitulation of the new elite takes place in *Death and the King's Horseman*. While the old order is victorious over the new elite, it must be stated that in such plays as *A Dance of the Forests* Soyinka has not written in any romantic desire for the past but rather he has composed "an elaborate attack on the gratuitous veneration of a romantic African past."[13]

The contestation in *Kongi's Harvest* is political. Kongi, the new Westminster prime minister of the country of Ismaland would like to incorporate his authority within the traditional format and so validate his hegemony. This might be because the foreign political formula does not evoke the awe of the populace as the traditional power structure does. The ritual that would make this possible is the festival of the New Yam. The Oba (king) is detained pending the time he would change his mind and hand over the ceremonial new yam to Kongi in public. When the prison camp superintendent stops the drums of the king's musicians who are allowed to keep the king company in prison, the Oba had this to say:

> Good friend, you merely stopped
> My drums. But they were silenced
> On the day when Kongi cast aside
> My props of wisdom, the day he
> Drove the old Aweri from their seats.
> What is a king without a clan
> Of elders? What will Kongi be without...
> Sarumi, what name was it again?[14]

Kongi had been undermining the old order. The final act of submission would be the receiving of the new yam from Oba Danlola. He had appropriated the mental support of the traditional ruler and renamed it 'The Reformed Aweri Fraternity' and filled it with western educated intellectuals instead of traditional elders. This body of western educated intellectuals mocks the Reformed Ogboni Fraternity that began to appear in

Yorubaland towards the end of the nineteenth century and the beginning of the twentieth century. These were secret cults based on the Ogboni tradition of authority in every Yoruba town and village. Oba Danlola sings the dirge of the times to be under this new order:

> DANLOLA (comes forward, dancing softly)
> This is the last
> Our feet shall touch together
> We thought the tune
> Obeyed us to the soul
> But the drums are newly shaped
> and stiff arms strain
> On stubborn crooks, so
> Delve with the left foot
> For ill–luck; with the left
> Again for ill–luck; once more
> With the left alone, for disaster
> Is the only certainty we know.[15]

In *The Road* we encounter the Professor who seems to be on the way to incorporating the traditional religious rituals of the Yoruba into his experience of Christianity. He had come back to the religion of his people through the failure, for him, of the church. Unfortunately, he does not convince those around him that his interest is not opportunistic, and is, therefore suspect. He fails and is killed.

Finally, in *Death and the King's Horseman* an educated Yoruba man plunges unapologetically into the rituals of Yoruba religion when his father fails to meet his responsibility to the society. Olunde, the son of the Horseman returns from England to Oyo, the capital of Yorubaland as soon as the news that the Oba had died reached him. He knew that his father would have to commit ritual suicide in order to accompany the departed king. In conversation with Jane, the wife of the District Officer, who considers Olunde a good example of the educated African, Olunde shocks her by his views of what is happening especially to his father:

> OLUNDE: Don't think it was just the war. Before that even
> started I had plenty of time to study your people.
> I saw nothing, finally, that gave you the right to pass
> judgement on other peoples and their ways. Nothing
> at all.[16]

Unlike the other plays where the representatives of the old order know their roles and know what to do, when Elesin Oba does

not fulfil his role, Olunde, in spite of the fact that he did not
know what to do, performs the outward act of suicide. It is
inconceivable that there should be no continuity in the life of the
community. It is therefore necessary that Olunde return to the
role of his family in spite of his western education. No foreign
religion could fulfil the ritual ceremonies of the community.

Looking back on these various permutations of the past and
the present, we find that in Achebe, those who stick to their old
ways fail albeit with dignity and much grandeur. Those who
abandon those old ways and try the imported western concepts
also fail but without arousing any respect for their failure. In
Soyinka, those who stick to the old ways sometimes succeed and
sometimes fail. But those who wish to combine both ways
always fail tragically.

Where does this conclusion leave the issue of creating something in the new times ushered in by the western European
encounter with Africa? I will attempt to answer this question in
some of the later chapters.

While Achebe's attitude is well known about the misrepresentation of the African past, Soyinka's seems not to have been as
well publicised. And because of the jibe at Negritude he has
even been accused by Chinweizu of not being concerned about
the issue of the African past. Soyinka's argument seems to be set
out in his Nobel Literature Prize lecture delivered in Sweden in
December 1986. Two issues are clear from this lecture. One is
that Soyinka does not lump colonialism with European misrepresentation of Africa and the African. For one thing, Arab documents are also not free of the negative representation of Africa
and the African. Such misrepresentation will not be corrected by
writing from the opposite direction, perhaps as Achebe does.
Rather, the episode of colonialism should be placed in its proper
perspective and addressed with the political and economic
instruments that alone can deal with it.

The second aspect is that Soyinka speaks generally of the misrepresentation of the 'Other' as problematic in all societies. What
is dangerous is the persistence of such misrepresentation in the
face of information refuting it. Soyinka continues by insisting
that this misrepresentation pre-dates colonialism and that it is
ingrained in the very ideas and ideals which sustain Europe. To
this end his lecture was entitled "This Past Must Address Its
Present". Looking back, as Achebe does, is like playacting and
he wants to know "When is playacting rebuked by reality?
When is fictionalising presumptuous? What happens after play-

acting?"[17] Speaking more directly to the issue of misrepresentation, he says:

> These narratives, uncluttered by impure motives that needed to mystify the plain, self–serving rush to dismantle independent societies for easy plundering, pointed accusing fingers unerringly in the direction of European savants, philosophers, scientists, and theorists of human evolution. Gobineau is a notorious name, but how many students of European thought today, even among us Africans, recall that several of the most revered names in European philosophy – Hegel, Locke, Hume, Voltaire – an endless list, were unabashed theorists of racial superiority and denigration of African history and being.[18]

There is no doubt that Soyinka's argument is sound as far as it goes. But Achebe's solution – to look back and thus empower Africans to see their own history positively no matter for how long European thinkers have had negative ideas about Africa and the African – has been more effective and has also achieved results.

Notes

1. *Myth, Literature and the African World*, "Ideology and the Social Vision" p. 91.

2. *The Trouble with Nigeria*, p. 48.

3. South Bank Lecture reprinted in *Okike* special edition on Chinua Achebe at Sixty, p. 11.

4. Chinua Achebe, *Hopes and Impediments*, Selected Essays 1965–1987. See especially the first two essays: "An Image of Africa: Racism in Conrad's *Heart of Darkness*" and "Impediments to Dialogue Between North and South" pp. 1–19.

5. Interview with Jonathan Cott quote by Ada Ugah in his book *In the Beginning... Chinua Achebe at Work* p.26. No source is provided for this interview.

6. First appeared in Chinua Achebe, *Morning Yet on Creation Day*, Essays, 1975, pp.3–18; the same essay is retained in the new publication *Hopes and Impediments*, Selected Essays 1965–87, 1988, pp.46–61.

7. *In the Beginning... Chinua Achebe at Work*, pp.28–29.

8. Robert Wren, *Achebe's World: The Historical and Cultural Context of the Novels of Chinua Achebe*.

9. ibid. p. 72.

10. Some of Professor Ayandele's epithets for them in his book *The Educated Elite in the Nigerian Society* include "deluded hybrids", "collaborators", "windsowers" who will never become new Nigerians.

11. Wole Soyinka, *Collected Plays* 2, p. 14.

12. T.M. Aluko, now in his seventies, trained as a civil engineer and published his first novel *One Man, One Wife* in Lagos through the Nigerian Printing and Publishing Co. Ltd. in 1959. This novel was reprinted in the Heinemann "African Writers Series"in 1967. His other novels, published in the "African Writers Series" are, *One Man, One Matchet* (1964), *Kinsman and Foreman* (1966), and *Chief, The Honourable Minister*, 1970. Although Aluko's novels take place in the Yoruba part of Nigeria, his characters cross ethnic national boundaries. The central character in *One Man, One Matchet*, for instance, is an Igbo newly arrived from England and appointed District Officer, a post reserved for the British until sometime in 1957 when the approach of independence made it necessary to begin to appoint Nigerian District Officers. The Yoruba among whom he works see him as a "black white man" rather than as Igbo.

13. Jeanne N. Dingome in "Soyinka's Role in Mbari", *African Theatre Journal* special issue on Wole Soyinka pp.8–14.

14. op. cit. p. 63.

15. op. cit. p. 69.

16. Wole Soyinka, *Six Plays*, p.196.

17. Henry Louis Gates Jr. *Black American Literature Forum*, Wole Soyinka Issue, Part 1, 1988, p. 431.

18. ibid. p. 437.

III
Pan-Africanism and the Nigerian Writer:

The Poems and Songs of Achebe and Soyinka

The first generation of modern African writers writing towards the end of colonial rule in Africa, wrote against the background of the pan-African movement, a blanket answer to pan-Europeanism. More than merely writing against this background, the writers also felt that it was their duty to defend Africa and the pan-African idea. Léopold Sédar Senghor, Sembène Ousmane, Camara Laye, Ayi Kwei Armah, Kofi Awoonor, Mongo Beti, Tchicaya U Tam'si, Ngugi wa Thiong'o and Es'kia Mphahlele are some of the writers from the African continent who have made the case for Africa from the point of view of pan-Africanism, while living with the reality of nation-states that are no more than geographical expressions still to acquire some personality.

The encounter of Africa with Europe, the trans-Atlantic slave trade (with nods in the direction of the Arab slave trade in Africa), the creation in the Western world of an African diaspora in North America, and the Caribbean have been their inspiration. Other large issues which have pre- occupied these writers are Europe's empire-building in Africa, European and North American colonisation and balkanisation of Africa into spheres of influence and later still into nation-states all divisions and additions which ignored Africa's pre-European contacts.

The case for African independence made on the basis of Africa's cultural validity and the humanity of Africans has also pre-occupied these writers. Léopold Sédar Senghor, born in 1906, in collaboration with the Caribbean poet and politician Aimé Cesaire, born in Martinique in 1913, founded the Negritude movement, a major arm of the pan-African idea. For Senghor,

Quite simply, negritude is the sum total of the values of the civilization of the African world.[1]

Senghor became, at the end, one of the guardians of the French language as a member of the Académie Française rather than a retriever of African culture. This example of Senghor indicates one of the two possible directions in which pan-Africanists can go: a total acceptance of Europe and things European, or a total return to the ethnic nationality and things to do with that particular ethnic nationality. Hanging out there between pan-Africanism and ethnic nationality, with no one to make a case for it, is the modern African nation-state. Little thought has been given to what its make-up should be. The writing block which has affected some writers has been caused perhaps partly as a result of their unwillingness to accept Europe and things European and their reluctance to go back to the ethnic nationality.

Sembène Ousmane, born in Senegal in 1923, began to write out of the experience of a dock worker in France. Involvement in trade unionism led him to write in what might be called socialist realism where the details of the social condition of Africans and the causes are exposed. Gradually, interest in historical causes of the African condition as well as the realisation that the masses of the people to address do not read has led Sembène Ousmane towards film-making. Film-making led to the use of Senegalese languages in his films even those based on previously published novels and short stories in French. From the generalized defence of Africa through pan- Africanism to the particular upholding of the history and cultural struggle of the peoples of Senegal against first, Moslem invaders, and then the French, has brought problems to Sembène Ousmane, the writer. Such problems are not unknown to other writers who have made the same journey as that of Sembène Ousmane. African governments, set up after the successful campaign of the pan-African struggle for African independence, have been the enemies of these writers. Sembène Ousmane has said:

I like to write and I like to film. A film obviously has more viewers than readers for a book, especially in Africa.[2]

Camara Laye, was born in Upper Guinea in 1928. While studying engineering in France, he wrote one of the most romantic memories of childhood in Africa entitled *L'enfant noir*, translated into English as *The Dark Child* in 1954 in the United States and as *The African Child*, in 1955 in Britain. With the independence of

Guinea in 1958 Camara Laye returned to Guinea and worked as an engineer. He had published his second novel *Le regard du roi* in 1954 with its English translation *Radiance of the King*, appearing in 1956. Twelve years later, Laye published *Dramouss*, his last novel. It appeared in 1958 as *A Dream of Africa*. With this book, he moved from fiction to a more direct social commentary.[3] *A Dream of Africa* is dedicated to the young of Africa and may be said to be one of the earliest examples of the African novels of disillusionment with the African governments. It includes a satire against Sekou Touré, the then President of Guinea Conakry, as 'Big Brute'. The process of the return to the ethnic nationality of the writer also includes the publication or performance of a poem, a novel or a play in this genre of disillusionment. Camara Laye's last book, before his death in exile in 1980, marks his return from the general Africa of pan-Africanism to the specific of the Malinke ethnicity. The book, *Le maître de la parole*, appeared in English, translated by the same person who had translated all his previous books, as *The Guardian of the Word* in 1981.[4] The book is the re- telling of the legend of Sundiata, already made famous by Djibril Tamsir Niane in his *Soundjata ou l'epopee mandique* published in Paris in 1960 and translated into English as *Sundiata: an Epic of Old Mali* in 1965.[5] Camara Laye's version emphasises the role of the griot, the traditional Madinke oral historian. He left Guinea Conakry for Dakar Senegal on exile where he died in 1980.

Ayi Kwei Armah was born in Takoradi, Ghana, in 1939. He studied in the United States of America and published his first novel *The Beautyful Ones Are Not Yet Born* in 1968. This novel is one of the most famous of the novels of disillusionment and both Kwame Nkrumah and Chinua Achebe have attacked it.

The Beautyful Ones Are Not Yet Born describes in what the Nigerian critic Charles Nnolim has described as pejorism – "implying that things are always moving from a better to a worse state" towards "corruption, decay, rot, decomposition;"[6]

The following is what Kwame Nkrumah wrote to June Milne on 14 April 1969 on finding an advertisement for the novel in his publication *Africa and the World*:

> I received from Rogers two copies of the April issue of *Africa and The World*. It was quite a good production. But I was disappointed with Heinemann's advert. Imagine advertising that book by Ayi Kwei Armah, *The Beautyful (sic) Ones Are Not Yet Born*. Fancy a Ghanaian writing about his own country and people in that way, and at a time like this. Rogers should have scanned through

it before accepting the advert. I have cabled him to that effect. I
hope he didn't get over-angry. All future adverts must conform
to the basic policy of the paper before they are accepted.[7]

In Chinua Achebe's essay "Africa and her Writers"[8] the following comments can be read:

> There is a brilliant Ghanaian novelist, Ayi Kwei Armah, who
> seems to me to be in grave danger of squandering his enormous
> talents and energy in pursuit of the human condition. In an
> impressive first novel, *The Beautyful Ones Are Not Yet Born*, he
> gives us a striking parable of corruption in Ghanaian society and
> of one man who refuses to be contaminated by this filth. It is a
> well-written book. Armah's command of language and imagery
> is of a very high order. But it is a sick book. Sick, not with the
> sickness of Ghana but with the sickness of the human condition.[9]

Like Camara Laye, Armah went on to publish what would
seem to be the next step in the process of the development of
those who refuse the European option – the recourse to the ethnic national option. *Two Thousand Seasons*, (Nairobi 1973;
London 1979) is a glorification of the collective performance of
the peoples of Ghana in the face of both Arab and European
invasions. *The Healers*, a historical novel of the fall to the English
imperialist, of Ashanti kingdom, was published in 1978 in
Nairobi and 1979 in London. Unlike the fantasy of *Two Thousand
Seasons* there is not much here for a positive representation of
Africa, now the main concern of pan-Africanism. Armah now
lives in Dakar Senegal and has not published a novel since the
appearance of *The Healers*. Neither the European option nor the
ethnic option seems to appeal to him. For the future, will he opt
for silence or for direct political writing and action?

Kofi Awoonor, who began to write under the name George
Awoonor-Williams, was born in Keta, Ghana, in 1935. The fact
of the change of name is important in the process which takes
the writer from the generalizations of pan-Africanism to the
specifics of the ethnic nationality. Kofi Awoonor is not alone in
this declaration of a definite African identity. The oral poetry of
the Ewe inspire and condition his poetry. His only novel, *This
Earth, My Brother* brings him into the era of the novels of disillusionment with African politicians and contemporary societies.
Writing of this novel Chinua Achebe says:

> There is a cumulativeness, indeed an organic, albeit bizarre,
> development towards the ultimate failure. But here is no existen-
> tial futility; at every stage there is a misty hint of a viable alterna-
> tive, of a road that was not taken, of a possibility that fails to

develop. The central failure is African independence, whose early promise is like the butterfly that the child Amamu caught in the fields of yellow sunflowers wide as the moon, and it flew away again.[10]

Kofi Awoonor has gone on to participate in the governance of Ghana as an ambassador to Brazil, then to Cuba and recently retired as the permanent representative of Ghana to the United Nations in New York. Is this the option for African writers – to capture the failure in beautiful images and help to make the good governance of the nation-state possible? This is definitely more positive than merely criticising politicians with little or no understanding of what problems they faced.

Mongo Beti was born in the Cameroon in 1932. He has spent most of his adult life in France and as a French citizen. All the same, the African condition as manifested by his native country has been his concern. As a result of what he has to say concerning his country, first in his publication, *Main basse sur le Cameroun*, (1972) a political study of post-independence Cameroon, and his journal *Peuples Noir/Peuples Africains*, his books have not been allowed to be circulated in Cameroon by the government of the country. *Main basse sur le Cameroon* was banned in France soon after it was published. This publication has been the inspiration for his subsequent novels such as *La ruine presque cocasse d'un polichinelle*, (1979), *Les mères de Guillaume Ismael Dzewatama Futur Camionnneur*, (1982) and *La revanche de Guillaume Ismael Dzewatama*, (1984) None of these novels have been translated into English. Mongo Beti finds himself in a unique situation where he has to fight both the government of post-independence Cameroon as well as the government of the country which colonised Cameroon, France. His energy is consumed in devising strategies to conduct this double struggle:

> I wanted to put into a novel form all the ideas I had written in essay form in *Main basse sur le Cameroun*. Why? Because in France there is a tradition of not seizing anything that is a novel, that is a work of art... [11]

Mongo Beti has had to suspend the publication of his journal for lack of funds and his attempt to return to Cameroon early 1994 was frustrated by government machinations. He went back to France.

Tchicaya U Tam'si, was born Gerald Felix Tchicaya in 1931 and went to France in 1946 where his father took up his seat as the Congo's first Deputy to the French National Assembly. His poetry has been influenced by both Aimé Césaire and Léopold Sédar Senghor. While he might have felt the need to hanker after Africa in the manner of Negritude at the beginning of his career, he seemed to have later preferred to write of

> this universe, this loneliness, sadness of man – man everywhere, whether he be black, white, yellow.[12]

This is a milder form of the European option taken by Léopold Sédar Senghor. Tchicaya U Tam'si died in France a few years ago.

Ngugi wa Thiong'o was born James Ngugi in Kenya in 1938. The most dramatic of African writers in terms of embracing the ethnic national option, his decision to stop writing in English received world-wide publicity and perhaps even acclaim as well. Ngugi's decision to change his name from James Ngugi to Ngugi wa Thiong'o is documented in Ime Ikiddeh's forward to *Homecoming: Essays on African and Caribbean Literature, Culture and Politics.* (1972)[13]

This volume of essays places Ngugi astride both the pan-African and the ethnic national options.

Whichever option an African writer takes beyond the victory of pan-Africanism and the failure of the nation-state which resulted from that victory, the European option can only mean total loss of the talent and capability of that writer to the African cause while the ethnic national option has possibilities for the future. Such possibilities do not include a romantic concept of ethnic nationality as Chinua Achebe points out at the end of his essay on Kofi Awoonor's novel:

> But of late many writers have been asking such questions: What then? What does Africa do? A return journey womb-wards to a rendezvous with golden-age innocence is clearly inadequate.[14]

The African writer must deal with the complexity of the nation-state the product of the pan-African struggle, a struggle which African intellectuals including writers supported.

Es'kia Mphahlele, being South African, presents a different side of the issue of the options for African writers after the independence of African countries. Born in Pretoria in 1919 Mphahlele published his first book, a collection of short stories entitled *Man Must Live,* in 1947.[15] He later lived in exile in Nigeria and Europe as well as the United States of America before returning to South Africa in 1977. Mphahlele touches the crucial issue which makes the South African writer "detribalized, Westernized, but still an African" somewhat different from writers from the rest of the continent in terms of the issue of pan-Africanism:

> These two ways of living, the African and the European, I think in South Africa are much more integrated than you will find outside South Africa...[16]

Mphahlele's return to a multi-ethnic, multi-lingual and multi-cultural South Africa seems to be the final choice of the African writer. That it has been easier for the South African writer to take this option has to do with the history of South Africa and the existence of an 'economous' state, by which I mean an autonomous economic structure to which all the different peoples of South Africa relate, an 'economous' state which becomes the hub of their community of sensibilities.

This term needs further explanation. The double-barrelled word *nation-state* needs to be broken down into its two constituents of *nation* and *state* to demonstrate its inadequacy. It is more realistic to speak of *nations* in order to reflect the multiplicity of languages and cultures of African countries. The state should be the new construction, the community of the various national sensibilities, the container of their economic collective effort, autonomous in its own rules and regulations administered by all for the benefit of all. This is what is meant by this term.

For someone who had realised for quite some time that "we have long exhausted the reserves built up by the early Pan-African congresses, and the need for frequent circuses has passed"[17] Mphahlele's decision to return to South Africa in 1977 must be seen now as an act of vision on his part.

Both Chinua Achebe and Wole Soyinka, in their different ways, have in their careers touched on all the options which have been spelt out by these writers.

With the achievement of independence from 1957 (Ghana) onwards, it seemed to have dawned on some of these writers that their politician-compatriots and fellow educated elites were not properly trained to bring into being the new nation-states, in spite of all their emotional investment in the programme. African writing which predicted heaven on earth the moment Africans began to run their own affairs shifted to writing which describes disillusionment, within a few years of independence. Ayi Kwei Armah's *The Beautyful Ones Are Not Yet Born* and Nkem Nwankwo's *My Mercedes is Bigger Than Yours* speak to

this era of disillusionment among many others. However justi-
fied the literary works which deal with the disappointment that
came after African independence, the writers did ignore some
difficult problems which the educated elite as leaders, as politicians, as writers and professionals faced from their former
European colonisers.

Europe had dismantled the political empire after the tragic
events of the Second World War only to set up an economic
empire which would be beyond the reach of the institutions of
an interventionist nation-state. Yet, all previous history taught
the African that these same institutions of the interventionist
nation-state were the instruments with which Europeans and
North Americans enriched themselves. For the educated elite of
Africa, all they had to do was to achieve political power and
everything, which the Europeans had, would be theirs.
Nowhere in the literature of anti-colonialism does one find the
mention of this important development and how it would affect
the impending African political independence.

Africans were going to be in government but they would not
be in power. The colonial government had been in government
as well as in power. The impact of the new arrangement was not
long in coming. African countries found that they could neither
determine the price at which they would sell their primary
products to European and North American consumers nor
could they say how much they would pay for the machinery,
medicines, aeroplanes, helicopters, handcuffs as well as consumer items and services they needed from Europe, North
America and Japan. All along, during the period before independence, the twin economic institutions of Europe and North
America, the International Monetary Fund and the World Bank
had been the advisers of these countries and they continue to
advise them today. Is there any reason why they should not
share in the blame for the failure of African countries? Of
course, the situation has not been helped by the unpunished corruption of the educated elite as well as their refusal to discipline
themselves. Whatever internal or external reasons are responsible for the retardation of African countries, few African writers
have attempted to understand the kind of pressures that African
politicians have had to bear.

Perhaps, it is as a result of the awareness of these pressures
and difficulties that African writers have begun to write more
and more from their specific ethnic national cultural backgrounds without feeling that they are betraying the aspirations

Achebe, 20th Century writer

Things fall Apart

writers such as
Va Thiong'o, have
history and social
nds. Achebe and
ent. Such a devel-
iow does Ngugi's
i is not the official
wards the commu-
irocess of bringing

;s of Achebe and

tural dimension to
ir songs celebrated
Its political ambi-
krumah's "Seek ye
be added to it"[18]
people, whose eco-
in elite against the
have survived, in

i shoot,

Bonus Bona Bonum
Boni Bone Bina
We want small Bonus
Bonus, Bo-Bonus!

Last year we say ner Flu
This year we call am Strike;
When all dem Coral[23] go,
Then Bonus, Sweet Bonus![24]

Here is a stanza of a poem entitled 'The Syrians' which was published in 1919:

> Grass he tells us we will eat,
> When with vengeance on rice did sit;
> Leaves and brooms and all he cornered,
> Farina, palm oil and kola;
> On the blood of the land.[25]

One 'poem' which seemed to have been popular among most people familiar with the struggles of pan-Africanism is the following entitled 'A Psalm 23'

> The European Merchant is my shepherd,
> And I am in want,
> He maketh me to lie down in cocoa farms;
> He leadeth me beside the waters of great need;
> He restoreth my doubt in the pool parts.
>
> Yea, though I walk in the valleys of starvation,
> I do not fear evil:
> For thou art against me.
> The general managers and profiteers frighten me.
> Thou preparest a reduction in my salary
> In the presence of my creditors.
> Thou anointest my income with taxes;
> My expense runs over my income.
> Surely unemployment and poverty will follow me
> All the days of my poor existence,
> And I will dwell in a rented house for ever![26]

Contemporary to the production of such songs and poems were the fulsome quotations from William Shakespeare in which the educated elite of the time revelled.[27]

In the meantime, songs in the local languages seemed to have been pre-occupied with a different concern from a different political attitude.

> Vikito-ria, Vikito-ria
> Aiye re l'awa nje
> O so gbogbo eru d'omo
> N'ile enia dudu.
>
> Victoria, Victoria
> What a life of ease we owe you!
> You turned all slaves into free beings.
> In the land of the black peoples.[28]

In passing, it is to be noted that Soyinka's father objects to the servility of the Yoruba to the British crown which this song indicates. Yet, it seemed to have been a view held generally, at this time, by the Yoruba about the accomplishment of the British in Yorubaland. The following comes from a Yoruba language auto-biography:

> Igba ti yipada fun gbogbo enia. Oyinbo ti o gun oke yi, yi ohun pupo pada; o yi igbesi aiye eni pupo pada; o so eru di ominira; o so olowo miran di talaka papa awon ti o je pe owo eru ni nwon se la.[29]

> (Times have changed for everybody. The ascendency of the white man has turned things around; it has turned the lives of many upside down, down side up; it has freed the slave and made the rich poor especially those who made their money from slave raid-ing and trading.)

The point can be made then that African songs and poetry begin from African imitations of hymns and biblical statements and should include the 'spontaneous' songs of protesting workers as well as the sentiments expressed about the society as a whole in the local languages. This is usually not the case with histories and accounts of African poetry.[30]

Such histories and accounts tend to begin with the imitations of classical English or French poetry. Yet, no complete under-standing of the products of African creative endeavour can be achieved without the inclusion of these aspects. In the case of Achebe and Soyinka, it is difficult to see how a proper analysis of their songs and poems can be done without an awareness of the songs and poems produced by the plight of workers in the history of the evolution of the nation-state of Nigeria and what was produced in Igbo and Yoruba.

Achebe's published poetry is centred around the civil war and the struggle of Biafra. The publication of the thirty poems in the USA edition under the title of *Christmas in Biafra and other Poems* (1973) seems to have been a deliberate attempt to keep the issue of Biafra in the public eye in spite of the fact that the war ended three years before. Recent studies of African literature has not given space to Achebe's poetry beyond the mentioning of it.[31] Achebe's poetry in Igbo has received no mention either in the treatment of his works. He has given effective performances of his poetry in Igbo and hopefully they will become available some time. The comment he makes on the influence of tradition-al Igbo poetry on his Igbo poems is important:

> The Igbo poem on Christopher Okigbo is actually structured on a traditional dirge format, the song that people sing when one of

their age-grade dies. The age-group goes around chanting. They
don't accept that he is dead yet, so that they are looking for him,
wondering whether he has gone to the stream, or to the forest. It
is a very old song, no doubt, and it's that form that I use in the
Igbo poem, expanding it and asking more questions than the traditional song would ask.[32]

Unlike Achebe's, Soyinka's songs and poetry have always constituted a major aspect of his creative work. In addition, his
expression in song and poetry have been spread over subjects
and spaces. Moreover, his songs and poems have been influenced by the struggles of African countries and peoples, the
classical songs and poems of English literature and by Yoruba
traditional ideas and forms.

The following two stanzas virtually became the Nigerian
national anthem for some television and radio stations in the
south-western part of Nigeria when the playing record of it first
appeared in 1983, a short time before the December elections of
that year:

> I love my country I no go lie
> Na inside am I go live and die
> I know my country I no go lie
> Na im and me go yap till I die
>
> I love my country I no go lie
> Na inside am I go live and die
> When e turn me so, I twist am so
> E push me, I push am, I no go go.[33]

The record is dedicated to the memory of The Great Ijemanze of
the band known as the Three Night Wizards "whose tunes the
ETIKA music was adopted"[34]

The poem 'Ujamaa' is written for Julius Nyerere, at the time
the president of Tanzania:

> Sweat is leaven, bread, Ujamaa
> Bread of the earth, by the earth
> For the earth. Earth is all people.[35]

Reference has been made earlier to Soyinka's collection of
poems entitled *Mandela's Earth and Other Poems*.[36]

Wole Soyinka's poem 'Gulliver' is an example of his deep
involvement with English literature:

> Once upon a ship-(of state)-wreck, where
> The sun had shrunk the world at last to a true
> Stature of deserving – the ant for unit –
> I lay on earth tide-flung, obtruding

> Miles of heart and mind, an alien hulk
> Into a thumb assemblage.[37]

One example of the influence of Yoruba forms of songs and poetry is the poem 'Malediction' explained as "for her who rejoiced". The poem is based on the form of *epe*, curse, and it seems to be one time when Wole Soyinka could not "suffer with 'enemy' as well as 'friend'".[38] The occasion for this poem was provided by a Yoruba woman living in Northern Nigeria during the killings unleashed on people of Igbo origin, who wrote to the then governor of the North thanking the people of the North through the governor that the targets of the murders had not been Yorubas.[39]

Ultimately, Soyinka's songs and poems leave a sense of joy and celebration in one's mind no matter what the subject matter. The plays are full of these songs and it would make sense in terms of literary analysis if they were published along with the other volumes of poetry because they – the songs and the poems – emanate from the same experiences.

Pan-African, Nigerian National and Ethnic Communal Agendas

If the Nigerian intellectual had been able to distance himself or herself from the immediacy of struggle for independence in order to provide a Nigerian alternative interpretation of the encounter between the Nigerian ethnic nationalities and the British (and consequently the Western world), perhaps the sorry condition of the Nigerian nation-state would not exist today. If the Nigerian intellectual had been bold enough to insist that the encounter between the West and Africa in Nigeria had both positive as well as negative possibilities, we would not be where we are today, still attempting to make sense of the nation-state and modernisation. If the Nigerian intellectual had been humble enough to accept that there were many ways in which the western life was qualitatively superior to the African way of life, the encounter with the West could have been the beginning of a renaissance in African life and in African re-development.

There is no doubt that much of the history of the encounter with the West is painful and humiliating for the African. Enslavement, unequal exchange, colonisation, racial disdain and continued harassment mark that history. But there are also some aspects of this encounter which Africans can in fact be proud of:

the great number of battles which African armies did win against superior western arms; the great number of African ritual objects stolen by westerners and the influence which these had on western artists and the continued existence of Africans on the African continent. Africans are in fact the only natives to have survived in large enough numbers to challenge Europeans and other settlers for the ownership of their land. The North American native, the South American native, the Canadian native, the Australian native and the New Zealand native have all been either completely displaced or else exist in ineffectual numbers compared with the European settlers in these places. Because it is the pain of African history that is more prominent, it is not surprising that the African has attempted to find compensation by valorising everything non-European.

Africans must be mature enough now to accept that while theirs was not paradise on earth, Europe did not come to them bearing the fruits of the Garden of Eden either. At the point of contact with the West, it is a fact that many African societies were near decay and stasis, whatever level of development they had achieved before this. Arab and European slave trading activities in Africa worsened the condition of Africans. The pain is made even more unbearable because Africans collaborated in this grievous material and spiritual damage to the African. Frequently these collaborators were the chiefs and princes and leaders of the Africans. As Soyinka's Chief Ogbugbu of Gbu puts it:

> When Africa was the white man's grave
> And none but fools came hither;
> I sold my subjects old or brave
> For beads and ostrich feather.[40]

The African elite learnt early in their encounter with the West to benefit materially from the encounter through the selling of their children, their brothers and sisters and their neighbours while at the same time condemning the Europeans for any act that would unite the elite with the ordinary people they were sacrificing to their new consumption style. With one hand the ruling elite collected western consumer products and with the other they joined in condemning the West for all manner of fancied evils.

Pan-Africanism provided African elites with the ideological justification for their hypocritical stand. Much has been written on the Pan-Africanist Movement and its influence on the political development of Africa. What has been little commented upon is the prominence of African-Americans and African-Caribbeans in the promotion of pan-Africanism, and also the role of African been-tos, Africans who had lived abroad, as against the virtual non-participation Africans who stayed at home and did not go to the United States of America or Europe to obtain some western education. Or, could it be that those Africans who did not travel overseas did play a role in the struggle for independence but have not been acknowledged anywhere on the continent? What do Africans who have no western education think of pan-Africanism? What role did they play in the movement? What role was there for African languages and African cultures in pan-Africanism? Why was it that pan-Africanism did not see fit that African languages had to be used to interrogate the process of the encounter with the West?

In many ways, the Africans of the Diaspora had no notion of African ways of life, spoke no African languages and so had no access to the body of ideas which must have informed the feelings of the Africans about the encounter with Europe. Most times, these Africans from the Diaspora regurgitated the attitudes of Europeans to Africans and despised the Africans for not being westernised. Africans in the Diaspora needed an instrument with which to flog their white compatriots, and like their African elite counterparts on the African continent, used the grievances of the total African population for this purpose.

In passing, it can be stated that few of the members of the Northern Nigerian political elite were apostles of pan-Africanism. Yet, when in 1964, the leadership of the African National Congress travelled through Africa, they were able to meet and receive financial help from Abubakar Tafawa Balewa, then the Prime Minister of Nigeria, while all kinds of obstacles were put in their way in their attempt to meet Kwame Nkrumah. They never met him and the excuse was that the Ghanaian president preferred the radicalism of the Pan-African Congress![41]

What were the intentions of Pan-Africanism in Africa? The most important agenda of the Pan-African Movement in Africa is the political liberation of the continent from the colonial rule of European powers. The method to be employed is the political mobilisation of the people of these African countries. The work of Kwame Nkrumah, his Convention Peoples Party and the movement for the independence of Ghana was symptomatic of

the way independence was to be won by many African countries. The political liberation of former Portuguese colonies in
Africa would be different from these French and British
colonies. Pan-Africanism's agenda was summed up in
Nkrumah's slogan:

> Seek ye first the political kingdom and all else will be added to
> it.[42]

As a slogan and a guide to action, it is apt and effective. It was
the product of the pan-African reading of the history of Europe
and North America in the last five or so hundred years. Through
political control and with the use of the coercive powers of
army, police, secret intelligence and other resources available to
all governments, Western Europe amassed to itself enormous
wealth from other peoples of the world, making itself powerful
in the process. The mineral wealth of South America, Africa and
Asia went into the coffers of western European countries
because these countries had the political power to steal such
wealth. Pan-Africanism read that history to the effect that if
Africa is to be as wealthy and as powerful as Western Europe
and North America, it must use political power the way
Western Europe had used it. Then Africa would have everything that Europe had. It is important to keep in mind the fact
that most non-European peoples consciously contemplating
modernisation in the way of the material consumer surplus of
Western Europe feared that such material wealth would make
Europeans of them. Even the Japanese, who have now perfected
the art of beating Europe at its material acquisition with the
hope of keeping their culture have had to accept defeat.
Professor Junzo Kawada says:

> As I have already stated, since the epoch of Westernization, the
> Japanese intellectuals opposed the *wakon* or 'Japanese spirit', to
> *yosai*, or 'Western learning' and the harmonious combination of
> these two had been thought to be desirable. But the Second
> World War was a severe trial. The war itself was led by a fanatic
> ultra-nationalistic ideology and during the war, the *wakon*, being
> stripped of all its garments of foreign origin, regressed in one
> leap to the period prior to the systematic introduction of Chinese
> civilization during the eighth century. Obviously, it is quite
> absurd to remove all elements of external origin in an attempt to
> seek an original Japanese culture, as human beings did not origi-
> nate in the Japanese islands. The surrender of Japan in the Second
> World War symbolized the defeat of *wakon* or 'Japanese spirit'
> combined with a hastily copied *yosai* or 'Western learning'. The

Japanese no longer had this slogan to encourage their cultural identity. But although the post-war Japanese had lost the slogan , in reality, in their efforts to reconstruct Japan, we can still find them making efficient use of these Japanistic values.[43]

So, speaking of the period soon after the Second World War, when the success of Japan was still decades away, it was not unusual for the intellectuals of Africa to inveigh against Europe and things European and call for the return of the African to things and ways African rather than allowing himself to be corrupted by the West.

Nkrumah's slogan showed an awareness of the behaviour of Western Europe in the past but it did not attempt to understand how Western Europe would behave in the future. It took for granted that Western Europe would not use other means to retrieve the political and economic power it was giving up in conceding independence to the colonies. With the benefit of hindsight it can be seen now that two processes were taking place and the Africans who were struggling for their independence should have taken note of both, not just one of them. The first process was that of decolonisation. The logic of capitalist advancement did not allow for the existence of colonies directly politically controlled by Western Europe. Times had changed and it had become necessary to uphold and even claim to defend the political rights of native peoples. As for upholding their economic rights, that was another issue altogether!

The other historical process taking place was the putting in place of multi-national and trans-national companies. As the western world dismantled their colonial empires, they were putting together an economic empire beyond the reach of political power. The experience of Ghana is relevant. Soon after Ghana became independent, the price of cocoa, the single source of most of Ghana's foreign revenue went down in the international market. Such has been the experience of every African country – getting less for what they sell to the West and paying more for what they buy from the West. They did find their political kingdom but not much was added unto them.

Literary production formed part of the struggle for the liberation of Africans. Aimé Césaire's *Return to My Native Land* is one of the most eloquent of this genre. Achebe's *Things Fall Apart* is another classic of this genre. The success of these works is based on their general appeal to a pan-African audience, an audience spread over the continents of the world.

Soyinka's initial response to this genre is well known through the already quoted Negritude–Tigritude quip. The point is that Soyinka had gone round to embrace the demand that African intellectuals help through their writing to retrieve the African past out of the denigrating arms of Western European scholars.

As pan-African sentiments failed to come to grips with the social and economic problems of African countries, African writers began to produce another genre, the literature of disillusionment.

While the literature of disillusionment concentrates on the failure of individual countries to carry through the agenda of pan-Africanism and realise the dream of having everything added unto them, it ignored the political and economic problems which occasioned the social problems that Africans were having to cope with. This is also the reason why novels such as *A Man of the People* and *The Interpreters* can make their point against the political elite without touching the core issues which made it impossible for the political leadership to provide the environment within which the talent of the group of interpreters was to come forth and bloom. The reason generally given for the continued failure of Africans to realise their pan-African dream is Western European colonisation, imperialism, racism, exploitation, anything but the reality of Africans attempting to modernise without paying attention to some specific aspects of the history and culture of Africa. The educated elite could not be specific because they had, through their pan-African ideology, generalised Africa.

It was left to revolutionaries such as Amilcar Cabral to point out the cultural specifics that should engage the attention of Africans. The important question was: what culture was to be retrieved? No two African cultures were at the same level of development. Different African cultures reacted to European presence differently as has been shown in the case of Nigeria. What then constituted African culture needing to be retrieved? Pan-Africanism did not make the distinction which Cabral was to make later:

> A people who free themselves from foreign domination will not be culturally free unless, without underestimating the importance of positive contributions from the oppressor's culture and other cultures, they return to the upward paths of their own culture.[44]

The problem was contained in the contradiction between the unanimity which pan-Africanism presented in its confrontation with European culture, European civilisation, European religion, European history, European values and the diversity and variety of African cultures. To every issue or topic or concept which the epithet 'European' could be attached, pan-Africanists felt it their duty to oppose an African counterpart. Yet, African cultures had not had the same space and the same length of time as the cultures of Europe to identify and take over contributions from their different peoples.

When we come to deal with the agenda of the new nation-states, we find some similarities as well as contradictions when compared with the pan-African agenda. The arbitrary nature of the boundaries determined for African peoples at the Berlin Conference of 1884–5 and confirmed by the Organisation of African Unity charter of 1963–4 has been the subject of many studies.

These boundaries corralled different ethnic nationalities into new nation states which had hardly got used to being called Yoruba before they are called Africans by the newly arriving Europeans who hardly recognised the differences between them and now they were to be called Nigerians. The Nigerian national agenda consisted of national unity, economic viability and development and the creation of social satisfaction.

National unity dreamed of having many people, one destiny, and one God and also one language. This aspiration ignored the reality of the composition of the Nigerian state and pushed ahead with the European concept of the nation-state. Along with the aspiration towards national unity was also the issue of cultural retrieval. Whose culture would be retrieved to represent the culture of the new nation state? To continue with the Yoruba example, Yoruba cultural practices and ideas have survived in parts of the Diaspora such as Brazil, Cuba, Trinidad and Tobago. A Yoruba modern nation-state would need to take cognizance of the residue of its culture overseas. A Nigerian nation that was serious about the cultures of its component members at home and in the Diaspora would also have had a cultural policy that gave this aspect some kind of recognition. This was not the case.

As for the economic agenda of the country, its failure demonstrates the weakness of the Nkrumah slogan. In the pursuit of the things to be added to political power, some African countries adopted what they called western type capitalism while others adopted what they thought to be socialism. All African economies ended at the door of the International Monetary Fund and the World Bank to be re-structured and adjusted to the detriment of the peoples of these countries.

In the cultural aspect of the national agenda, there was hardly
a departure from the pan-African prescription; anti-imperialism
and anti-colonialism, anti-oppression and anti-exploitation are
transformed into anti-Europe and anti-white and anti-anything
that has to do with whatever positive contribution European
culture could have made to African specific cultures.

In many ways, ethnic agendas contradict both pan-African as
well as nation-state agendas. Yet, the source of expression of
some of the general agendas of pan-Africanism is the ethnic cultural dynamics. When Achebe atttempts to retrieve the past of
the African for the African, it is through the medium of Igbo history and Igbo culture that he successfully does this. When
Soyinka proposes an alternative to Aristotelian tragedy in the
name of Africa, it is through Yoruba theatre history and theatre
practice that he does this. Thus, the base of both pan-African
and nation-state cultural agendas is the ethnic national cultural
agenda. Yet, it is this ethnic base that is so casually criminalized
by pan-Africanism.

Outside of cultural issues, political and economic competition
between the ethnic nationalities have been the cause of social
instability. It is the failure to convert the cultural positives of
these ethnic nationalities towards the resolution of these social,
economic and political problems that damns the educated elite
of the African countries. The greatest achievement of our writers
has been the ability to translate their ethnic cultural specifics
into the generalities of pan-Africanism. Their greatest failure is
the inability to use those cultural specifics for the creation of a
community of sensibilities in a new Nigerian nation-state.

Notes

1. John Reed and Clive Wake, eds. *Senghor: Prose and Poetry*,
London,1965, re-issued 1976. p. 99.

2. Sembène Ousmane, 'Denoncer la nouvelle bourgeoisie' *Afrique-
Asie*, no. 79, 24 March 1975, p. 64, as quoted in *A Reader's Guide to
African Literature*, Hans Zell, Carol Bundy & Virginia Coulon, eds.,
1983. p. 459

3. quoted by *A New Reader's Guide to African Literature*, from A.C.
Brench, p. 405.

4. Camara Laye, *The Guardian of the Word*, (translated from the
French by James Kirkup) Glasgow: Fontana/Collins, 1981.

5. D.T. Niane, *Sundiata, An Epic of Old Mali*, (translated from the
French by G.D. Pickett) London: Longman, 1965.

6. Charles E. Nnolim "Dialectic as From: Pejorism in the Novels of Armah" in *African Literature Today* no. 10, 1979, pp. 207 – 223.

7. *Kwame Nkrumah – The Conakry Years: His Life and Letters* compiled by June Milne, p.303.

8. Chinua Achebe, *Morning Yet on Creation Day*, pp. 19 – 29

9. ibid. p. 25

10. See "Kofi Awoonor as a Novelist" in *Chinua Achebe, Hopes and Impediments – Selected Essays 1965 – 87*, p. 83.

11. 'Entretien avec Mongo Beti' *Peuples Noir/Peuples Africains*, no. 10, July – Aug., 1979, p. 105, quoted in *A New Reader's Guide to African Literature*, p. 364.

12. Tchicaya U Tam'si interviewed by Edris Makward during the African Studies Association Conference held in Montreal, October 1969, *Cultural Events in Africa*, no. 60, 1969, pp. ii, iii, iv as quoted in *A New Reader's Guide to African Literature*, p. 504

13. "I am not a man of the Church. I am not even a Christian." Those were the stunning words with which James Ngugi opened his talk to the Fifth General Assembly of the Presbyterian Church of East Africa in Nairobi in March 1970, reproduced in the collection as *Church, Culture and Politics*. He had hardly ended his address when a wry old man visibly choking with anger leapt to the floor, and, shaking his walking-stick menacingly towards the front, warned the speaker to seek immediate repentance in prayer. The old man did not forget to add as a reminder that in spite of his shameless denial or his blasphemy, the speaker *was* a Christian, and the evidence was his first name. Ngugi had never given serious thought to this contradiction. p. xii.

14. op. cit. Chinua Achebe, p. 86.

15. By African Bookman of Cape Town in *A New Reader's Guide to African Literature*, p. 419.

16. ibid. p. 420.

17. Es'kia Mphahlele, *The African Image*, p. 122.

18. David Rooney, *Kwame Nkrumah – The Political Kingdom in the Third World*, p. 43.

19. Refers to Kaiser Wilhelm of Imperial Germany.

20. Refers to Viscount Milner, Secretary of State for the Colonies.

21. Barker was the Acting General Manager of Sierra Leone Railway whose workers went on strike over the bonus question.

22. R.A. Maude, Attorney-General of the Sierra Leone Government.

23. The Lebanese traders are called 'corals' along the West African coast because of the coral beads and other cheap articles they used to hawk around the streets and markets when they first appeared as petty traders.

24. This was known as "The Bonus Song" and was sung during the Great Strike and Peace Celebration, July 18th to 22nd 1919. The song and the above notes are from J. Ayodele Langley, *Pan-Africanism and Nationalism in West Africa 1900 – 1945*, pp. 211–212.

25. *Sierra Leone Weekly News*, Freetown, 13th .September 1919.

26. From WASU (*West African Students Union*, a publication by and for West African students in London) in which this 'poem' appeared with the following Editor's note: "This psalm was written by a Gold Coast (now Ghana) soldier on active service and was passed by the military censor No. 4212. It is being reprinted as it appeared in *The African Morning Post*, in Accra on Saturday, September 2nd, 1944". This information is from J. Ayo Langley, *Ideologies of Liberation in Black Africa 1856 – 1970 Documents of Modern African Political Thought from Colonial Times to the Present*. pp. 415–416.

27. ibid. p. 299 where the speaker, Rev. Ndabaningi Sithole, (1920 –) quotes from *The Tempest*; and p. 434 where another speaker, S.R.B. Attoh Ahuma, quotes from Othello.

28. Wole Soyinka, *Isara – A Voyage Around Essay*, p. 108. Wole Soyinka's translation.

29. Oloye I.O. Delano, *L'Ojo Ojo Un*, p. 20. See Bibliography for the works of Oloye Delano.

30. See, for instance, in the most recent publication on African literatures the accounts on poetry in Oyekan Owomoyela (ed.) *A History of Twentieth Century African Literatures*, 1993, chapters 4, English-Language poetry, and 7, French-Language poetry.

31. Owomoyela's *A History of Twentieth Century African Literatures*, referred to above, says nothing about Achebe's poetry.

32. Jane Wilkinson, *Talking With African Writers*, pp. 49–50.

33. On the back of the sleeve of the record "Unlimited Liability Company" with Music and Lyrics by Wole Soyinka.

34. Front of sleeve of "Unlimited Liability Company".

35. Wole Soyinka, *A Shuttle in the Crypt*, p. 80.

36. More is said about this collection of poems in chapter viii.

37. Wole Soyinka, *A Shuttle in the Crypt*, p. 23.

38. Eldred Durosimi Jones, *The Writing of Wole Soyinka*, Revised Edition, p. 159.

39. Wole Soyinka, *Idanre and Other Poems*, p. 55.

40. Wole Soyinka, *Before the Black Out*, p. 6.

41. See Kole Omotoso, *Season of Migration to the South*, pp. 70–1. This narration comes together through personal interviews with John La Rose of London and Port of Spain Trinidad, and President Nelson Mandela and Joe Mathews of South Africa.

42. According to David Rooney's *Kwame Nkrumah: The Political Kingdom in the Third World*, this slogan was first popularized by the Accra Evening News, p.43.

43. Kawada, Junzo, "Development and Culture – Is Japan a Model?" in *Development and Culture*, 1988, p. 58.

44. Amilcar Cabral, *Unity and Struggle*, p. 143.

IV

Achebe, Soyinka and the Gods and Goddesses of their Ancestors

Both Chinua Achebe and Wole Soyinka have always been aware of the central position of the Christian religion in the undermining of Africa and the African. Western European empire builders, Western European missionaries working in Africa and converting Africans, and Western European anthropologists ensured that they undermined the African way of life by condemning the polytheism and the paganism of Africans. Everywhere these people went they fought with unnatural enthusiasm to destroy the so–called idols of the Africans. Nothing was spared, not money, not even lives, to convince the Africans that they were wrong in worshipping idols. As if their efforts were not enough, they brought in returning African–freed slaves to preach to their kith and kin. Such returnees as Bishop Ajayi Crowther and his descendants in the service of the Church Missionary Society are representative of these African missionaries. To hear the message of the Christian God from one's own brother's mouth must have had its effects.

Everywhere in the Yoruba country and in Igboland carvings and other symbols of traditional religion were either burnt or looted and taken to Europe and North America to be sold as works of art. After the British attack on Benin in 1897, more than a thousand items of ritual objects were stolen from the palace of the Oba of Benin, including the ivory carving of a Benin princess which was the symbol of the Festival of Black and African Arts and Culture which took place in Lagos in 1977.

Given this situation of the African religion it is not surprising that writers determined from the beginning to help Africa and Africans to retrieve their glorious past and show genuine interest in the religion of their peoples. Unfortunately, the education and upbringing of these young future writers did not include

traditional religion. Worse still, they were positively prevented
from getting to know this religion at first hand. The narrator of
Chinua Achebe's *Anthills of the Savannah* has this to say about
one of the major characters of the novel:

> Beatrice Nwanyibuife did not know these traditions and legends
> of her people because they played but little part in her upbring-
> ing. She was born as we have seen into a world apart; was bap-
> tized and sent to schools which made much about the English
> and the Jews and the Hindu and practically everybody else but
> hardly put in a word for her forebears and the divinities with
> whom they had evolved. So she came to barely knowing who she
> was.[1]

In spite of the fact that so much has been written about Chinua
Achebe and his works little has been written about his use of
Igbo traditional religion, his understanding of it, and his wish to
do something about giving the beliefs of his people the recognition and the respect they deserve. He has commented on this
neglect in the only essay to date that he has written on the issue
of belief among the Igbo:

> Without an understanding of the nature of *chi* one could not
> begin to make sense of the Igbo world– view; and yet no study of
> it exists that could even be called preliminary. What I am
> attempting here is not to fill that gap but to draw attention to it in
> a manner appropriate to one whose primary love is literature and
> not religion, philosophy or linguistics. I will not even touch upon
> such tantalising speculations as what happens to a person's *chi*
> when the person dies, and its shrine is destroyed.[2]

In dealing with the issue of religion and religious belief
among the Igbo, this chapter relies heavily on this one essay of
Achebe's and on references to religious belief in *Anthills of the
Savannah*. Achebe insists, early in this essay, that those interested in studying the beliefs of the Igbo must do it according to the
dictates of the Igbo:

> Since Igbo people did not construct a rigid and closely argued
> system of thought to explain the universe and the place of man in
> it, preferring the metaphor of myth and poetry, anyone seeking
> an insight into their world must seek it along their own way.

> Some of these ways are folk–tales, proverbs, proper names, ritu-
> als and festivals.[3]

Achebe then goes on to emphasise the central position of duality
in Igbo thought. He says:

> Wherever something stands, something else will stand beside it.
> Nothing is absolute.
>
> *I am the truth, the way and the life* would be called blasphemous or
> simply absurd for is it not well known that a man may worship
> Ogwugwu to perfection and yet be killed by Udo?[4]

This duality is seen clearly in the idea that a person's *chi* is the
person's double and lives in the world of the spirits while the
person lives in the world of the living. Achebe ends the essay
with the following statement:

> And finally, at the root of it all lies that very belief we have
> already seen: a belief in the fundamental worth and indepen-
> dence of every man and of his right to speak on matters of con-
> cern to him and, flowing from it, a rejection of any form of abso-
> lutism which might endanger those values.[5]

An important aspect of the position of gods and goddesses
among the Igbo is that they are created and they are also
destroyed according to the will of the people. Molly Mahood
quotes an Igbo proverb: "If a god becomes perky, we will show
him what wood he is carved from."[6] She also quotes the fate of
the deity of the people of Aninta as mentioned in *Arrow of God*
when that deity failed the people. "Did they not carry him to the
boundary between them and their neighbours and set fire on
him?"[7]

Molly Mahood quotes from one of her informers,
B.I. Chukwukere, who has written on gods in Igbo society:

> A village group possesses a guardian deity in the same way that
> each village, each family and individual has one. Therefore one
> would assume that Igbo religion postulates a pantheon of gods.
> The paradox of this phenomenon, however, is that there is no
> hierarchical ordering of the pantheon in the "action sphere" of
> Igbo people's relationship with these gods and other spiritual
> beings. Here the semblance of religious unity implicit in the fact
> of a common village–group guardian deity forcefully, as it were,
> gives way to an atomistic 'organisation' of gods, each manipulat-
> ing its relationship with Igbo mortal beings in order to secure
> more power and influence in the very same way that the latter
> themselves manipulate their own social relationships for material
> and spiritual benefits.[8]

One central issue raised by this lack of a hierarchy, of an ordinal
organisation of society both of the gods and of human beings, is
this: to whom or to what is the Igbo man or woman finally and
ultimately answerable? Who or what sanctions the body of

ideas, formulas and codes by which relationships are regulated between men and men, and between women and women and between men and women? And finally, between human beings and their makers?

If these issues are so rudimentary among the Igbo, on what basis then can a depiction of this society be generalized into being valid for the rest of Africa?

Wole Soyinka, in commenting on Chinua Achebe's hero in *Arrow of God* makes the statement which other critics outside of the Nigerian cultural milieu have termed 'controversial' without saying why it is so.[9] Soyinka makes the point that because Achebe situates the conflict between Ezeulu and Winterbottom on a secular basis rather than on a moral and consequently a religious basis, Ezeulu was bound to lose the contest. Says Soyinka:

> Can we really, from the presentation so far of Ulu and his priest, read Ezeulu's mind and understand him as saying 'I cannot serve God and Man?' It does not appear so. All that has preceded this confrontation negates such an interpretation... Achebe, deliberately or not, avoids any spiritual dimensions in the priest's experience of exile.[10]

After reading what Achebe and other Igbo intellectuals have to say about religion among their people, it is clear that Soyinka is asking Achebe to do what religion among the Igbo does not prepare Achebe to do: which is that he should place the priest of Ulu in a morally superior position to the administrative triteness of a Winterbottom. Soyinka is assessing the action of the priest not from the point of view of religion among the Igbo but from the point of view of religion among the Yoruba, a point of view which Soyinka takes in his own writing, especially in *Death and the King's Horseman*. Here Soyinka portrays the British colonial officer and his wife as people incapable of understanding the mysteries of the ritual that the Horseman was being asked to perform.

To go back to an earlier issue raised, Igbo intellectuals do make much of their people's republican institutions and political praxis. But research that has been done does not indicate that there existed a centralized constitution which becomes the point of reference for all and sundry. If God resides in everyman, to whom does everyman owe the final accounting?

Perhaps this is also the occasion to deal with Achebe's much loved quote from the work of Cheikh Hamidou Kane whom he calls a Moslem writer. Referring to *Ambiguous Adventure*, Achebe contrasts Kane's conscious depiction of African contestation of European intrusion into their space with Joseph Conrad's assumption that the forest was empty of human beings and without human existence in his *Heart of Darkness*. But Hamidou Kane does more than merely present the human presence of the Diallobe authorities. He does what Soyinka had asked Achebe to do in terms of the contestation with Winterbottom: place the issue at the moral level. While Achebe's Ezeulu sends his son to go to the white man's school to bring back to him whatever material gain was available, Hamidou Kane tells the son of the Diallobe to "go to learn from them the art of conquering without being in the right."[11]

In proceding to what Wole Soyinka has made of the religion of the Yoruba, we are on firmer ground. In Achebe's essay already quoted, he makes the point that

> In Yoruba cosmology the Supreme God, Olodumare (one of whose titles is, incidentally, Owner of the Sun) sent the god Obatala, on a mission of creation of man. The Igbo are not so specific about Chukwu's role in the creation of man, ...[12]

With a different religious inheritance, Wole Soyinka has been able to do more in the process of retrieving the moral instruments with which to propose new African possibilities through the medium of African deities. When the British occupation of Yorubaland became a fact, the compromise of the Yoruba educated elite was phrased in the following terms:

> With the establishment of the British Protectorate over Yorubaland a new era dawned upon the country. It marked the close of the fourth and the beginning of the fifth period. What the distinguishing feature of this new era will be, and how long it will last, are questions which only the future can answer. When we have allowed for the difficulties of a transition stage, the advantages that must of necessity arise by the application of rules and ideas of a highly civilized people to one of another race, degree of civilization, and of different ideas, we should hope the result will be a distinct gain to the country. But that peace should reign universally, with prosperity and advancement, and that the disjointed units should all be once more welded into one under one head from the Niger to the coast as in the happy days of Abiodun, so dear to our fathers, that clannish spirit disappear, and above all that Christianity should be the principal religion in the land paganism and Mohammedanism having had their full trial – should be the wish of every true son of Yoruba.[13]

This quote recognises the superiority of the civilization of the British compared with that of the Yoruba. It also shows that the Yoruba educated elite expect to benefit from the British conquest,and that the Yoruba expect to abandon their traditional religion for the religion of their conquerors. All these differ from the Igbo attitude to the presence of the British among them. In the circumstance the Yoruba writer would hardly speak in terms of a culture clash as has been the case among Igbo writers. The encounter with the British and the Europeans is already slotted into the march of the history of the Yoruba and there an end. Witness Wole Soyinka's disclaimer in the author's note to *Death and the King's Horseman*:

> This play is based on events which took place in Oyo, ancient Yoruba city of Nigeria, in 1946. That year, the lives of Elesin (Olori Elesin), his son, and the Colonial District Officer intertwined with the disastrous result set out in the play... The factual account still exists in the archives of the British Colonial Administration... The bane of themes of this genre is that they are no sooner employed creatively than they acquire the facile tag of 'clash of cultures', a prejudicial label which, quite apart from its frequent misapplication, presupposes a potential equality *in every given situation* of the alien culture and the indigenous, on the actual soil of the latter. (In the area of misapplication, the overseas prize for illiteracy and mental conditioning undoubtedly goes to the blurb writer for the American edition of my novel *Season of Anomy* who unblushingly declares that this work portrays the 'clash between old values and new ways, between methods and African traditions!'). It is thanks to this kind of perverse mentality that I find it necessary to caution the would–be producer of this play against a sadly familiar reductionist tendency, and to direct his vision instead to the far more difficult and risky task of eliciting the play's threnodic essence. One of the more obvious alternative structures of the play would be to make the District Officer the victim of a cruel dilemma. This is not to my taste and it is not by chance that I have avoided dialogue or situation which would encourage this. No attempt should be made in production to suggest it. The Colonial Factor is an incident, a catalytic incident merely. The confrontation in the play is largely metaphysical, contained in the human vehicle which is Elesin and the universe of the Yoruba mind – the world of the living, the dead and the unborn, and the numinous passage which links all; transition.[14]

Soyinka makes the above statement against a history and a projection which already created space in its own self–awareness for the consciousness of the new conquerors. That awareness of the new situation is conditioned by the religious past of the Yoruba.

The major source for this religious past is the poetry of the Ifa corpus, the complex system of divination which developed among the ancient Yoruba. The Ifa corpus has been compared to the Bible and the Koran, to any of the bodies of sacred knowledge revealed to the initiated of the race. Within its poems and verses are contained the cumulative historical, geographical as well as other forms of knowledge which the Yoruba have acquired in the course of their existence and in their encounters with other cultures.

One of the interesting incidents in Yorubaland during the nineteenth century must be the encounters between the Yoruba *babalawo* on the one hand and the Christian missionary on the other. Sometimes these encounters were also complicated by the presence of the Moslem Imam. From the various records which exist in the archives of the Church Missionary Society in London, it can be seen that these encounters were debates between representatives of these different religions.

John Peel of the School of Oriental and African Studies in London has done research in this area and published some of his findings.[15] The missionaries distinguished the Ifa priest from the common run of fetish priests who deceived the people. They argued with them and attempted to convince them to change from their Ifa cult and become Christians. On their side, the *babalawo* were curious about what Christianity meant. This is what Reverend Townsend, a missionary in Abeokuta, had to say:

> Two priests of Ifah came to me with this question: What does the Law of God command? They have attended our services several times and appear much interested in what they heard... I read to them the Ten Commandments making a few explanatory remarks.[16]

The challenge which confronted Ifa from these two world religions, Christianity and Islam, was to purge itself of the charge of idolatry from these religions and then to take over their ideas. Peel believes that the way the Yoruba dealt with Islam was a pointer to the way they would wish to deal with Christianity once they had overcome their initial surprise. Islam among the Yoruba is unique compared to its existence in other parts of the world where it took root. Islam is supposed to be both a religion and a political system in all other places. Among the Yoruba

only the religious aspect survives while the political aspect suc-
cumbed to the Yoruba political practice. Outside of Ilorin which
the Sokoto Caliphate took from the Yoruba during their jihad
into Yorubaland in the late eighteenth century, Islam did not
make any inroad into the political ideas of the Yoruba. On the
other hand, the Yoruba traditional religious terminology got
into the Yoruba practice of Islam. More than this, the Ifa corpus
produced its own explanation of the origin of Islam!

After the initial enthusiasm of the Yoruba for Christianity,
there followed a cooling off period. This was especially so when
the discovery of quinine as cure for malaria fever made it possible for whites to live for longer periods in West Africa and led to
white men being made to replace Africans in the service of the
churches that had been established. The Yoruba educated elite
accused the missionaries of hypocrisy and they began to found
their own African churches.

Knowledge of other non-monotheistic religions such as
Shintoism and Buddhism also encouraged some traditional
priests to work towards founding a new Ifa church. The moder-
ation which this movement brought made it possible for the
Yoruba society to now insist on practising Christianity without
giving up the veneration they had for their own religion especially the knowledge which was contained in the Ifa corpus.

Wole Soyinka was at the head of a movement at the
University of Ife in the late 1970s and early 1980s to build a
place of communion with the Yoruba deities, a place to be
known as *Orile Orisa*. In the process he rendered some of the
messages of the Ifa Divination into English. One example will
suffice:

> Obatala fulfils. Purity, love, transparency of heart. Stoical
> strength. Luminous truth. Man is imperfect; man strives towards
> perfection. Yet even the imperfect may find interior harmony
> with Nature. Spirit overcomes blemish – be it of mind or body.
> Oh, peace that giveth understanding, possess our human heart.[17]

When Wole Soyinka writes or speaks in defence of African religion, then, he does so against the background of one African
religion which has had the daring to take on both Islam and
Christianity. He writes from a body of knowledge which is veri-
fiable in the Ifa corpus, a system of divination which has given
rise to many publications by both western and African anthropologists.

Soyinka, like Achebe, has attacked the dogmatic claims made on behalf of Islam and Christianity by their devotees. He says:

> I seize every occasion to call attention to the resilience and vibrancy of these religions... Their validity remains unchanged and, they repeat a necessary warning against unrepentant in this stubborn reiteration of the nothingness credo against African spirituality. Let those who wish to retain or elevate religion as a twenty–first century project feel free to do so, but let it not be done as continuation of the game of denigration against African spiritual heritage.[18]

From the foregoing, if anyone was to carry out what Achebe considers the first duty of the African writer, which is to show that

> African people did not hear of culture for the first time from Europeans; that their societies were not mindless but frequently had a philosophy of great depth and value and beauty, that they had poetry and, above all, they had dignity.[19]

That writer had to be Wole Soyinka. He was born into a culture of celebration, public and private, a culture of dance and song in such a variety it could be bewildering. But also he had been born into a culture that had always made a virtue of taking from others what it thought useful for its continued self–expression and survival.

Notes

1. *Anthills of the Savannah*, p. 105.
2. *Morning Yet on Creation Day*, p. 93.
3. ibid. p. 94.
4. ibid. p. 94.
5. ibid. p. 103.
6. C.L. Innes and Bernth Lindfors, eds. *Critical Perspectives on Chinua Achebe*, p. 183.
7. *Arrow of God*, p. 33.
8. *Critical Perspectives of Chinua Achebe*, p. 183.
9. Simon Gikandi's *Reading Chinua Achebe*, p. 54.
10. *Myth, Literature and the African World*, p. 94.
11. *Ambiguous Adventure*, 1972 edition, p. 37.
12. *Morning Yet on Creation Day*, p. 99.
13. Johnson, Reverend Samuel, *The History of the Yorubas – From the Earliest Times to the Beginning of the British Protectorate*, London: Church Missionary Society, 1921. pp. 641–642.
14. Soyinka, *Six Plays*, pp. 144–145.

15. Peel, John, "The Pastor and the Babalawo: The Interaction of Religions in Nineteenth Century Yorubaland" *Africa* vol.6, no.3, 1990, pp.338–368.

16. *Africa* p.346 quoting W. Townsend Journal to 25 June 1847.

17. *The Credo of Being and Nothingness*, p.33.

18. *The Credo of Being and Nothingness*, pp.16–17.

19. *Morning Yet on Creation Day*, p.45.

V
Towards a Community of Sensibilities

In his article for the London *Guardian* series entitled 'Writing Home' in which various writers from different parts of the world write about literature and their countries, Chinua Achebe says:

> Our 1960 national anthem, given to us as a parting gift by a British housewife in England, who had called Nigeria 'our sovereign motherland'. The current anthem, put together by a committee of Nigerian intellectuals and actually worse than the first one, invokes the father image. But it has occurred to me that Nigeria is neither my mother nor my father. Nigeria is a child. Gifted, enormously talented, prodigiously endowed, and wayward.[1]

It is easy to see, against the background of this statement that the contemporary multi–ethnic, multi–lingual and multi–cultural African nation–state has no existing example to follow. For three decades the example of the Soviet Union of Socialist States as well as Yugoslavia were attractive models for many African political and intellectual leaders such as Kwame Nkrumah and Sekou Touré. Unfortunately these nation–states did not create

> major central institutions, government, law, learning, religion and literature – which lead to the emergence of a reasonably common language among men drawn from various parts of the region to take part in these central activities.[2]

Thus by the time the Soviet Union and the Yugoslavia federation broke up into their various ethnic nationalities and sectional concerns, the failure of the African nation-state had become obvious. Most governments had been unstable owing to ethnic competitions for political power and economic advantages. Laws had been outlawed because of corruption and there was no learning to be had in the educational institutions whose infrastructure had decayed. The failure of the nation-state to be responsible for all its citizens led individuals to seek protection under the still surviving ethnic structures of their particular nationalities. Labelling the 'struggle' against British imperialism as 'nationalist' needs to be questioned. The basis for the struggle in Nigeria was not one Nigerian nation. Rather, the 'struggle' was waged on the basis of liberal ideals of self-determination, freedom of organisation and the scrambled pan-African ideals of anti-racism, and anti-imperialism. At no time during the 'struggle' was any serious thought given to the idea and the nature of the Nigeria to be established.

The succession of dictatorships – civilian or military, malevolent or benevolent, competent or incompetent – made it impossible to discuss the concepts which should underlie the new nation. It is only recently through national conferences taking place in different parts of the continent that serious thought is now being given to the idea of the nation in its multi-ethnicity, multi-lingualism and multi–culturalism. The failure of the nation-state is best demonstrated in the failure of the countries of Africa to produce a middle class cutting across ethnic and language boundaries. The struggle for independence against British imperialism had co-opted the struggle of the workers for a decent wage. Sometimes, the struggle had even been predicated on the fate of the workers. But independence was handed over to the educated elite in the words of Nnamdi Azikiwe, the first Nigerian President and Head of State "on a platter of gold". After independence the plight of the workers was forgotten by the educated elite. Nothing was done about the rural population. Corruption destroyed the meagre infrastructure that the British left behind. Within six years Nigeria was engaged in a civil war for its survival.

Assuming that there was in fact a nation-state in existence in Nigeria, writers – especially Chinua Achebe and Wole Soyinka – lambasted their fellow members of the elite, to the amusement of the international community, for their failure to provide good leadership. In the meantime the political arm of the elite which had 'fought' and won the war for independence saw the narration of the 'struggle' as sufficient achievement in its own right.[3] There had been little else to show for the struggle for independence.

The intellectual elite on the other hand, including the writers, tried to write on the existing situation without adequately confronting the issue of ethnic rivalries in the country. From the experience of other formerly oppressed nations such as Ireland and Egypt, the past before the imposition of colonisation and the future of imagined freedom always play important roles in rallying the people for collective action against the coloniser. In the case of Nigeria, there was no shared past. Each of the ethnic nationalities which made up the new nation-state of Nigeria were 'pacified' by the British at different times in the past. They were at different levels of collective development. Treaties and agreements had been made with each ethnic nationality alone, no matter how large or how small. Perhaps, not sharing a common past could have been overcome if there had been a shared future to look forward to. Here, Nigeria presents one of its usual exceptions.

Two broad aspirations arose out of the encounter with the British in Nigeria. There were those mainly from the predominantly Moslem North of Nigeria who defined themselves in terms of the Islamic past and saw the prospect of a westernized future as a threat to their Islamic past. This is perhaps one of the reasons why some Southern educated elite have labelled their Northern counterparts as being uninterested in being independent of the British.

The second broad group is the Southern educated elite who defined themselves in terms of making amends for the past through assimilating western concepts, western ideas and western technology to achieve their new and supposedly superior future. Instability has been the result of the merging of these two different concepts and there has been no possibility of these Nigerians creating a soul for their people.

Nigerian writers have generally ignored this task of the need for a soul for the people. When they have dealt with the assumptions of such a concept, they have generally written negatively rather than positively, spoken of the Chief Nangas rather than of the Mandelas. While the attempt of the post civil war generation of Nigerian writers such as Femi Osofisan[4], Festus Iyayi[5] and Tunde Fatunde[6] to incorporate the working class, the variously identified masses and the ordinary man on the street into the national ideal, is not the subject of this study, their effort needs to be mentioned, at least in passing.

In plays such as *Once Upon Four Robbers* by Femi Osofisan, novels such as *Violence* by Festus Iyayi, and pidgin English language plays such as *Oga na Tief Man* by Tunde Fatunde these writers have attempted to restore the worker to the centre of the nation-building enterprise. While the Southern elite snub these efforts, the Northern elite dismiss them by saying that their workers are not the same as the Southern workers.

It is against this background that this study investigates in greater detail here, the contrasts and the similarities in the works of Chinua Achebe and Wole Soyinka in their attempts to write towards a new community of sensibilities in Nigeria.

From Old to New Communities

First in *Drama from Ibsen to Eliot* (1954) and later in *Culture and Society 1780 – 1950* (1958) and *The Long Revolution* (1961) Raymond Williams[7] describes some important issues in the existence of a *community of sensibilities*. One statement is relevant here:

> But at all times, the community between the artist and audience which seems to matter is the *community of sensibilities*. The artist's sensibility – his capacity for experience, his ways of thinking, feeling and conjunction – will often be finer and more developed than that of the mean of his audience. But if his sensibility is of the same kind, his language and the language of his audience will be closely and organically related; the common language will be the expression of the common sensibility.[8]

Two traditions of thinking through the issue of 'community' can be found in western European philosophy.[9] The liberal tradition, taking its source from the Renaissance and the Reformation makes the individual the principle of existence and the community the derivative. This liberal tradition has been the dominant of the two traditions. It ensures that the community guarantees the rights of the individual through the system of common life, the condition of common life, and the framework of common life.[10]

The other tradition, to which Africans can relate more naturally, makes the community the principle and the individual the derivative. The creation of the community as the greatest invention of the human being and as the place of the individuals greatest achievement becomes the duty of the individuals.

For African writers and artists, the failure to contribute towards the creation of a new community of sensibilities stems from the concept and practice of *making the community the principle and making themselves as individuals the principle as well* in a situation where either the community or the individual must, of necessity, be subordinate to the other. Examples can be provided to demonstrate the implication of this statement. In the meantime, it is necessary to deal with the issues raised by (i) the framework of common life, (ii) the system of common life, and

(iii) the condition of common life in terms of the process of creating a new community of sensibilities.

Whatever role is given to the community or the individual, fundamental to human existence is the economic system. In modern terms this translates into the founding of a corporate state. In their roles as individuals and members of a community, writers can contribute towards the founding of that corporate state especially in the process of choosing paradigms for the new state.

For historical reasons idealism has dominated this aspect of African existence. An African post-independence government did not wish to maintain the conditions of the colonial economy whereby the colony produced what it did not consume and consumed what it did not produce. Rather, a socialist economic system was proclaimed as the target of the new government. The failure of this economic system has been one of the reasons for the sobering re-assessment that is going on in Africa today.

The issue of the relationship between economic practice and cultural consequences must be seen as a passing discourse. It used to be assumed that the cultural manifestation of capitalist economic practice is a culture of oppression between capital and labour, between workers and management and between high brow and low brow. There is a growing possibility that economic practice could in fact become irrelevant to cultural practice. The rituals of our daily existence, out of which we create our arts, could be carried through with little or no effect from our economic practice. Perhaps the example of a Moslem making his annual holiday to coincide with the pilgrimage prescribed by Islam to Mecca and Medina might be seen as not important enough; yet there is no doubt that from such a small example others can be identified and developed.

The implication of this possibility is that, for the first time in human history, the economic condition for the creation of a community of sensibilities exists. A community of sensibilities implies a multi-lingual, multi-ethnic and multi-religious community. The expression of the common sensibility would be the totality of the ideals of the various languages, ethnicities and religions which make up the community. Unfortunately, it has been impossible for African writers to discover the language of that expression because at the same time that they insist on the primacy of the community they also insist on the primacy of their individuality.

Any African writer will do to demonstrate the negative outcome of this position: Ama Ata Aidoo[11] has published plays,
poetry and novels. Her play *Anowa* (1970) deals with the relationship of Anowa and her husband Kofi Ako and the story is
supposed to have taken place sometime in the 1870s. Within the
play as well as the logic of the play, it is possible to assume that
Ama Ata Aidoo places greater importance on the community
than on the individual. Anowa rebels against the norms of the
community, chooses her husband and goes away with him. The
couple work and make money together. Kofi Ako decides he
would buy a few slaves to help in their work. Anowa objects
and will have nothing to do with slavery. Kofi Ako persists and
the relationship begins to collapse until both of them commit
suicide at the end of the play. Anowa's pursuit of her individuality precipitates the collapse of their relationship, the failure of
the individual and the triumph of the community.

What can be said about the relationship of Ama Ata Aidoo,
playwright, to this play? She is a progressive western educated
individual who has been a university professor as well as a minister of state in Ghana in charge of education. She is also a person who would oppose the subjugation of women in the expression of their individuality. What does the failure of Anowa's
marriage say to the liberal assumptions of the playwright? If,
Ama Ata Aidoo as the writer, accepts that African societies must
be renewed and reformed, who are to do these duties of renewal
and reformation? Can the communities, this time as abstrac-
tions, renew and reform themselves? At the end of Ama Ata
Aidoo's play, the community at Yebi is no better for the existence of Anowa. My suggestion is that if the writer maintains
the importance of the community at the same level as his or her
own importance as an individual, his or her possibility of writing towards a new community of sensibilities is almost non-
existent.

One other crucial issue in the problems involved in creating
new communities of sensibilities in Africa has to do with the
way and manner in which writers using European languages
tend to write mainly what is politically correct in terms of the
pan-African agenda of the educated elite on the continent. It has
been mentioned earlier that the position of the Yoruba in terms
of the experience of British colonial imposition in Nigeria is
complicated and not always antagonistic. In this way it would
seem as if writers writing in Yoruba would be closer to the position of their community. There is an interesting example of this

in one of the novels of D.O. Fagunwa.[12] *Irinkerindo Ninu Igbo Elegbeje* (Irinkerindo in Elegbeje Forest) was first published in 1954. Nigeria was still under the British colonial rule but the agitation for independence had begun and the example of India had been incorporated into the struggle for Nigerian independence. The novel deals with the journey of Irinkerindo at the head of fifty master hunters in pursuit of the fruit of wisdom that would revolutionize their society. On the way to the source of that fruit they came to the city of Edidare where everything was done contrary to Yoruba customs of doing things. Parents obeyed their children, women ordered their husbands around and subjects ruled their kings. Irinkerindo objected to this way of life and fought the people of the city. After they had conquered them, they came to an arrangement with them:

> I hope you would like to know what we did with the king, whether we appointed another king or we left the king to continue to rule. In fact, we did not appoint another king. What we did was to appoint one of us as governor over them, the person's name being Apata-igbehin. We told him to take care of the city, while we went on to the Forest of Elegbeje. By the time we would be returning we hope that the people of the city would have been civilized. The reason we appointed Apata-igbehin as their governor was because he was a no-nonsense person who would not permit the people of Edidare to misbehave.[13]

This is the classic system of indirect rule used by the British in both Yorubaland and in the Hausa states of Northern Nigeria. Fagunwa does not present this as a parody or a satire on the system of indirect rule. The hunters who institute this system on the city state of Edidare believe that it will work to the good of the people of the city in the same way that British colonial occupation would benefit the Yoruba after a period of time. Here, the fictional characters seem to be one with the author that the community benefits from a period of colonial occupation. The individual works for the good of the community because the community here is more important than the individual. There is nowhere in all African literature in European languages where an example such as the above can be found.

Writing African literatures in English or any other European languages was not going to be the dead end of these literatures as Obi Wali had feared in his now famous article in *Transition* magazine in 1965.[14] If anything, Africans are writing better and more accomplished in European languages than ever before. There are outlets in Europe that distribute African writing and publishing, just as there have developed markets locally in many African countries, and definitely in Nigeria, for African writing. What was to bring African literatures to a dead end in whatever languages it cared to be written was the continuation of pan-African themes in these literatures, the continuation of Africans writing about themselves as victims (of imperialism, colonialism, neo-colonialism, etc) when their subject-matter should have changed to that of victors with institutions to build, with a new history to make.

Pan-Africanism was kept alive as long as there still existed on the continent African countries which were still under the heel of direct colonial authorities such as was the case in the Portuguese colonies of Angola, Mozambique and Guinea-Bissau. And also as long as South Africa continued its racist minority government of apartheid. Pan-Africanism provided the umbrella under which action could be united and focused on these evil doers. The Organisation of African Unity provided the institutional point from which to begin. Both the United Nations Organisation and its affiliates were to be used in dealing with these enemies of the Black continent. Pan-Africanism also provided a handle for African descendants in the Diaspora, such as those in the USA and the Caribbean, with which to respond to the victories and the failures of the peoples of the continent. Looked at in this manner, one can not dismiss the pan-African movement. It did some good. The problem was not to have recognised, by the time of independence, the limitations of pan-Africanism. Or else, not to have re-defined its objectives at the local level.

While pan-Africanism still responded to the 'Other' in terms of victim, ethnic nationalities had already re-defined their objectives in the light of the defeat they had suffered at the hands of the British, for instance, in Nigeria. Even the Hausa-Fulani who had rudely rejected the hand of friendship which Lugard extended to them before he undertook their pacification had been humiliated through the pursuit and assassination of their Sultan and his replacement with someone conducive to the objectives of the British, had bided their time, accepted British rule and worked it in such a manner that they came out on top of the other ethnic nationalities competing for political power within the boundaries of Nigeria. It is this victory that some southern intellectuals such as Achebe and Soyinka have mistaken for Hausa-Fulani collaboration with the British colonial government and an unwillingness to be free of colonialism. It is like saying that the Japanese were not fighting for their own future when they went into wholesale modernisation.

Thus, at the ethnic national level, it was not possible to write from a total vision of society when writing in English or in the local indigenous languages. In between these two parallels – the pan-African agenda and the ethnic national agenda – hung the new nation's own agenda. This agenda, understandably, parodied the pan-African agenda and, unfortunately, criminalised ethnicity and the ethnic agenda. Kwame Nkrumah, a good example of this dilemma, in his usual inimitable manner, dedicated the freedom of Ghana to the total liberation of the African continent. He would consider the freedom of Ghana as not yet achieved as long as there was one single country left on the African continent still under foreign rule. Other African countries were to follow suit and many, especially those countries which bordered the racist Republic of South Africa, were to lose much in this struggle.

The failure of African intellectuals has been their inability to convert the slogans of pan-Africanism, with the realism of the ethnic national agendas, to the higher duty of making of Nigeria a new community of sensibilities for all Nigerians. As the country failed to live up to the expectations of all, and one violent succession of government followed another, writers were the first to express their disillusionment with politicians such as Nkrumah, supposedly responsible for the destruction of the dream of the new nation-states.

The implications of emphasising the community while insisting on the individuality of the writer in the same breath show in the works of Chinua Achebe and Wole Soyinka and virtually make the process of their writing towards a new community of sensibilities in Nigeria difficult.

It is obvious that Chinua Achebe does not approve of the 'victory' of the community made up of the six villages of Umuaro over their Chief Priest, Ezeulu. The writer here does not lend his belief in the primacy of the community over the individual to shore up the community. Here is Achebe's final comment, as author of *Arrow of God*, on the choice that the community had made and on the feeling of the community that their God was with them in that choice against their Chief Priest:

> If this was so then Ulu had chosen a dangerous time to uphold that truth, for in destroying his priest he had also brought disaster on himself, like the lizard in the fable who ruined his mother's funeral by his own hand. For a deity who chose a moment such

as this to chastise his priest or abandon him before his enemies
was inciting people to take liberties; and Umuaro was just ripe to
do so.[15]

It is necessary to remember that Umuaro was founded on the
reformation and renaissance idea that the community would
defend the individuals against their enemies and the interests of
the community of Umuaro would over-ride the interest of the
individual six villages which make up Umuaro. While the community here is logical, Achebe, who calls it into existence, rejects
the implications of that logic. His position does not help him to
pursue his declared objective of writing towards a new community of sensibilities in Nigeria.

The choice which the people of the six villages of Umuaro
make would seem to prove the point which Lamin Sanneh
argues in his book *Translating the Message: The Missionary Impact
on Culture*.[16] The main argument of the book, which is relevant
here, is that adopting African languages for the spread of the
Christian gospel, "was tantamount to adopting indigenous cultural criteria for the message, a piece of radical indigenization
far greater than the standard portrayal of mission as Western
cultural imperialism."[17] To this extent, Achebe misses the point
that the clash of cultures was not the culture of the white man
and the culture of the black man, but rather the culture of the
traditional elite and the culture of those who were attempting to
escape that traditional authority. Perhaps the reason that
Soyinka is less strident than Achebe on the issue of culture clash
is because he sees more of an intra-Yoruba clash of cultures than
inter-Europe-Yoruba clash of cultures.

No Longer at Ease demonstrates even more dramatically the
impossibility of giving equal priority to both the community
and the individual in the same breath. Obi Okonkwo was educated at the expense of the community towards the amelioration
of the condition of the community in the way and manner in
which the community perceives that enterprise of amelioration.
When the final rift comes between Obi Okonkwo and the
Umuofia Progressive Union branch in Lagos the career of Obi
Okonkwo the individual is given continued attention while the
loss of the community is ignored.

Wole Soyinka's position might be different in detail, but the
end result is the same as in the case of Chinua Achebe: the community stagnates and the individual is powerless to effect
change.

In *Death and the King's Horseman*, collective opprobrium finally forces Elesin to commit suicide. But it was already too late since his suicide follows only after he had been told that his son had died in his place. Elesin's attempt to insist on his individual destiny – as different from the community – fails. The suicide of his son makes the possibility of development within the community problematic. These two issues make *Death and the King's Horseman* a tragic celebration of communal and individual loss.

The Interpreters assumes a community that is ill-defined. The positive characters of the novel are concerned with erecting what might be termed the framework of common life. Those who oppose them want things to remain the way they are. The way things are is perhaps the present condition of the community. The novel does not detail this present condition while detailing the struggle of the individuals against that condition. At the end the individuals are destroyed and all that is left is the painting of them lifting them to the position of ancestors and deities. Soyinka's novel then stands in the position of the narration of African epic struggles for freedom which is then followed by post-independence stasis. The narration of the struggle becomes the only achievement. The telling of the epic struggle of Haiti dwarfs the pitiable use to which the independence born out of that struggle has been put.

A further stage is reached when these two writers turn their powers of satire on the puny efforts of those who would attempt to create the new community. In Achebe's *A Man of the People* it is the ministers of state while in Soyinka's *Kongi's Harvest* it is the president of Ghana himself, Kwame Nkrumah.

Here is how a discussion goes among Kongi's Reformed Aweri Fraternity:

FOURTH: We might consider a scientific image. This would be a positive stamp, one very much in tune with our contemporary situation. Our pronouncement should be dominated by a positive scientificism.

THIRD: A brilliant conception. I move that we adopt it at once.

SIXTH: What exactly is positive scientificism?

THIRD: Whatever it is, it is not long-winded proverbs and senile pronouncements. In fact we could say a step has already been taken in that direction. If you've read our leader's last publication...

FIFTH: Ah yes. Nor proverbs nor verse, only ideograms in
            algebraic quantums. If the square of XQY(2bc) equals
            QA into the square root of X, then the progressive
            forces must prevail over the reactionary in the span
            of .32 of a single generation.[18]

Compare the tone of the above dialogue with the following :

Since, according to philosophical consciencism in its embracing of
philosophical dialectical materialism, a change can only result
from an operation of forces, in order to liberate a colony a dialectical moment needs to be introduced in (na>pa)g to transform it
to (pa>na)g. Hence a liberated territory arises under the condition lib.g ⟷ [D(na>pa)g ⟶ (pa>na)g] [19]

Chinua Achebe and Wole Soyinka, in response to the pan-
African wishes of the history of black people, wrote to defend
the continent against those who had spent their lives denigrating the people of Africa. Achebe and Soyinka had done this
empowered by their ethnic national cultures. But somehow they
had failed to use the same culture to build the small unit of
Nigeria for many reasons some of which we have already dealt
with before now. This failure can be expressed in the idea that
while these two writers were able to write from the old communities of their ethnic nationality, they were unable to write
towards a new community.

How does a writer write from an old community towards a
new one? Were we to take the German existentialist Karl Jaspers
seriously, we would despair of the possibility of creating new
communities of sensibility. He was quoted by Nadine Gordimer
thus:

Community is a historical concept. Each separate community is
unique, rooted in an unfathomable past that has determined it,
and that has been handed down through oral teaching, books,
usages, customs, habits and above all, through the institutions of
the family and religion. Community is something that grows, that
cannot be planned; it may be preserved but it cannot be created.[20]

When we add the following so-called 'forces of cohesion' – a
common language, a sense of ethnic kinship, geographic unity
and contiguity, common historical experience, common frame of
political thought, a common area of economic mutuality, the
fear of a common foe, shared future possibilities and hopes and
expectations and shared present programme and concern – it is
impossible not to despair of the possibility of creating a new
community of Nigerian sensibility.

The only common language is English and in spite of writing in English both Achebe and Soyinka claim to be Igbo and Yoruba writers respectively. Achebe had tried to allocate to Nigerian national literature the English language while calling what is written in indigenous languages as ethnic literature. This linguistic delimitation does not work. English should have been used to express the common historical experience of Nigeria rather than for the expression of the ethnic cultural experiences of the ethnic nationalities. That is, writing in the indigenous languages could have been the process of writing from the old communities while writing in English should have been the process of writing *towards* the new community.

There is no sense of ethnic kinship to speak of. But what sense of kinship could be created through inhabiting the same geographic unit, contiguity, the common historical experience of pre-colonial encounters, the encounter with Europe, the experience of the slave trade, the colonial experience and the struggle to throw off the burden of oppression?

Finding a common frame of political thought should not have been too difficult either. Nor for that matter would one have had to stretch one's imagination to accept the idea of a common area of economic mutuality. The fear of a common foe, shared future possibilities and hopes and expectations, as well as shared present programme and concern could not be said to be impossible to create.

Yet, after over thirty years of writing from Nigeria, a writer of the calibre of Soyinka can say that he is a Yoruba writer rather than a Nigerian writer. And a critic of the reputation of Ernest Emenyonu can come out proudly to declare that Achebe, in spite of his writing in English, was in fact an Igbo writer. Was Nigeria not worth writing towards? The answer is that no nation, new or old, was worth working for. The later part of the twentieth century has not been the most favourable time for nationalism of the German type. Intellectuals in particular have found it difficult not to share the position of their European and North American counterparts that any form of nationalism is in fact some kind of jingoism around which one must not be found to sit. Yet these same intellectuals shared the aspirations of the struggle for the liberation of Africa. What did they expect after that liberation? Did they expect that African countries would revert to their ethnic units as the basis of nationalism in the modern times?

Nobody seems to have thought through this aspect of African existence and what would happen in the future. Since there could not be a vacuum, it is not surprising that the previously existing ethnic national agendas easily took over. And this is so in a situation where the leadership could not speak with a common voice and provide a common aim for the country as a whole.

Notes

1. *Guardian,* May 7, 1992, review section, p. 21.
2. Raymond Williams, *The Long Revolution,* p. 240. I have opted for interpreting 'language' more extensively than merely a tongue.
3. The narration was also usually cast in mythic terms such as the classic example provided by Dr. Nnamdi Azikiwe in his autobiography entitled My Odyssey. He is Jason and the other educated members of the elite are the argonauts venturing the seas in search of the golden fleece with which to liberate their nations.
4, 5
and 6. See complete list of the publications of these writers in the section of the Bibliography devoted to the works of African writers cited in this work.
7. Raymond Williams, *Drama from Ibsen to Eliot,* p. 31.
8. Raymond Williams, *The Long Revolution,* pp. 93–6.
9. ibid. p. 94.
10. ibid. p. 95.
11. Ama Ata Aidoo: see Bibliography.
12. D.O. Fagunwa: see Bibliography.
13. *Irinkerindo ninu Igbo Elegbeje,* pp.53 – 4; my translation.
14. Obi Wali *Transition,* 'The Dead End of African Literature', no. 10, September 1963, pp.4 – 14.
15. *Arrow of God* in *The African Trilogy,* p. 555
16. Sanneh, Lamin, *Translating the Message: The Missionary Impact on Culture,* Maryknoll, NY: Orbis Books, 1989.
17. ibid. p.3.
18. *Collected Plays 2,* pp.71–72.
19. Kwame Nkrumah, *Consciencism,* p.109.
20. *Times Literary Supplement,* 11 August 1961, pp.520–523.

VI

The Agendas of the Big Three

The three main ethnic nationalities in Nigeria, usually referred to as the Big Three, are the Hausa-Fulani, the Yoruba and the Igbo. The argument of this book is that the writers from these nationalities have laboured more for the production of literatures which represent their ethnic national agendas rather than for the agenda of the nation-state Nigeria. Apart from the fact that an understanding of their various languages as well as their particular attitudes to the coming of the British into their world help us to understand this peculiar situation, the writers themselves have made statements supporting such a conclusion – that they have advanced their ethnic agendas rather than writing towards a new community of sensibilities in Nigeria.

In this chapter, three Nigerian writers are dealt with: Alhaji Sir Abubakar Tafawa Balewa,[1] the first prime minister of independent Nigeria, who was assassinated in January 1966 when the first coup d'etat took place; Zaynab Alkali;[2] one of the few women writers to come out of the North; and Ibrahim Tahir,[3] from Bauchi in the North-East who writes from the point of view of the Hausa-Fulani power elite of the Sokoto Caliphate.

Abubakar Tafawa Balewa was born in Bauchi in 1912. He was a teacher, becoming a member of the Northern House of Assembly from where he was asked to go to the Federal House of Representatives by the Northern Peoples Congress, of which he was then the deputy leader to Sir Ahmadu Bello. He was known as a keen reader of modern novels especially detective novels. His only novel *Shaihu Umar* was written in the Hausa language and translated into English by Mervyn Hiskett and published in 1967.[4] As the translator says in his introduction, the novel is "a statement of the values and philosophy of orthodox Islam."[5]

The story of the novel takes place towards the end of the nineteenth century although the Sokoto Caliphate had been at war

with the Yoruba southwards and had taken some of their territory. This novel does not mention the Yoruba. The style of the
novel is influenced by the form of narration in Arabic writing of
the time. It begins with the customary acknowledgement of
Allah and carries on in the first person to tell the story of the life
of the Shaihu. A film of the novel has been made.

Zaynab Alkali was born in Maiduguri of Christian parents but
her books are steeped in the Islamic environment of Northern
Nigeria. She teaches at the Yola campus of the University of
Maiduguri where her husband is a professor of History. She has
published two novels both directed at teenage readers. *The
Stillborn*, (1984) deals with the anxieties of a young married
woman. Her equally young husband has been drawn from their
little rural village to the big city. The dilemma of the young wife
is whether she should follow him or wait until he sends for her.
When tradition is mentioned in this novel and her other one, *The
Virtuous One*, (1987), it is the tradition of the Hausa within the
animist and Islamic syncretism that has taken place in the
North.

> She was playing to the tune of a traditional courtship. A woman
> was not supposed to show interest in a man on their first meet-
> ing. His seriousness would only be determined by how well he
> took a rebuff and how persistently he pursued his woman.[6]

The second novel *The Virtuous Woman* deals with the doubts of a
disabled young girl as she meets the person she feels she would
wish to marry. Unlike the other novel, and unlike Tafawa
Balewa's and Ibrahim Tahir's fiction, this novel tries to deal with
the modern problems of the country as a whole. The young girl
is going to a secondary school in Ilorin, the capital of the area of
Yorubaland conquered by the Sokoto Caliphate. All the same,
old prejudices persist. Someone Nana Ai, the central character in
the novel, meets on the train to Ilorin exclaims:

> 'By God, its a long way down south and you girls can travel by
> yourselves?' 'No we can't. We have an old man as escort,' she
> gestured towards the sleeping man.[7]

Towards the end of the novel, Bello, Nana Ai's boy friend makes
the following remark about the nation:

> 'No Nana, we will have to have mercy on ourselves first. God has
> other priorities than to help a nation that is bent on destroying
> itself', Bello replied vehemently.[8]

Ibrahim Tahir, like Zaynab Alkali, and unlike Tafawa Balewa writes in English and he is one of the most important collaborators with the jihadists of the Sokoto Caliphate. Achebe and Soyinka are not unique among the writers of the main ethnic nationalities for writing within the agenda of their ethnic nationalities. Tahir is dealt with here to complete the troika of ethnic nationalities and demonstrate their similarities.

The Last Imam published in 1984, is Ibrahim Tahir's only novel up to date. He was educated in a traditional Islamic *madrassa* before going to a western type primary school and then on to secondary school. He finished his secondary education in Britain and went on to do his undergraduate work as well as his doctorate in political science in Cambridge. While in Britain he worked for the BBC Hausa Service and began to write as well. Dr. Tahir taught for some time at the Ahmadu Bello University before getting into politics where he rose to be a minister in the cabinet of President Shehu Shagari, the NPN the National Party of Nigeria government terminated in December 1983 for, among other reasons, massive corruption.

The Last Imam, is based in Bauchi. Alhaji Usman, the Imam of the title is a descendent of the Shehu Usman Dan Fodio, the founder of the Sokoto Caliphate. His family has occupied the Imam's position in Bauchi for generations. The crisis of the novel begins with the challenge to his authority because of his presumed partiality, by his wives in the house, then by his peers in the mosque and finally by the Emir. Imam Usman has four wives as allowed by his religion, as well as four concubines as permitted by the practice of his faith. But his mind and soul are captured by his concubine Hasana, who dies at the beginning of the novel, and Kasim, their son. Although he has other children from the other women in his harem, we do not get a single glimpse of any of them. As for the other wives, even in death, Hasana monopolises the attention of the Alhaji. At the beginning of the novel, he makes a visit to her grave and laments her death. He promises to do everything for their son, Kasim. Soon after this visit to the grave of Hasana, A'isha, the first wife leads the other wives in revolt. She does not have a child of her own and although she is supposed to act as the mother of Kasim, she confesses that she cannot control him. When she reports his misbehaviour to the husband, he does not punish him, which only encourages Kasim to indulge in more misbehaviour. The ultimate – that the Imam would ever beat his son because of A'isha – happens when A'isha, wrongly accuses Kasim of stealing a shilling which he had been asked to give to the miller grinding the family corn. Kasim protests his innocence and throws a stone that hits A'isha on the forehead. When his father canes him for this misbehaviour, Kasim runs away from home.

The month of the Moslem fast is approaching. The wives and concubines of the Imam take this opportunity to refuse to cook for their husband as a way of registering their anger against their ill-treatment over the years. At this point the problem assumes new dimensions. In Borno, the figure of the man abandoned, for whatever reasons, by his wives at the onset of the month of fasting is a figure of fun, to be ridiculed in public play performances throughout the town. Knowing what is coming to him, Imam Usman takes the opportunity of his Friday sermon in the mosque to the faithful to denounce this ancient custom and declare it a sin.

The common people grumble but they can do nothing to change the dictate of the Imam. As if this is not enough, Imam Usman also preaches against the acceptance of bastards, children conceived through concubines, in the society. In doing this, he was indirectly condemning not only himself but also his own father, the Imam before him, who had fathered bastard children through his concubines. In fact, when Kasim ran away from home, he went to his uncle, whom Imam Usman knew to be a half-baked Islamic scholar, but did not know was also the son of his father and therefore his half-brother. When Imam Usman preaches in the mosque calling these children bastards, his peers revolt and the Emir calls him to question:

> There was nothing amiable about the Emir. If anything, he looked slightly anxious.
>
> 'Nothing troubles you, I hope my lord',Usman said. It was a long time before the Emir spoke.
>
> 'I have called you here about your sermon, the last one', he said.
>
> 'Ah, that was nothing, my lord. I did only the work of Allah as it needs to be done. I can only hope you did not find it wanting'.
>
> 'In the work of Allah nothing is wanting.'
>
> 'In the work of Allah nothing is wanting but perhaps the discharge of it occasionally exceeds bounds'.[9]

The two men argue for quite some time and it becomes more and more apparent that the Emir had lost confidence in his Imam:

If you had only said that! Even if you did have to say more it would surely have been enough just to warn them against the sin of nuptial injustice and to have left it at that. Even now, Alhaji, I find it difficult to understand what could have happened to you. What madness – standing there revealing the most intimate secrets of your life to men who could have little sense of it! Did you realise that to the people you are a legend, that you have always been something of a god who did not belong to the world of ordinary men. They suggest nothing, but they know and I know that your father, the late Imam, knew what could and could not be done, what should or should not be left to the will of God but to the wisdom of men.[10]

As the crisis deepens and more and more people in the capital begin to object to the way the Imam was using his position to justify himself and attack others, the Emir has no choice but to call him once more and for the last time:

What your ancestors and especially you, have done for this king-dom and for us all, is impossible to measure or recount. Your reward is with Allah and there is no doubt He will give them to you when the time comes. We can only express our gratitude. However, from this moment, Alhaji Usman, you are untur-banned. You are no longer the Imam.[11]

To compound the irony of the situation, the Emir appoints Alhaji Usman's half-brother, the one he would want to see as a bastard, the one to whom his son ran for shelter, as the new Imam.

The Last Imam is a fundamental text of the Hausa-Fulani ethnic nationality of Nigeria, the same way that Chinua Achebe's *Arrow of God* is fundamental to the Igbo ethnic nationality and Wole Soyinka's *Death and the King's Horseman* is fundamental to the Yoruba ethnic nationality. A whole study could in fact be made of these texts, especially at a comparative level. *The Last Imam* deals with the past and the present of the Hausa-Fulani. The novel also makes a statement about the future of this peo-ple.

The following is the link which the novel makes between Bauchi, the capital of Borno emirate, and the Sokoto Caliphate:

His father's couch was here and he, a young boy, was lying beside it listening to his father boasting to him about his line.

'Oh, yes, they are a very long line. Fulani herdsmen who lived on their cattle and went wherever the land was rich and grass was green and free from tse-tse fly. Then the Jihad of Usman Dan Fodio came and the emirs of Hausaland received their flags from

Shehu Usman. But they were not all learned enough to give the
people spiritual guidance and those who were, spent too much
time in the wars. Our Emir in Bauchi at the time heard of them
and their great learning and devotion to religion and he invited
their leader to become Imam. Since then, my son, the Imam has
always come from amongst them. I am Imam today and when I
die one of my sons will be Imam after me. Who knows, it may be
you.[12]

One of the major themes of Achebe and Soyinka is the
retrieval of the past. In their various ways they attempt to
retrieve the past from the calumny of white writing and to
restore it to the African. Ibrahim Tahir does not have to answer
western denigrations of Islam and Islamic ways. Moslems and
Arabs the world over have been doing that for over a thousand
years. What we find here is the appropriation of Arab-Islamic
history as part of the history of the Hausa-Fulani. According to
classical Islamic and Arab historical practice, what happened in
Arabia prior to the coming of Prophet Muhammad in 622 A.D.
is consigned into what has come to be known as the 'age of
ignorance', the Jahilliyah. The history of Arabia is demarcated
by the period of Ignorance and the Period of Islam. This historical practice has also been imposed on the local history of the
places to which Islam spread. In some places, the practice does
not hold, as for instance in India and among the Yoruba. In
other places, such as the North of Nigeria, this historical practice
is accepted. Thus, Ibrahim Tahir can see the past of Bauchi in the
following terms:

> Yet only three hundred years ago, and maybe less, the Word of
> God and God Himself had not existed for the people who inhab-
> ited the land. For Bauchi then was no more than a rocky trough
> in the mountainous country of the wild savannah no prophet
> land of pagan tribes, each with its shrine sheltering behind a
> rocky grove. And the gods who had lived in those shrines were
> no abstract beings like the God Alhaji Usman seemed to the
> pagans' successors to have known so well, but real solid gods,
> concrete to sight and touch, moulded in grotesque shapes in
> mud, wood and stone. For three hundred years they had lived
> the ways of this new God until by now it had fossilised and
> become their real nature – not as something capsulated and desic-
> cated but alive like the ways and times of their pagan ancestors
> when life and ritual were one and the same.[13]

With the appropriation of the past of Islam as their history and folklore, the people have a different pre-occupation from those of the Yoruba and the Igbo:

> They did not understand the words because most of them did not understand Arabic. But they had faith, they had memory, the memory of fragments of information gathered from their scanty education about earlier days, the days of the struggles of Mohammed and the victories and glories of Islam, and the memory of something more deeply buried, things they themselves did not know and had never seen, things which demanded more demonstration than Islam; and this memory and the excellence, the pathos, of Usman's chanting of the Holy Koran would bring tears to their eyes.[14]

If these people have any awareness of the other ethnic nationalities in the country, or awareness of their rivals the Igbo and the Yoruba, such awareness is dim and the stuff of legends and rumours. There are examples of these legends in the novel. Here, a maiden dreams of her future love:

> My love, my prophet come with me
> To our chamber of love, out here I am cold.
> Feed me honey, feed me cream,
> And anoint my chest with the scents of Araby.
> Cover my body in the silks of the East
> And drape me in the prints of Yorubaland.
> Then I shall give you what you want
> And you will give me what I want.[15]

When Kasim ran away from home, he spent a night in the forest before he is found the following day and rescued by his uncle. The wives and concubines of his father are sorry for what they have done:

> They thought of the animals in the wild which could kill Kasim and of the robbers who were no less dangerous than the beasts. Child thieves, too, were lurking in the jungles, ready to pounce on any stray child and sell him to the men of the South, the Asaba as they were called.[16]

There is no doubt that Ibrahim Tahir's people have no problem with their past. They do not see the West as their hope and possibility into the future as do the Yoruba and the Igbo. Neither do they aspire to sending their children to their schools and their churches. When the British came, as previously mentioned, they did not wish to have anything to do with them. Compared with the crisis in *The Last Imam* the crisis of *Arrow of God* is caused by

the intrusion of the white man into the affairs of the Igbo. Unlike
Bauchi, Umuaro lacks the central authority with political stabili-
ty and spiritual calm of the community in mind to call the priest
of Ulu to order the way the Emir could call the erring Imam to
order. While the world of the Igbo and the Yoruba fragment
and, in the words of Elesin's Praise Singer 'leaves its course and
smashes on boulders of the great void', the world of the Hausa-
Fulani does not suffer such a tragedy. The Hausa-Fulani are pos-
sibly the only one who can say that the presence of the white
man has not mattered to them as much as it has mattered to the
others in the country.

Stylistically, *The Last Imam* bears some similarity to both
Achebe's *Arrow of God* and Soyinka's *Death and the King's
Horseman*. Tahir locates part of the action of the novel in the past
and writes sometimes obviously for the benefit of the outsider.
He uses figures of speech from the Borno past and validates
popular practice among the people. For these and the other similarities already pointed out *The Last Imam* is a fundamental text
which helps one in understanding the Hausa-Fulani of Northern
Nigeria.

Looking in Different Directions

From the foregoing and from the earlier chapters dealing with
the backgrounds of Chinua Achebe and Wole Soyinka it is clear
that the three largest ethnic nationalities of Nigeria – the Igbo,
the Yoruba and the Hausa-Fulani looked in different intellectual
directions. The Igbo and the Yoruba, both located in the south of
Nigeria, occupying the East and the West respectively, looked to
Europe and the United States of America for their visions of
their future. The Hausa-Fulani, on the other hand,looked to the
Arab-Islamic world for their vision of their future. Western education was the way out for the southerners and their regional
governments encouraged it. First the Yoruba Western Region
instituted free education in their region in 1954, a few months
into self-rule in the regions. The Igbo Eastern Region followed
the Western Region a couple of years later. Communities and
villages in the South put their resources together to send deserv-
ing young men among them for further education even up to
university in the United Kingdom. Obi Okonkwo, of *No Longer
at Ease* was a beneficiary of such a scheme:

> Six or seven years ago Umuofians abroad had formed their Union
> with the aim of collecting money to send some of their brighter

young men to study in England. They taxed themselves merci-
lessly.[17]

These community schemes were also widespread in the Yoruba
area. This cannot be said of the Northern part of the country.
There was, in fact, a general unwillingness on the parts of parents to send their children to western type schools since it was
seen as a sure sign of losing them to Christianity.

While a few writers from the South such as Cyprian Ekwensi
have located their novels or plays in parts of the North and used
characters from that part of the country, the references to the
North and to Northerners are few and far between in the writings of Chinua Achebe and Wole Soyinka.

Generally, references to other parts of the country by Yoruba
writers writing in Yoruba have never been particularly positive.
The following is from the first page of a Yoruba novel *Alosi
Ologo* (The Left-Handed Detective) by E. K. Akinlade:[18]

> Ajeji alailenia ni Jolaade fe, A ko mo ile tabi ona re. Nje lona
> Asaba lohun ko ni nwon so pe ilu okunrin naa wa? O se! nibiti
> talaka lasanlasan ti nri enia atata fe omo re, alarinkiri kan saa ni
> Arigba ri fi omo tire fun.

> (Jolaade married a total stranger without relations. No one knows
> from where he came. Was is not said that the man came from
> somewhere on the way to Asaba? What a tragedy! In a place
> where poverty-stricken men marry into wealthy families, a rich
> man such as Arigba goes and gives his daughter to a mere wan-
> derer!)[19]

It should be no surprise then if one finds the following argument between Dehinwa, the female among the interpreters in
Wole Soyinka's novel of the same title, and her mother:

> Are men so short in town? Eh? Tell me Dehinwa, are good-look-
> ing, decent men so hard to find that you must go with a
> *Gambari*?[20] Don't you know what your name is that you even let
> yourself be seen with a *Gambari*?[21]

Dehinwa begins mildly by telling her mother not to listen to
such talk, but the mother, with encouragement of the aunt,
intensifies her objection. She insists that she did not slave to
send her to England to study only for her to hand herself over to
a Northerner. Dehinwa gets angry and promises to pay her
mother back so that she can see whoever she may wish to see.
Obi Okonkwo of *No Longer at Ease* reacts the same way when he
broke with the Umuofia Progressive Union, Lagos Branch. He

would pay them back the money they spent on him while he studied in England.[22]

The issue of the relationships between ethnic nationalities in reality and in literature are important for the formation of the community of sensibilities which was mentioned earlier. Writing towards this new community would mean that an attempt would be made to explore and lay bare the hidden igno-rance which make these types of comments possible among citi-zens of the same country. Anyone committed to creating a new community of sensibilities would not have simply reflected the reality if indeed this is the reality. It would have had to be tran-scended.

Notes

1, 2
and 3. See the section of the Bibliography devoted to the works of African writers mentioned in this book.

4. *A New Reader's Guide to African Literature* gives the publication date as 1968 and spells the first name of the translator as Mervin.

5. Tafawa Balewa, *Shaihu Umar*, p.4.

6. Zaynab Alkali, *The Stillborn*, p.18.

7. Zaynab Alkali, *The Virtuous Woman*, p.45.

8. ibid. p. 79.

9. Ibrahim Tahir, *The Last Imam*, p. 195.

10. ibid. p. 200.

11. ibid. p. 240.

12. ibid. p. 12.

13. ibid. p. 121.

14. ibid. p. 17.

15. ibid. p. 49.

16. ibid. p. 65.

17. Chinua Achebe, *No Longer at Ease*, p.7.

18. See Bibliography for the list of the publications of E.K. (also Kola) Akinlade.

19. E.K. Akinlade, *Alosi Ologo*, p. 1.

20. The glossary at the end of *The Interpreters* gives the following explanation for Gambari: "local slang for a Hausaman (pejorative)" p. 253, first edition 1965. Obviously, the locality of this slang must be spe-cific to Yorubaland rather than Hausaland.

21. Wole Soyinka, *The Interpreters*, p.37, first edition 1965.

22. Chinua Achebe, *No Longer at Ease*, p. 83: "I am not going to listen to you any more. I take back my request. I shall start paying you back at the end of this month. Now, this minute! But don't you dare interfere in my affairs again."

VII
Minority Voices and the Nigerian Civil War

The pan-African nature of the discussion of politics and economics in Africa has almost always prevented the mention of the power (political and economic) of the majority ethnic nationalities in relation to the limited power or even powerlessness of the minority ethnic nationalities. From time to time the violent outcome of these power relationships burst into the international media and then dies out as has been the case in Burundi in Central Africa, and as is the case in Mauritania in West Africa. Yet, the relationship between these ethnic nationalities is often volatile, antagonistic and hardly ever friendly and mutually beneficial to them.

In the particular case of Nigeria, it is even possible to say that the minority ethnic nationalities kept the Nigerian federation together. Having no ethnic agenda of their own, minority ethnic nationalities have tended to work for the only institution which guarantees them a space of their own, and this institution is the Federation of Nigeria. At particular times in the history of the federation, each of the major ethnic nationalities had been prepared to end the federation or else break away from it if they could not control it. At each critical time, it has been the effort of the minority ethnic nationalities which had made it possible for the federation to survive. No one has written about the works of Nigerian writers from ethnic minority nationalities from the point of view of their contribution to the survival of the federation. The tradition of lumping all writers together as either Nigerian or African and leaving them as such has led to this neglect.

Ben Okri[1] mentions, in an interview[2] the fact that his father, a lawyer practising in Lagos, could never get the big cases since these were the preserve of the ethnic giants of the country, found himself practising among the petty criminals of the Ajegunle ghetto of Lagos.

Obafemi Awolowo[3] was one of those political leaders of the independence movement in Nigeria who addressed the issue of ethnic nationalities in the country and what should be done to ensure that each national group could keep its language and culture and at the same time participate in the life of the federation. In endorsing an ethnic rather than a pan-African solution to the nation- building agenda, Awolowo could be said to have been helping the British colonial powers to achieve their divide and rule tactics in the country. The political leadership of the North also went along with this solution. This endorsement of ethnic development is one of the reasons why Chinua Achebe labels Awolowo a "tribal leader only".[4]

The British colonial government did attempt to resolve the position of the minorities within the Nigerian federation before the granting of independence. A minorities rights commission, The Willink Commission of Inquiry, was set up in 1957. This was scuttled by the politicking of the major ethnic nationalities by promising that they would rather have independence and then deal with the issue of the minorities after. The British government was then obliged to grant independence to the Federation of Nigeria on the promise that the issue of the alleviation of the fears of the minority ethnic nationalities would be attended to as soon as possible. The history of the federation in its state creation aspect can be seen in the fact that, from four regions in January 1966 when the first coup d'etat took place, Nigeria now has thirty states. Again, because of the manipulation of the process by two of the three major ethnic nationalities, that is the Hausa-Fulani and the Yoruba (the Igbos had been effectively eliminated because they lost the civil war) the creation of states has not benefited the minority ethnic nationalities as it would have been expected to do. Put simply, the creation of new states became a means of cornering for each ethnic nationality more and more of already over-exploited national cake, especially after the concentrated exploitation of petroleum products. Before then, federal fiscal policy insisted on places of derivation of any economic product being the major beneficiary. With the coming of the Petro-Dollar after the civil war, fiscal policy shifted to 'equitable' distribution of available financial resources. This arrangement favoured the three big ones and the sources of these resources suffered.

The first mass creation of states just before the civil war delimited the area of the former Eastern Region confining the Igbo in their own area, far from the oil producing areas of the region. It is against this background that the more directly political writings of two Nigerians from minority ethnic nationalities are examined here. The two writers are Elechi Amadi[5] and Ken Saro-Wiwa.[6]

Elechi Amadi was born in Aluu near Port Harcourt in 1934. After graduating in mathematics and physics from the University of Ibadan, he joined the Nigerian Army Educational Corps. He resigned from the army a few months before the first coup d'etat of January 1966. While his major novels deal with communities untouched by westernisation, his plays and essays deal with the Nigeria of today and the possibilities of its survival. For sometime during the civil war he was detained by the Biafran authorities for his being involved in demanding a state for his minority people. But for the victory of the federal army, there is no doubt that Elechi Amadi might have been executed. Here, it is necessary to quote at length from his civil war diary entitled *Sunset in Biafra* (1973)

> Who were the minority groups? In what is now the Southeastern State we have Efik, Ibibio, Annang, Ogoja and Ekoi tribes. The tribes in present Rivers State are more numerous, smaller and weaker politically. They are: Ijaw, Kalabari, Okrika, Ogoni, Etche, Ekpeye, Engeni, Abua, Ogba, Egbema and Ikwere – to which I belong. Perhaps difficulties in communication in riverine areas gave rise to these numerous distinct tribal groups... Some thirty years ago, the Ibos began to move in to trade in the riverine areas. Eventually many settled and by sheer force of numbers began to dominate the smaller tribes. Igbo came to be so widely used that certain tribes practically lost their mother tongue. It is a fact that one or two riverine tribes can hardly speak their own language now, and have to make do with a peculiar Igbo pidgin highly amusing to the Ibos. A determined effort is now being made to remedy the situation. In some areas this cultural imposition was very pronounced. Igbo was officially taught and spoken in schools. It could hardly be otherwise, since most teachers were Ibos. As the Bible had not been translated into the minority languages, the Igbo Bible and prayer books were used in schools and churches. However, cultural domination in Nigeria also implied political and economic domination. The smaller tribes were not aware of this fact until the fifties, when party (tribal) government became established. Jobs, contracts, scholarships and other privileges were awarded on a tribal basis. The bigger minority tribes like the Efiks, Ibibios and Tivs reacted by fighting to get a few of their men into key positions.[7]

Sunset in Biafra accuses the Biafran state, and one could say by extension, the Federal Republic of Nigeria, of political, economic and cultural imposition of the major ethnic nationalities on the more numerous minority ethnic nationalities. This is how Amadi states the issues in the economic argument:

> An independent Eastern Nigeria with its manpower resources and the revenue from oil could develop into a robust state which could in a short time compete with the developed nations in economic and technological advancement. This argument was not far-fetched. Its one big flaw was that it never took into consideration the will of the minorities who wanted the creation of states for the same reason that the Ibos wanted secession. Very few Ibo men of real influence conceded that the minorities should have a say in the determination of their own future.[8]

Nowhere in the writings of Chinua Achebe would a reader find the representation of this aspect of the 'trouble' with Nigeria.

Saro-Wiwa has made a reputation with his Basi and Company sit-com television series. He has also written one of the most moving novels of the civil war, *Sozaboy* (1985), as well as publishing collections of short stories and plays for stage and radio. As in the case of Elechi Amadi, Ken Saro-Wiwa's thematic concerns are about Nigeria, especially the social malaise. He has made the theme of 'get rich quick' his own through the television series Basi and Company, the scripts and stories of which have been published for both children and adults. *Sozaboy* is an exploration of the failure of, or inability to control, language and the frightening consequences of the impossibility of communication. A young man who convinced himself when the civil war began that he must go to the war as a soldier, partly to impress the girl he loved, finds himself thrown from one side of the conflict to the other. At the end of the civil war he finds that he had lost all he had fought for – the comfort of his mother and his girl-friend.

At the time of writing this, Ken Saro-Wiwa is being detained for his campaign for justice for the minorities of Nigeria in general and the Ogoni in particular. Three of his pamphlets are relevant in this connection. They are The *Ogoni Nationality Today and Tomorrow*, (1968), *Letter to Ogoni Youth*, (1983) and *Ogoni Bill of Rights presented to the Government and People of Nigeria*, (1990). As in the case that Elechi Amadi makes, Ken Saro-Wiwa accuses the major ethnic nationalities of internal colonisation of the minority ethnic nationalities. The *Ogoni Nationality Today and Tomorrow* documents the political experience of the Ogoni within Nigeria. Saro-Wiwa identifies the major defenders of the Ogoni at the 1957/58 Willink Commission of Inquiry into the wishes of the minorities, and the victimisation they experienced from the Ibo government of Eastern Region as a result of their wish to go along with the people of the Rivers if a state or region of their own was going to be created. Elechi Amadi mentions oil in his book. Saro-Wiwa gives details:

> In the late fifties, oil was struck in commercial quantity in the Ogoni nationality; first, it was so-called Afam which is actually Ogoni soil; then it was the Bomu oilfields. The company? Shell-BP.[9]

He quotes a popular song about oil and Shell and the consequences of oil exploration for the Ogoni:

> The flames of Shell are flames of hell
> We bask below their light
> Nought for us save the blight
> Of cursed neglect and cursed Shell.

For the people of Ogoni, Biafra was nothing other than Biakpara which means they, the Ogoni, were to remain poor forever as long as the Ibos were in charge of things. The choice of the Ogoni in the civil war was clear. In large capitals Saro-Wiwa proclaims in this pamphlet:

> It is small nationalities such as ours who have had the worst of everything since Nigeria became independent. It is such nationalities as ours that Yakubu Gowon has saved from extinction.[10]

In *Letter to Ogoni Youth* Saro-Wiwa explains the politics of Nigeria to a younger generation of Ogoni who would not have had the benefit of such information in their history lessons. He attributes the failure of development for the Ogoni people to the "vagaries of Nigerian politics".

> Let me explain what I mean by the vagaries of Nigerian politics. The movement for Nigerian independence gathered momentum after the Second World War. Prior to 1914, Nigeria had been administered in two distinct units – the Protectorate of Northern Nigeria and the Protectorate of Southern Nigeria (for all practical purposes the Colony of Lagos belonged to the South). In 1914, both Protectorates were amalgamated and subsequently split into provinces. Differing administrative practices in both areas led to different attitudes towards British rule as well as independence. These differences are drawn on the basis of the North and the South. As independence began to look like a distant possibility, it became obvious that the country would not continue as a unitary

State divided into provinces. A federal arrangement was therefore worked out.[11]

The fact that the situation has hardly changed for the better
keeps Saro-Wiwa still writing, but also becoming impatient with
the political as well as the intellectual leadership of the country.
He was arrested and detained in June 1993 without trial for his
advocacy of the case of the Ogoni and other minorities in the
country. He accuses the intellectuals who come mainly from the
majority ethnic nationalities of being silent on the plight of the
minority peoples of the country, of ignoring the ecological
tragedy that is the consequence of irresponsible oil exploration
in the riverine areas of the country. The situation is so desperate
that Saro-Wiwa and the Movement for the Survival of Ogoni
People is proposing to take Nigeria to the United Nations on the
charge of genocide against the minority ethnic nationalities,
especially the Ogoni people.

As has been pointed out in the last chapter, Chinua Achebe
and Wole Soyinka hardly pay attention to the northern parts of
the country in their writing; and whenever they do mention it, it
is usually in a pejorative manner. We must remember that the
Hausa-Fulani constitute the third leg of the tripod which has
dominated the politics of Nigeria since amalgamation in 1914. If
for some reason these two Nigerian writers ignore the northern
rivals of their own ethnic nationalities, they would have no time
for smaller units such as the minorities. The positions which
Achebe and Soyinka took during the Nigerian civil war opposed
the rights of the minorities in what was to be the Republic of
Biafra in the case of Achebe, and found no place for the minorities in the case of Soyinka.

The political crisis which began sometime in 1962, or 1964 or
1965, or 1966 (any of these dates would do since one crisis merely repeats the last) developed into a shooting war between the
people of Eastern Region of Nigeria and the rest of the country.
The civil war was to last thirty months.

In 1962, the leader of the Yoruba, Obafemi Awolowo was
jailed for attempting to alter the political arrangement which
had been handed over to the country in the independence constitution of 1959. In 1964, a political crisis was avoided when the
president of the country, Nnamdi Azikiwe, was virtually forced
to call on the Prime Minister to form a new government after an
election characterised by thuggery and widespread rigging. In
1965, the Western Region exploded into a near civil war when

the premier of the region was considered to have rigged the election with the support of the federal government which was in the hands of the Northern region. In January 1966, five majors of the Nigerian Army staged a coup d'etat which ended in their failure to achieve political power. Instead, older and more senior officers took over power. The Southern regions had rejoiced at the staging of the coup d'etat while the Northern region was in mourning. Statistics were later manipulated by those who felt aggrieved to show that the majority of those responsible for the staging of the coup d'etat were of Igbo Eastern region origin. In July 1966, officers of Northern origin in the Nigerian Army staged what was a revenge coup d'etat and killed mainly officers of Igbo Eastern region origin. The killings spilled over into the community generally and the Igbos could no longer be safe anywhere other than their own area of the country. The military leader of the Eastern region appealed to his people to come back home to the East and they responded in thousands, tens and hundreds of thousands. When no agreement could be reached that would guarantee the safety of the Igbos, the state of Biafra was declared as a breakaway country from Nigeria.

Nigerian writers had begun to organise themselves in the Mbari Club in Ibadan soon after independence, and although they did not constitute some kind of school of writing, they had a healthy attitude to each other's individual creative efforts. As a result of the disturbances throughout the country, both Christopher Okigbo and Chinua Achebe moved to Enugu from Ibadan and Lagos respectively. Christopher Okigbo died in the war. While Achebe and Soyinka found themselves on the side of Biafra for different reasons – if in fact it could be said that they were both on the side of Biafra – J.P. Clark, another important member of the group from their Ibadan University days, was firmly on the side of the Federal government. Years were to pass before these former friends and fellow writers were to sit together again, reconciled.

How did Chinua Achebe and Wole Soyinka explain this political crisis in the life of their country? Achebe, in a paper at a political science seminar at Makerere University College, Kampala, Uganda, in August 1968,[12] confronts political scientists of Africa with the issue of Biafra. He begins by insisting, rightly, that any African writer who ignores "the social and political issues of contemporary Africa will end up being completely irrelevant"[13] He then goes on to show that decolonisation did not really take place, at least not in Nigeria, where, according to Chinua Achebe:

> The British... made certain on the eve of their departure that power went to that conservative element in the country which had played no part in the struggle for independence.[14]

This, of course, is a gross mis-representation of the role of the Northern region in the struggle for independence, especially when it is realised that the political party based among the Igbo, Chinua Achebe's people, allied itself with the Northern party in that first independent government of the country. That same Igbo-based political party continued to ally itself with the Northern party in all the future governments of Nigeria before and after the civil war. Achebe characterises this government as being made up of "a bunch of black stooges" ready "to do the dirty work" of the white man "for commission".[15] As far as Achebe is concerned, then, the cause of the civil war in Nigeria had to do with the manipulation of the Nigerian leadership made up of Northerners who had not wanted independence in the first place. This is not the truth. No matter what the initial manipulation of the Nigerian political leaders by the colonial officers might have been in the process of putting together the independence constitution, the final product was agreed to by all, Northeners, Easterners and Westerners, all. In fact, these main ethnic nationalities were so anxious to be rid of the British that they agreed not to deal with the issue of the minority ethnic nationalities in spite of the fact that it would have paid them to wait and settle that particular issue. If Achebe could not say why the civil war came about, could he say why Biafra failed? Being a realistic writer and seeing that the reality that emerged from his experience of Biafra had nothing heroic about it, nothing of grandeur about it, Achebe has written precious little about the Biafran episode in the history of Nigeria.

In the title short story in the collection *Girls at War* we see the process of the degeneration of the idealism which initially buoyed Biafra, to sheer survivalist materialism. Another short story, not included in the first collection of the short stories in the 1972 edition but included in the 1977 edition, speaks even more damagingly about the elite in Biafra and what they thought they were about. 'Sugar Baby' the short story in question, is about Cletus who reduced everything in the enclave to the unavailability of sugar because of the Biafran struggle to free itself from the clutches of the Nigerian hordes. It is left to a white man to rebuke him. He had gone to beg for sugar of a reverend father in charge of the distribution of relief food. This is how the reaction of the white reverend gentleman is described:

> He seized Cletus by the scruff of his neck and shouting wretch! wretch! shoved him outside. Then he went for me; but I had already found and taken another exit. He raved and swore and stamped like a truly demented man. He prayed God to remember this outrage against His Holy Ghost on Judgement Day. Sugar! Sugar!! Sugar!!! he screamed in hoarse crescendo. Sugar when thousands of God's innocents perished daily for lack of a glass of milk! Worked up now beyond endurance by his own words he rushed out and made for us. And there was nothing for it but run, his holy imprecations ringing in our ears.[16]

Chinua Achebe has nothing to say about the plight of the minorities within or without Biafra who, more than others bore the brunt of the civil war.

What about Wole Soyinka? How does he explain the cause of the civil war? Soyinka's *The Man Died* is a personal record of his imprisonment for eighteen months, fifteen of these in solitary confinement during the civil war. In spite of being a personal record, it also includes political speculations. Soyinka believes that the aims of the January 1966 coup-makers were genuine enough, only that things did not work out as they had planned. They lost power to a conservative senior group of officers within the army and it was only a matter of waiting for the blackout of the civil war. According to *The Man Died*, the condition of the civil war was ideal for following through an idea mooted by Victor Banjo. This idea was called The Third Force. Soyinka saw in this "a truly national, moral and revolutionary alternative"[17] to the set-up both in Nigeria and Biafra. The plan of the Third Force was to hijack Biafran power at the point of its final victory over the Federal forces.

Again, like the explanation that Achebe has for the cause of the civil war, Soyinka's explanation is not the truth. It ignores what is on the ground, the reality of the country. Soyinka recommends a socialist resolution of the problems of Nigeria at a time when the constituent parts of the country were looking into their different histories in search of a local solution. But because Soyinka's vision is cast in mythic, rather than realistic terms, it is easier for him to universalise the issues of the immediate crisis – the greed of the elite for political power along with all the material advantages which power carries.

Both Achebe and Soyinka, then, do distort the political reality in the country. One can only say that they did this for their own political reasons. It cannot be said that they did not know of the political and economic rivalries of the three main ethnic nationalities, rivalries which have been responsible for the instability in the country.

Soyinka's literary responses to the civil war have been in the form of a collection of poems, *A Shuttle in the Crypt*, (1972), a play, *Madmen and Specialists*, (1971), and a novel, *Season of Anomy* (1973). Each bears the imprint of being propped up with the aid of ideas from cultures near and far, including European and Asian ones. Some commentators on these works have complained about this involvement of foreign ideas generally in the writings of Wole Soyinka.

Referring to this aspect, Dan Izevbaye writes in his review of *The Man Died*:

> Referring to the more explicit references and allusions in *The Man Died*, a reviewer criticises Soyinka for his heavy reliance on non-African thinkers. With reference to *Season of Anomy*, many of our writers borrow myths from 'white cultures'. It is true that the use to which Soyinka puts the Orpheus myth shows his alienation. But the problem takes us back to early attempts to reduce all world cultures to mere variations of Greek and Roman culture. Frobenius found Prester John at Ife, Nadel discovered another Byzantium in Bida, Fraizer's dying gods also died in Benin, and Robert Graves can locate Yoruba evidence that the lost Atlantis is no myth. Africans too have collaborated by tracing cultural sources to Egypt and the Middle East, using similarities of names and structural features as proofs of cultural diffusion.[18]

Soyinka has defended himself against this charge in the interview published in this same booklet:

> I've read widely in the world's literature, European, Asiatic, American, there are Buddhist reference points and mythologies in my poetry too. In other words, I cannot cut off and will not attempt to cut off what is my experience and what is after all, the world's experience. There is a great deal of intercommunication in the world.[19]

With whatever material Soyinka decides to interpret the situation of Nigeria ("I borrow alien lands/To stay the season of the mind"[20]) and the causes of the civil war, he has ignored the situation as it exists on the ground. And like Chinua Achebe he fails to explain the failure of the Biafran enterprise.

Their failure to provide an adequate explanation of the causes of the civil war in Nigeria does not prevent the two writers from calling attention to the danger that threatens the health of the community if incidents which led to the civil war are not properly explained by those who call themselves the intellectual and political leaders of the community.

The children's book *How the Leopard Got its Claws* written by Chinua Achebe, John Iroaganachi and Christopher Okigbo expresses, quite movingly, the sense of communal danger posed by the type of action taken by the rest of the country against the Igbo in the years and months leading up to the civil war. Here is the poem which Okigbo contributed to the story:

> O Leopard our noble king,
> Where are you?
> Spotted King of the forest,
> Where are you?
> Even if you are far away
> Come, hurry home:
> The worst has happened to us
> The worst has happened to us...
> The common shelter we built
> The cruel dog keeps us from it.
> The common shelter we built
> The cruel dog keeps us from it.
> The worst has happened to us
> The worst has happened to us.[21]

In *How the Leopard Got its Claws* animals once lived together with the Leopard as their king. Leopard called upon all the animals to build a house to which they could always repair in times of danger. They all cooperated, except Dog who insisted that he was satisfied with his cave. Then, one day, there was a great storm and all the animals were forced to seek shelter in their newly completed House of the Animals. Leopard was not in the village at the time, having gone visiting. Dog abandoned his cave and occupied the House of the Animals before everybody else. He then kept all the other animals out of the House. Why was he able to do this? He was the only animal who at this time had sharp teeth which he used to keep the others out in the storm. The animals sent a message to their old king Leopard, asking him to come back but they need not have worried. Dog soon convinces them to declare him their king, then sends out his guards to search everywhere and bring Leopard back to justice for desertion! Fortunately for Leopard, he is able to escape after some mauling from the guards of the new king. When his wounds heal, he goes about arming himself for the ultimate confrontation with Dog and the fickle-minded community of animals. He goes to the most talented blacksmiths in Awka for the sharpest teeth and the best honed claws that their skill could provide. Once the teeth and the claws are in place, Leopard goes to Thunder and begs a little of his voice. Thus equipped Leopard goes back to the House of the Animals. Dog cannot withstand the new Leopard and flees. Leopard is so angry and disappointed at the fickle-mindedness of the animals that he does not resume his position as king. Instead, he disbands the village and destroys the House asking all the animals to return to their individual ways forever.

Achebe's disillusionment, first with Nigeria and then Biafra, was to keep him from composing another work of fiction for almost fifteen years. Herein lies the great importance of his *Anthills of the Savannah* which appeared in 1986 and constitutes his reconciliation with Nigeria. As a result of his world-wide reputation, and expectations from some quarters that his novel would be about Biafra, *Anthills of the Savannah* became one of the most eagerly awaited publications in the history of Nigerian literature. It was clear to me though that the novel could not be about Biafra, since Biafra had been a replay of Nigeria in the most negative aspects of the similarity. The short story 'Sugar Baby' expresses Achebe's anger against the elite of Biafra the way he had never permitted himself to so clearly state in fiction. Neither could the novel be about the fleshing out of the position of Leopard, no matter the correctness of Leopard's analysis that everyone should go back to bear their father's names rather than the name of Nigeria. This would have been against the pan-African commitment of Chinua Achebe. It would have been politically backward. What then would *Anthills of the Savannah* be about? The main action of the novel revolves around a change of guards within the military government, a coup d'etat by the military against the military as has been the case in Nigeria a number of times: July – August 1966, July 1975 and August 1985. But this is the least important issue in the novel. Achebe does settle a few scores with, for instance, the very positive presentation, or re-presentation, of one of the female characters Beatrice, as well as a little more explicit description of adult sexual relations than hitherto available in his other novels and short stories. The major achievement of *Anthills of the Savannah* is that for the first time Chinua Achebe deals with people from all parts of the country. In novels such as *No Longer at Ease* in which most of the action takes place in Lagos, the heart of Yoruba urbanisation, Obi Okonkwo seemed not to have made friends across ethnic boundaries. Awareness, not only of other people from other ethnic nationalities, but also of the usefulness of getting to work with them is one of the major aspects of this novel:

> He was something else, that boy Emmanuel. Why did we not cultivate such young men before now? Why, we did not even know they existed if the truth must be told! We? Who are we? The trinity who thought they owned Kangan as BB once unkindly said?[22]

The trinity are, of course, the Igbo, the Yoruba and the Hausa-Fulani for whom nobody else exists in the country.

Another aspect of this novel which showed Achebe's political development from the days of *A Man of the People* is the fact that there is more criticism here of the system than of persons and individuals. Not only is Achebe or the intervening voice in the novel more respectable to the head of state, the other characters in the novel expect their head of state to be treated properly. Here is Beatrice at a small dinner dance at the palace of the head of state:

> If I went to America today, to Washington DC, would I, could I, walk into a White House private dinner and take the American President hostage. And his Defence Chief and his Director of CIA?[23]

In terms of the probing of the sources of the problems of the state the clowning of politicians no longer suffice for explanation:

> The prime failure of this government began also to take on a clearer meaning for him. It can't be the massive corruption though its scale and pervasiveness are truly intolerable; it isn't the subservience to foreign manipulation, degrading as it is; it isn't even this second-class, hand-me-down capitalism, ludicrous and doomed; nor is it the damnable shooting of striking railway-workers and demonstrating students and the destruction and banning thereafter of independent unions and cooperatives. It is the failure of our rulers to re-establish vital inner links with the poor and the dispossessed of this country, with the bruised heart that throbs painfully at the core of the nation's being.[24]

But the most Nigerian aspect of this novel is the way and manner in which the most important character meets his end which incident ends the novel:

'You go report me for where? You de craze! No be you de ask
about President just now? If you know commot for my front now
I go blow your head to Jericho, craze-man.' 'Na you de craze,'said
Chris. 'A police officer stealing a lorry-load of beer and then
abducting a school girl! You are a disgrace to the force.'

The other said nothing more. He unslung his gun, cocked it,
narrowed his eyes while confused voices went up all around
some asking Chris to run, others the policeman to put the gun
away. Chris stood his ground looking straight into the man's
face, daring him to shoot. And he did, point-blank into the chest
presented to him.

'My friend, do you realize you have just shot the
Commissioner for Information?' asked a man unsteady on his
feet and shaking his head from side to side like an albino in
bright sunshine.[25]

This is not the traditional end of a story in any of the oral traditions of the country. It is not the way and manner a novel termi-
nates the earthly life of its central character. Only a writer who
has observed with superhuman keenness the waste of human
life that is modern Nigeria could have devised this end for the
novel. The ultimate comment of the novel is that life as it is lived
in Nigeria has no meaning.

Achebe makes two other related points in the novel. These are
the primacy of the story and the need for the story teller to withstand any temptation to join the fray. Both points have to be
contested if the argument of this book is to stand. The
spokesperson of the Abazon delegation insists that Recalling-is-
Greatest.

It is the story that outlives the sound of war-drums and the
exploits of brave fighters. It is the story, not the others, that saves
our progeny from blundering like blind beggars into the spikes of
the cactus fence.[26]

If a story ends in mindless and meaningless death, of what use
is its telling? It would seem like the situation which demands
that the telling of stories be suspended while human existence is
corrected.

As for the need for the observer not to tarnish his reputation
by joining the fray such advice simply makes it possible for the
system to continue without any possibility of reformation and
renewal.

I believe I was about to tell the fellow that there was no need for
him to have said that. But I am glad I didn't in the end, because

there are things which an observer can only see if he resists the
temptation to jump into the fray and become an actor himself.[27]

What happened to the writer as teacher? If the teacher does not
join the fray who can do so? At one and the same time, *Anthills
of the Savannah* pointed to a new direction in the work of Chinua
Achebe while back-peddling on his previous commitments.

Soyinka's fears for the health of the community is expressed
in the sentence: "The man dies in all who keep silent in the face
of tyranny." This then is the message of *The Man Died* and the
book documents the tyranny of Gowon's government which
Soyinka felt had to be unseated. Gowon's soldiers fought under
the slogan: "To keep Nigeria one, is a task that must be done".
Soyinka parodies this and says: "To keep Nigeria one, Justice
must be done".

While Soyinka's forte is the theatre, he, from time to time, for-
ays into the prose form. The novel that came as a result of the
civil war is *Season of Anomy*. It is within this novel that Soyinka
presents his ideal of what Nigeria could be without tyranny and
with justice for all. In spite of the overbearing position of the
Orpheus myth in this novel, the structure is based on the example of the apostolic Christian communal village of Aiyetoro in
the riverine areas of Yorubaland in the fifties and early sixties.
Unlike Achebe's vengeful story *How the Leopard Got his Claws*,
Soyinka's is a utopian, behind which the likes of Dentist, a character in the novel, must help to rid the community of the rotten
teeth in it. Like all liberal utopian dreams, this is not easily real-
isable.

The last issue to deal with here is the extent of danger to the
persons of these writers during the civil war. The simple reason
for calling attention to this aspect of the civil war is to speculate
why these writers would endanger their lives and livelihoods
for the concepts and ideas that they believe would benefit either
Nigeria or Biafra or both and fail to put these concepts and ideas
into their writings which would live forever.

There is no fear of exaggeration to say that it was a matter of
life and death for both of them. Chinua Achebe describes the
bombing of his house and the loss of his relations, not to mention his papers, in the short piece which introduces the volume
of poems dedicated to Christopher Okigbo entitled *Don't Let him
Die* (1978) to which Soyinka also contributed.

Here is how Achebe describes his last meeting with Okigbo
who had come to commiserate with him at the bombing:

Okigbo's exit was, for me, totally in character. I can see him clearly in his white 'gown' and the cream trousers among the vast
crowd milling around my bombed apartment, the first spectacle
of its kind in the Biafran capital in the second month of the war. I
doubt that we exchanged more than a sentence or two. There
were scores of sympathizers pressing forward to commiserate
with me or praise God that my life and the lives of my wife and
children had been spared. So I hardly caught more than a
glimpse of him in that crowd and then he was gone like the mete-
or, for ever.[28]

This incident seemed to have been partly responsible for
Achebe's moving to Ogidi.

Fear for his personal safety was a continuing condition of
Soyinka's detention throughout the period and especially during the last months spent in solitary confinement. In the outside
world, there were always rumours that Soyinka might have
died in prison. Achebe mentions this rumour in his presentation
to the political science meeting in Kampala, Uganda.[26] Soyinka
himself describes his fears in *The Man Died*:

I was framed for my activities in gaol. I was framed and nearly
successfully liquidated because of my activities inside prison.
From Kirikiri I wrote and smuggled out a letter setting out the
latest proof of the genocidal policies of the government of
Gowon. It was betrayed to the guilty men; they sought to compound their treason by a murderous conspiracy.[29]

The failure of both writers to effect any change in the way things
were being run underlines their wrong analysis of the causes of
the civil war, at the end of which, Nigeria was kept one but
Justice was not done.

What is the problem in Nigeria which prevented and still pre-
vents the creation of a community of sensibilities in the country?
Basically, it is that the three major ethnic nationalities found no
positive common cause to which to channel the energy of the
people of the country and the resources of their land. The artists
of the country found it difficult to speak on behalf of those not
from their ethnic nationalities. The abiding image has been provided very vividly by Akinwunmi Isola, a Yoruba writer who
has also done translations of Wole Soyinka into Yoruba.[30] He
speaks of the small pots of the ethnic nationalities being brought
together and the contents poured into the big Nigerian pot.
Thereafter, the dilemma of the ethnic nationalities is to keep
their pots and attend to their care or else break them and con-
centrate their energy towards replenishing the national pot

together. The wisdom of ethnicity would dictate that ours is ours but mine is mine. Only the resolution of this dilemma can solve the problem of creating a community of sensibilities in Nigeria. The logic of keeping ours as ours and mine as mine is that everybody must be part of the supervision of what is ours while everybody else must ensure that mine does not impinge on ours. In terms of governance, this means that the winner-take-all tradition of democracy taken over from Westminster must give way to an all inclusive form of democracy where nobody is deemed to be in opposition or else in government.

Notes

1. See Bibliography for the writings of Ben Okri.
2. ICA – Guardian Conversations (Video) Ben Okri with Edward Blishen, 1988.
3. See Bibliography for Obafemi Awolowo's publications.
4. Chinua Achebe's quoted comment after the death of Chief Awolowo in 1987.
5
and 6. See Bibliography for the list of the works of these writers.
7. Elechi Amadi, *Sunset in Biafra*, pp.20–1.
8. ibid. p.41.
9. Ken Saro-Wiwa, *The Ogoni Nationality Today and Tomorrow*, p.7.
10. ibid. p.17.
11. Ken Saro-Wiwa, Letter to Ogoni Youth, p.3.
12. Chinua Achebe, "The African Writer and the Biafran Cause", in *Morning Yet on Creation Day*, pp.78–84.
13. ibid. p. 78.
14. ibid. p. 82.
15. ibid. p. 82.
16. Chinua Achebe, *Girls at War* (2nd edition), 1977, p. 97.
17. Wole Soyinka, *The Man Died*, p. 94.
18. John Agetua, *When the Man Died*, p. 13.
19. ibid. p. 35.
20. Wole Soyinka, 'Massacre October '66' in *Idanre & Other Poems*, p. 52.
21. Chinua Achebe and John Iroaganachi, *How the Leopard Got Its Claws*, p. 18.
22. Chinua Achebe, *Anthills of the Savannah*, p. 191.
23. ibid. p. 81.
24. ibid. p. 141.
25. ibid. p. 215.
26. ibid. p. 124.
27. Chinua Achebe, *Hopes and Impediments*, p. 77.

28. Chinua Achebe, "The African Writer and the Biafran Cause" in *Morning Yet on Creation Day*, p. 83.

> "The white man killed my father
> My father was strong
> The white man raped my mother
> My mother was beautiful

David Diop unfortunately died young. He would have known that the black man can also murder and rape. Wole Soyinka, if he is alive, knows it."

29. Wole Soyinka, *The Man Died*, p. 19.

30. See Bibliography for the works of Akinwunmi Isola.

VIII

Achebe and Soyinka and the World Beyond Nigeria

Nothing demonstrates the contrast between these two writers better than their attitudes to the world at large, the world outside of Nigeria. Both writers recognise that whatever has happened and is happening in Africa has happened before in the past and in other places. Furthermore, it follows that for Africa to reform and renew itself, it must borrow from the experiences of the rest of the world. To what is borrowed will be added whatever can be retrieved from Africa's past, especially that past before the encounter with Europe to achieve a renaissance of Africa. Any African who accepts this position could not consider the encounter between Africa and Europe as totally negative . Another African, who feels strongly that Africa has nothing to learn from Europe as a result of the encounter, is likely to end up dispirited and disillusioned.

The need to learn from Europe becomes even more urgent when it is realised that the structure of the organisation of African society after the encounter with Europe is the nation–state. The European example of the nation-state has dominated world history since the second half of the eighteenth century until now. The Berlin Conference (1884–5) in which Africa was divided into areas of European influence, which later became colonies of such European countries, is as much part of European history as it is of African history. The Organisation of African Unity upheld the nation-state boundaries agreed at that conference.

However sophisticated African states might have been before their encounter with Europe, there is nothing to show that they were as advanced as the European nation-states which conquered them and colonised them. If Africans were serious about making a success of the nation-state system on the continent, it stood to reason that not only must they retrieve something from their past but also borrow something from the European experience of the nation-state.

Looking at the works of these two writers it is clear that they have different attitudes to the world out there in the rest of Africa and the world at large especially the world of Europe and North America.

Achebe and Africa

Chinua Achebe began to write as a conscious reaction to what he considered the misrepresentation of Africa and the African by European writers. His two examples are Joseph Conrad and Joyce Cary.[1]

> I did not know that I was going to be a writer because I did not really know of the existence of such creatures until fairly late.[2]

A little later in the essay from which the above is quoted, Achebe has the following to say about his decision to become a writer:

> At the university I read some appalling novels about Africa (including Joyce Cary's much praised *Mister Johnson*) and decided that the story we had to tell could not be told for us by anyone else no matter how gifted or well-intentioned.
>
> Although I did not set about it consciously in that solemn way, I now know that my first book, *Things Fall Apart*, was an act of atonement with my past, the ritual return and homage of a prodigal son.[3]

Achebe assumes that his personal experience is the experience of other Africans and other Nigerians.

> Later, when I got to know that the European stories I read were written by known people it still didn't help much. It was the same Europeans who made all the other marvellous things like the motor-car. We did not come into it at all. We made nothing that wasn't primitive and heathenish.[4]

This enlargement of one African experience as the totality of all African experience easily permits the missionary commitment with which Achebe assumes the defence of Africa. Like the pan-African ideology to which his work gives validity, the detailing of the experience of each African ethnic nationality becomes suspect and even criminal. European critics who would not dare to call a French writer a European writer do not hesitate to label Achebe an African writer.

There is hardly an awareness of Africa in the works of this African writer. *Anthills of the Savannah* had begun an awareness of Nigeria. Hopefully Achebe's future works will project the experience of being Igbo in a changing Africa, rather than making the Igbo experience the paradigm of all African experience. There is a statement in the delightful essay "Onitsha, Gift of the Niger"[5] which typifies Achebe's basic relationship with the world outside of Nigeria:

> In its 2,600-mile journey from the Futa Jalon Mountains through savannahs, scrublands and desert and then southwards through forest, finally losing itself in a thousand digressions in the Bight of Biafra, the River Niger sees many lands and diverse human settlements, old and new, picturesque and ordinary: Goa and Timbuktu of medieval fame; Lokoja created by British zealots of 'legitimate commerce' one hundred years ago and ridiculed by a sceptical Charles Dickens as so much 'Borrioboola-Gha'; Bussa, passive witness of an explorer's disaster in 1805 now itself sunk beneath the waters of a gargantuan hydro-electric lake. By the time the River Niger gets to Onitsha it has answered many names, seen a multitude of sights; it is now big, experienced and unhurried. Its name is simply Orimili or 'plenitude of waters'.[6]

The entire destiny of the River Niger is the founding of the market town of Onitsha. Whatever else happened on its course towards the coast of what was to become Nigeria was in preparation for that major role of building Onitsha. There is no doubt that the peoples and places along the course of the river may not share such a self-centred interpretation of their river. I once read an article in an Arabic journal published in Cairo in which the River Niger was referred to as one of the rivers of Islam.

It is the same internalising process which makes Achebe marvel at the absence of 'tribalism' in Tanganyika, now Tanzania.

> As a West African I was amazed at the total absence of tribalism in Tanganyika. In this respect the territory is unique in Black Africa.[7]

Achebe goes on to speculate about the reason for this, suggesting that perhaps the tribes here "were too fragmentary and small". The fact of the matter is that in East and Southern Africa wherever there had been white settlements, or attempts at white settlements, all the ethnic nationalities had usually found themselves against white racism. All had been discriminated against in favour of Indians, coloureds and whites that there was really nothing for the ethnic nationalities to fight themselves about. Achebe records in this same piece the rather brusque behaviour

of the receptionist at the British Council when he went there to
check on some people. He also records the complaint of an
Asian:

> Some days later I visited the home of a rich and good-natured
> Asian (with children in expensive public schools in England) who
> complained bitterly that in spite of the large sums of money he
> had contributed to African charity he was neither appreciated nor
> trusted. 'I was born here,' he said,'I have no other home.'[8]

Somehow, Achebe does not comment on this Asian's complaints
and nothing is stated further on the issue of racialism in East
Africa. But the most noteworthy effect of this particular travel to
East Africa is that it makes Achebe accept for other Africans
what he refuses to contemplate for the Igbo people – the acceptance of the need for change in the direction suggested by
Europeans. Commenting on the Wachagga who live on the
slopes of the Kilimanjaro, Achebe concludes:

> Personally, I think the future belongs to those who, like the
> Wachagga, are ready to take in new ideas. Like all with open
> minds they will take a lot of rubbish. They will certainly not be a
> tourist attraction. But in the end life will favour those who come
> to terms with it, not those who run away. I was not surprised to
> find that although the Wachagga had no tradition of art they
> have produced East Africa's best known painter Sam Ntiro, and
> one of its best sculptors.[9]

If this personal opinion is seriously held why does it not affect
the way and manner Achebe writes about the Igbo?

Soyinka, Africa and the World

Soyinka's experience of books and writing differs from that of
Chinua Achebe. Wole Soyinka was born in Abeokuta where,
about a hundred years earlier, the first newspaper in what was
to become Nigeria, was founded. *Iwe Irohin*, literally *newspaper*,
began in 1834. Soyinka's father and his group of friends
watched a performance of *Faust*,[10] and he might have even con-
templated doing some writing himself. He was in touch with
D.O. Fagunwa,[11] the Yoruba novelist, whose first novel *Ogboju
Ode Ninu Igbo Irunmole* Soyinka (fils) was to translate into
English later as *The Forest of a Thousand Daemons*. Soyinka (père)
had reported to his enterprising friend, Sipe, that Fagunwa was
looking for a publisher for a pamphlet he wanted to write
explaining the origins of the Second World War to Nigerians.

Sipe was sceptical doubting that such a publication could be as popular as the man's novels to which Soyinka (père) responded:

> Even from the pen of a famous writer like Fagunwa? And he plans to do it bi-lingually you know, English and Yoruba. And that is only to start with. Later, it will have other bi-lingual versions – English-Ibo, English-Hausa, maybe even Tsekiri and one or two other languages.[11]

Besides growing up in this atmosphere of writing and publishing, Wole Soyinka's father and the Rev. I.O. Ransome-Kuti, the father of the famous Nigerian musician and social critic Fela Anikulapo-Kuti, fought for the inclusion of Yoruba music in Christian church services:

> Daodu (Rev. Ransome-Kuti) also swinging the Union (Nigeria Union of Teachers) fully behind him on the matter of local composers... 'On the banks of Allan waters' must now compete with 'E se rere o'. That's all we ask, let all melodies contend![12]

In the context of all melodies contending, Wole Soyinka took his Yoruba culture to the international arena and insisted that it was as good and valid as any other culture in the world. While Achebe seemed to have assumed that there was only one Europe to which one Africa had to respond, Soyinka recognised the existence of the variety in human cultures and human cultural expressions. The European attempt to down-grade the cultures of Africa was not the whole story of the encounter of Africa with Europe. If it had any importance at all, it was the importance of a particularly virulent single incident in the history of the people.

Thus, Soyinka would not make any special pleading for the nastiness of European imperialism in Africa. Rather, he would insist that because the relationship was that of one weak people and one strong people, it would have been strange if in fact the resulting oppression did not take place. He would further insist that if Africans had the same chance they would also have done the same thing to Europeans.

This is not the position that Achebe takes. When he speaks of Joseph Conrad's *Heart of Darkness*, it is as if he would wish that Joseph Conrad had written the novel to favour Africans. Joseph Conrad was not writing for Africans. He was writing for Europeans. That Africans would one day read his novel perhaps never even occurred to him as a possibility. Achebe's position leads him to write to European culture, not to believe the spokespersons of European culture. Obviously it has not worked, given the continuous complaints of Achebe against racist critics of his novels.[13]

Bearing the shield of Yoruba alternatives to whatever Europe had to offer, Soyinka takes the whole world as his oyster. His first major play was to be one on the Black struggle in South Africa.

At Leeds University, he had joined the University Officer corps:

> At the beginning, mind you, I did believe that our battle front was Southern Africa... And then one stumbled into the huge emptiness of mind of those first-come politicians, a bottomless pit filled with nothing but penkelemes... [peculiar mess] Then you knew the task would have to begin here; [in Nigeria][14]

Only the title of the play, *The Invention*, has survived. But his concern for the struggle in South Africa was later to re-surface in the powerful poems collected in the volume *Mandela's Earth and Other Poems*.[14]

Soyinka's other artistic interventions in Africa include two plays – *Opera Wonyosi*[15] and *A Play of Giants*.[16] Through these two plays, Soyinka ridicules the dangerous inanities of Idi Amin Dada of Uganda, Emperor Bokassa of the Central African Empire and Nguema of Equatorial Guinea.

Soyinka's position seems to assume that whatever the European world thought about Africa it would have thought better of it if it knew about the details of such African peoples as the Yoruba. Ignorance in the first instance would seem forgivable but in spite of the proliferation of information about the plastic and verbal arts of the Africans with such examples as the Yoruba, European thought has hardly budged from positions originally taken out of ignorance. In such a situation only a celebration of those valid alternatives to what Europe has to offer in all its conquering invasion can restore the sanity of the African. Such alternatives exist in the details of the ethnic national cultures of African peoples.

> I have long been preoccupied with the process of apprehending my own world in its full complexity, also through its contemporary progression and distortions – evidence of this is present both in my creative work and in one of my earliest essays, *The Fourth Stage*, included in this collection as an appendix. The persistent thread in the more recent lectures stems from this earliest effort to encapsulate my understanding of this metaphysical world and its reflection in Yoruba contemporary social psyche.[17]

As mentioned earlier, *Anthills of the Savannah* indicate the beginning of a new direction for Chinua Achebe. For the first time in his creative work, he offers an aspect of Igbo culture to the world and permits the young to enact new rituals to meet the new ways of life.

> What must a people do to appease an embittered history?[18]

> She called the little assembly to order and proceeded to improvise a ritual.[19]

> Do you know why I am laughing like this? I am laughing because in you young people our world has met its match.[20]

The offer to the world of aspects of Igbo culture is done boldly in the lecture "African Literature as Celebration."[21]

> I offer to you as one illustration of my pre-colonial inheritance – of art as celebration of my reality; of art in its social dimension; of the creative potential in all of us and of the need to exercise this latent energy again and again in artistic expression and communal, cooperative enterprises.[22]

Chinua Achebe and Wole Soyinka come to the world of writing from different directions. They go to the world from different directions and for different reasons. These differences affect what they write and as such must affect how what they write is understood and re-presented.

Notes

1. Joseph Conrad and Joyce Cary. See Bibliography for their works.
2. Chinua Achebe, "Named for Victoria, Queen of England", in *Morning Yet on Creation Day*, p. 69.
3. ibid. p. 70.
4. ibid. p. 70.
5. in *Morning Yet on Creation Day*, pp.90–2.
6. ibid. p.90.
7. "Tanganyika – jottings of a tourist" p.73 in *Morning Yet on Creation Day*.
8. ibid. p.71.
9. ibid. p.75.
10. Wole Soyinka, *Isara – A Voyage Around Essay*, p.101.
11. ibid. p.153.
12. ibid. p.53.
13. See for instance the essay "Colonialist Criticism" in *Hopes and Impediments*, pp.46–61.

14. Wole Soyinka, *Mandela's Earth and Other Poems*, Ibadan: Fountain Publications, 1989. Also London: Methuen, 1988.

15. *Opera Wonyosi*, first performed in 1977.

16. See Bibliography.

17. Wole Soyinka, *Myth,Literature and the African World*, p. ix. "The Fourth Stage" appeared first in *The Morality of Art: Essays Presented to G. Wilson Knight*, ed. D. W. Jefferson, published in London by Cambridge University Press in 1973.

18. Chinua Achebe, *Anthills of the Savannah*, p.220.

19. ibid. p. 222.

20. ibid. p. 227.

21. in *Chinua Achebe: A Celebration*, eds. Kirsten Holst Petersen and Anna Rutherford, pp.1– 10.

22. ibid. p.3.

IX

Achebe and Soyinka and their Critics

Everyone involved in the enterprise 'African Literatures', like everyone involved in literatures produced by territories formerly colonised, acknowledges the peculiar nature of this product.The writers, even when they write in African languages, write from a multi-lingual, multi-ethnic and multi-cultural background. Their critics, especially those from Europe and North America, usually write from a mono-lingual and mono-cultural background. The inadequacy of this background has always been veiled by the conception that African literature is one single unit and that multiplicity and variation in African cultures do not exist. This means that the influence of these cultures and their languages on the writers are not acknowledged. Wole Soyinka has in fact spoken of this "ignorance of the cultural variants on the African literary products"[1] If the critics of African literatures have been unwilling to acknowledge these cultural variants, the writers themselves, and particularly those writing in European languages, have also been wary to expose their foreign readers to the full blast of African cultures and African cultural norms. Some African writers have even been adamant in insisting that they were simply writers, not 'African' writers.

Three main peculiarities have set African literatures apart from previous literatures. While the language of composition determined the nomenclature previously – English literature, German literature etc, – the coming of colonies and colonial societies brought into existence literatures which have carried geographical specifications. One of these peculiarities is that Africans are writing in languages other than their mother tongues. While the validity of the complete truthfulness of this situation has been questioned by both critics and writers, little has been done to pin down the limitations of such a practice. Even where writers such as Ngugi have gone on to virtually

denying their previous writing, in this case in English, no critics
have come forward to work on what limitations are placed on
the English language in doing what Achebe believes that
African writers could make the language do, which is to carry
the burden of the African experience.[2] Does the English language, for instance, contain the totality of the African experience?

A second peculiarity is that most of this writing was largely
published in Europe and North America. This peculiarity cries
out for explanation, especially in Nigeria where there had been
publication of fiction in English locally long before Amos
Tutuola's *The Palmwine Drinkard*[3] was published in London in
1952, and Chinua Achebe's *Things Fall Apart* was published, also
in London, in 1958. All of Cyprian Ekwensi's [4] shorter fiction
was published at Onitsha to begin with, and T.M. Aluko[5] had
published his first novel *One Man, One Wife* in Lagos as well.
Perhaps, one of the reasons for the need to publish overseas
could have been the sparse attention paid to these publications
by European and North American critics. However, these local
publications which were in English had a readership. In addition, there were books and readers in the Nigerian languages,
such as Yoruba and Hausa. In time, a critical tradition would
have evolved.

The third peculiarity seems to be a result of this need for local
critics. This peculiarity is that the critical response to African literatures has been based on critical understanding of European
and North American literatures in the various European languages. The literary tradition of Europe which began to inform
the interpretation of African literatures comes from the development of Humanism since the period of the Renaissance in
Europe. Humanism aspired towards the creation of an aggre-
gate of human values to be housed in the word 'universalism'.
The result of this idiosyncrasy is that most African literary criticism tends to be done by means of title analysis of each author's
output, something that would not be done if the critics were
dealing with the literary output of a French or German writer.
Usually such writer's output is considered against the background of the sociology, the philosophy, the politics and the literature of France or Germany, as the case of the writer may be.
The fact that many African writers writing in these languages
called upon the Humanist tradition, and sometimes wrote
against and with the express attention to European and North
American texts, made it mandatory for the critics of Europe and

North America to respond, and do so from their own antecedents. Achebe's case is well known in the sense that his first novels were deliberately written to counter some of the novels of Joseph Conrad and Joyce Cary.

As for the criticism of African literatures, three trends can be identified. The great tradition of humanist universalism is the first one. For reasons obvious from what has been said earlier, this kind of criticism has not usually paid attention to the African languages and cultures which have influenced the works of the African writers being considered. Such practice of criticism has been either as a result of ignorance, or out of a feeling that such detailed consideration did not matter or was not necessary. From the various protests which have emanated from writers such as Ayi Kwei Armah, Chinua Achebe and Wole Soyinka, it is obvious that such consideration of the various cultural influences was important for the understanding of the works of African writers.

The second trend in the criticism of African literatures began in the 1970s. Given the parlous state of the socio-economic condition of African countries, which led both self-declared radical as well as conservative governments to the doors of the International Monetary Fund and the World Bank with begging bowls, it was only natural that writers and their writing would be subjected to a more radical set of critical values. Radical critics from the Russian Revolution as well as Euro-Marxists became the guides at this period. Universalism and its parent notion of Humanism were labelled as bourgeois and the idea of art for the sake of art was dismissed. Criticism began to dictate to literature how to make itself an instrument, a weapon of the much needed African revolution. Here also, little attention was paid to the tradition of radicalism in the countries from which the writing and the writers came.

The third trend – and perhaps the most recent – is the Deconstructionist, Semiotic, Post-modernist criticism of which little is going to be said here. Much of African literary criticism, because of its refusal to pay attention to the cultural variants that Wole Soyinka has mentioned, is not only incomplete, it is also inadequate. Within the first ten years of the appearance of the first major work of African fiction to get noticed in Europe and North America, African writers were already complaining about the type of criticism their works were receiving.

In two early essays, Chinua Achebe takes on both foreign and African critics of African literatures. He condemns, for instance, the insistence of some of these critics to valorise universalism since it seemed to demand that the African writer must write what European critics consider to be universal, thus denying African product its African origin. The two essays – "Colonialist Criticism"[6] and "Where Angels Fear to Tread"[7] castigate the ignorance of Africa displayed by some of these critics and literary journalists. But Achebe is also aware of the African writer's intellectual entanglement with European culture and literature. He points out:

> The first big point to remember is that Nigerian writers cannot eat their cake (or eba or whatever they eat) and have it. They cannot borrow a world language to write in, seek publication in Europe and America and then expect the world not to say something about their products, even if that were desirable.[8]

While Achebe's anger has been against universalists, that of Soyinka has been focused on self-styled radical critics. The group of critics who have felt this anger most are the triumvirate of Chinweizu, Jemie and Madubuike, as well as the Ibadan-Ife based socialist critics. To this latter group of critics are to be added European and North American critics such as Gerald Moore and Bernth Lindfors and a drama critic writing in the *New York Times* in 1989. Gerald Moore, Soyinka insists, hides behind local Nigerian Marxist critics to question some aspects of his works. Moore for instance reads *Season of Anomy* as Soyinka's attempt to foist on the rest of Nigeria, the feudalistic system of the Yoruba. What Soyinka does, according to Moore, is to locate the action of the novel about the Nigerian civil war in a Yoruba experimental community. Although this is a historically correct thing to do it would seem to disturb Gerald Moore.[9]

Bernth Lindfors' offence is worse since he is accused of publishing inaccurate information about Soyinka. Dubbing Lindfors as 'Hagiographer Extraordinary' Soyinka says (commenting on Lindfors's essay "The Early Writings of Wole Soyinka"):

> "...every page contains at least one inaccuracy of time and place and a series of absurd attributions."[10]

Soyinka is even angrier though with the local Marxist critics.

> When the critics gather themselves together at the Annual Leftocratic Convention in orgies of ideological puritanism, they seem unaware of a process of attrition in the actual productivity of a potential generation of authors. Perhaps no literature is better than certain kinds of literature; that is quite possible. I only ask that they understand the negative, sterilising effect which a

misuse of critical notions, a misplacement of their own socio-critical situating now has both on the quality and actual quantity of output among students from their captive audience in the lecture-room.[11]

Soyinka is angriest with Chinweizu and his co-authors of the article and the book which claimed to be helping towards 'decolonising' African literature.[12] Their case against Soyinka is that he is obscure in his poetry and not African in his prose writing. At the same time these critics hold up Achebe as the best example of African writing: simple and African. How Soyinka goes about debunking their arguments is one of the best examples of misunderstandings brought about by critics not taking into consideration the cultural variants in existence in Africa. Soyinka illustrates his argument with the compactness of African carvings and with the complexities of the Yoruba Ifa Divination poetry.

> It is most magnificently, overwhelmingly expressed in African sculpture, especially those specimens which suggest a technique of impacted planes to which the term cubism is sometimes given... This reading is of course both specifically and assertively mine. It is subjective, but it is based also on an immersion in the *dialectics of continuity* so inextricably interwoven into the poetry of Ifa divination, proverbs, riddles, the 'iwi' of masquerades and even oral history.[13]

Is Chinweizu capable of understanding where Soyinka is coming from without an understanding of Ifa divination poetry and its various roles in Yoruba language and culture? Does Chinweizu valorize a divination system in his Igbo language and culture? Does such a system of divination and poetry exist in Igbo language and culture? It can only be inadequate for a critic, African or foreign, to assume that because Soyinka writes in English, the critic who happens to read English, would understand him completely.

The caution that needs to be heeded then is not that non-Africans, or that non-Yoruba or non-Igbo, cannot criticise Nigerian writing and writers, but that whoever wants to interpret these writers must understand the multi-lingual, multi-ethnic and multi-cultural background from which they spring: Western European, British, African, Nigerian, Yoruba, Igbo and so on and so forth in all their complexities and multiplicities. African writers are not simply the renaissance men and women they have often been called. They are today the most eligible cit-

izens of the global village. They speak various international languages, they are aware of various world cultures, but all these
only make them men and women of their own languages and
cultures when they write.

Perhaps a survey of European and North American critics and
criticism today would show that non-African critics of African
literatures have grown up and matured beyond the initial reactions of their elders of the 1950s and the 1960s. Or perhaps what
might be revealed is that interest in things African has so waned
that it really does not matter. What matters, then, are the works
of individual critics of European and North American origin
such as the French critic Alain Ricard who has written extensively about the concert party in Togo and on Wole Soyinka;
and Richard Bjornson who has written one of the most detailed
studies of Cameroonian writings. The abundance of details
which earlier foreign and African critics omitted is available in
these studies. Unfortunately, it is not true to say that the pattern
of criticism found in the writings of Alain Ricard[14] and Richard
Bjornson[15] has become the norm in the criticism of African literatures.

Richard Bjornson was professor of French and Comparative
Literature at the Ohio State University as well as editor of
Research in African Literatures before his sudden death in 1992. In
his *The African Quest for Freedom and Identity: Cameroonian
Writing and the National Experience*,[16] he tackles the issue of the
Cameroonian nationality as portrayed by literary writing in
French and English. Some of his comments are not irrelevant to
the issues dealt with in this book:

> A major impetus for Cameroonian writing during the colonial
> period was the desire to challenge European misrepresentations
> of Africa by portraying African realities from an African point of
> view.[17]

Bjornson concludes correctly that:

> Yet the term national literature is like any other schema that is
> used to describe a complex, ambiguous reality. It can reveal only
> a portion of that reality. In the case of the Cameroon, it does not
> do justice to the ethnically based oral literature that still shapes
> the dominant universe of discourse for millions of people.[18]

While agreeing with Bjornson about his conclusion, there is
the need to add that the critic who wishes to capture the totality
of that particular African reality needs to look at the material
written in the local languages, especially the local languages

spoken by the various writers he or she is dealing with. Invariably, the reality presented in writings in the European languages is not only a portion of the total reality but also differs from those in the African languages if not even contradicts them.

Alain Ricard is at the University of Bordeaux and one of the editors of *Politique Africaine*. His doctoral thesis had been on a comparative study of Wole Soyinka and Le Roi Jones and later published *Théâtre et Nationalisme: Wole Soyinka et LeRoi Jones*.[19] Unlike Bjornson, Ricard deals with the Yoruba background of Wole Soyinka both in its oral form and in the literature written in Yoruba. It is as a result of this that Ricard can conclude that:

> Une nouvelle culture doit naître de la rencontre entre l'Occident et les cultures africaines. Wole Soyinka souhaite intégrer son heritage yoruba dans une culture nigeriane composée d'un heritage africain et d'une contribution occidentale[20]

> (A new culture must grow as a result of the encounter between the West and African cultures. Wole Soyinka attempts to integrate his Yoruba culture with a Nigerian culture made up of African heritage and some western contribution)

Few North American and European critics have bothered to so study the details of the oral and written texts of African languages. It is for this reason that three important issues must be raised here, issues which affect the proper understanding of African literatures.

The first issue is the paradox of European concepts such as humanism expressible in a European slogan such as 'liberty, equality and brotherhood'. Europeans and North Americans are justly proud of their tradition of such concepts and speak glowingly of the struggle to achieve these ideals in their societies. African intellectuals have been brought up in this celebration. At the same time, these same Europeans and North Americans in their differing guises as missionaries, travellers, administrators and politicians stand these ideals on their heads once they are in Africa or the Caribbean or anywhere else but Europe and North America. The African intellectual, including the African writer, becomes the means of preaching the ideals of Europeans and North Americans to the very same Europeans and North Americans. The African writer then shares the intellectual history of Europe and North America along with its ideals, but does not see these ideals being put to practice in the actions of Europe and North America on the African continent.

The second issue is that of the transition from oral to a written form of artistic expression and the implications for the position of the writer. The artist in African societies, perhaps like in all exclusively oral societies, because of the immediacy of his audience, tended to deal with things communal. He becomes even the voice of the community and speaks in their name. The artist in the western tradition of writing which has been the main influence on us, tends to work alone, away from his potential audience. The African writer combines both worlds, speaking on behalf of his community but at the same time using the tactics of the Western and North American writer. Perhaps in the not too distant future there will be African writers who would wish to write from their individual and particularist angst. For now such personal angst is subsumed under the collective agenda of clans, tribes, ethnic nationalities, etc.

The third issue is that European and North American readers of African literatures must acknowledge the diversity of African cultures. In some ways, African writers themselves have encouraged the tendency of blurring the cultural lines. Coming as they do from multi-cultural backgrounds and writing from these cultural backgrounds, European as well as African, they are likely to object when their writing is judged according to only one of these cultures alone.

Notes

1. Wole Soyinka, *Art, Dialogue and Outrage*, p. 266.
2. Achebe in "The African Writer and the English Language" in *Morning Yet on Creation Day*, pp. 55–62.
3. See Bibliography for the list of Amos Tutuola's writing.
4. See Bibliography for the list of Cyprian Ekwensi's writing.
5. See Bibliography for the list of T.M. Aluko's writing.
6. "Colonialist Criticism" in *Hopes and Impediments*, pp. 46–61.
7. "Where Angels Fear to Tread" in *Morning Yet on Creation Day*, pp. 46–8.
8. ibid. p.46.
9. Wole Soyinka, *Art, Dialogue and Outrage*, p. 167.
10. ibid. p. 168.
11. ibid. p. 165.
12. Chinweizu et al in *Transition* magazine 1974, and *Towards the Decolonization of African Literature*.
13. Wole Soyinka, *Art, Dialogue and Outrage*, pp.105–106.
14. See Bibliography for the list of Alain Ricard's writing.

15. See Bibliography for the list of Richard Bjornson's publications.

16. Richard Bjornson, *The African Quest for Freedom and Identity: Cameroonian Writing and the National Experience*, Bloomington and Indianapolis: Indiana University Press, 1991.

17. ibid. p. 457.

18. ibid. p. 460.

19. Alain Ricard, *Théâtre et Nationalisme: Wole Soyinka et LeRoi Jones*, Paris: Présence Africaine, 1972. The book has been translated into English by Femi Osofisan as *Theatre and Nationalism: Wole Soyinka and LeRoi Jones*, Ile-Ife: University of Ife Press, 1983.

20. ibid. p. 175.

X

Achebe, Soyinka and the Languages of African Literatures

The language debate in African literatures can now be considered in terms of the activities of three individuals over the last three decades: Obi Wali and the celebrated article he published in *Transition* magazine in September 1963;[1] Wole Soyinka's declaration, through the Union of the Writers of African Peoples meeting in Accra that Swahili be adopted as one common African language in 1975 and the repetition of the same suggestion at Festac in Lagos in 1977;[2] and the well-publicised decision of Ngugi wa Thiong'o first to change his name from James Ngugi in 1972 and to thereafter stop writing in English and write only in Gikuyu and Swahili in 1986.[3] Wali's point was that if African writers persisted in the use of European languages in the expression of African sentiments and culture they would end in a cultural cul-de-sac. The implication that was obvious in his essay was that unless African writers used African languages to create African literature there would be nothing to be called African literature.

At the particular time that Obi Wali wrote this article everything seemed to be working for Africa. The disillusionment was still to come. The spate of military governments that would be the blight of the sub-Saharan region was just beginning with the possible suggestion of a positive alternative. It is therefore not surprising that reaction to Obi Wali was quick and not particularly sympathetic:

> Although he (editor of *Transition*) had predicted that Wali's article might 'cause some anxious heart-searching among the young writers of this Continent' (p. 3 of that issue) the reaction must have surprised even Neogy by its stridency and persistence. The uproar, in fact, did not die down until two years later.[4]

Wole Soyinka's response to Obi Wali's article was to insist on the right of the writer to choose whichever language he/she felt comfortable enough to write in:

> I learn a great deal about my opinions every day and it was a new revelation that I do not consider Yoruba suitable for any of my plays. But what about Ibo? May I know what Obi Wali has done to translate my plays or others' into Ibo or whatever language he professes to speak?[5]

Chinua Achebe did not respond until almost two years after the appearance of Obi Wali's article. "English and the African Writer", Achebe's response, was later re-published in his first collection of essays *Morning Yet on Creation Day*.[6] Achebe's defence is less cavalier than that of Soyinka and goes along with the two best known arguments: firstly, that English is the language of national unity in Nigeria, as European languages are in other multi-ethnic and multi-lingual African countries. This convenience must not be underestimated. This first argument is still heard from country to country, for instance as in the case of the adoption of English as the national language of independent Namibia. The second argument, which Achebe also deploys, is that writing in African languages is not practicable. European languages, it is argued, give African writers a hearing at an international level as well as providing a living. Beyond these two arguments Achebe then demonstrates how an African writer, combining the strengths of his or her African language, with the non-racialist possibilities of English or any other European language can achieve success in expressing African culture in a European language.

By the time Wole Soyinka made his suggestion that Swahili be adopted as the continental language of Africa in 1975, Africa had gone through some sobering experiences. Nigeria had gone through a debilitating thirty-month civil war and most sub-Saharan African countries were under military rule. The economy of the continent was stagnant if not deteriorating. The novels of disillusionment, such as Ayi Kwei Armah's *The Beautyful Ones Are Not Yet Born* and Chinua Achebe's *A Man of the People* had appeared and encouraged a school of writing which saw little hope for the African situation. Perhaps it was time to consider radical alternatives. The issue of language once more became paramount.

The inaugural meeting of the Union of the Writers of the African Peoples took place in Accra, where Wole Soyinka was living at the time, in 1975. Another meeting of the Union took place in Dakar, Senegal, hosted by then President Leopold Sédar Senghor, in 1976 at which Tchicaya U Tamsi was elected president and Wole Soyinka Secretary-General.

The first two aims of the Union as published in a statement from the Secretariat in Accra are as follows:

1. To encourage and promote the literature of Africa in all languages in use on the continent.

2. To give especial encouragement to the literature of Africa in the indigenous languages and at the same time promote the adoption of a single language for the continent of Africa, as an instrument and symbol of the unity of African peoples everywhere. It must be understood that this language is intended to be a common means of expression and communication accessible to all, not a replacement of existing languages.[7]

It is important to note that Swahili is not mentioned in this statement although it came up in the discussions, in which I participated, and which preceded the framing of the aims of the Union.

The Second World and African Festival of Arts and Culture, commonly known as Festac '77, provided an opportunity for Soyinka to propose Swahili on his own personal authority. In his contribution to the Colloquium which accompanied Festac '77, entitled "The Scholar in African Society" Wole Soyinka, according to Professor Moyibi Amoda,

seems to be (making) a cultural nationalist argument, a neotraditionalist argument. But this is not where he wishes to lead us. The question is what has happened to the world of our fathers, for we are not immediately our fathers' sons. How are we to speak with the integrity and autonomy of our fathers in a world context where we are woefully trapped?[8]

The Working Group Two of the Festac '77 Colloquium, whose brief had to do with 'Black Civilization and African Languages', recommended the

teaching in African languages literacy campaigns for the masses in African languages; the use of African languages in public life, publication and dissemination of literary and scientific works and the development of information in African languages; collaboration in teaching and research on African languages.[9]

Again, there is no mention of Swahili but at a press conference which Wole Soyinka held soon after Festac '77, he suggested that Swahili be the language of continental Africa. Chinua

Achebe's reaction to this suggestion was that Soyinka was only further burdening Nigerians, who had over two hundred languages to choose from with one additional language.[10]

Ngugi's decision to change his name in 1972 was followed with a period of work in Kenya especially in the theatre in Limuru. The effectiveness of working in the language of the majority of the people taught him that the use of Gikuyu was the only logical road to literary relevance, and so in 1986 Ngugi wa Thiong'o published his book *Decolonising the Mind: The Politics of Language in African Literature*. It is in this essay that Ngugi stated his case for deciding to write only in Gikuyu and Swahili rather than in English.

Before dealing with the present situation in Nigeria, whereby Achebe seems determined to stick with English but able to explore the use of Igbo language for poetry and drama, and Soyinka is having many of his publications translated into Yoruba, it is necessary to go back to the language situation of Nigeria during the period of Christianisation and the beginning of colonial rule. The question which needs to be asked is: was English imposed on Nigerians, or did the Nigerian elite find it necessary to impose English on themselves and on their children?

The English language came into Nigeria as the language of the missionaries, the tongue of the merchants and the medium of communication of the empire builders. The missionaries wanted the Africans to internalise the message of Jesus Christ through their mother tongues and so insisted on learning the languages of the Yoruba and the Igbo. The merchants were prepared to bargain and in the process pidgin English evolved. Only the empire builders and the colonial administrators refused to change their language. English it had to be.

Two developments were to further this situation and make English the desirable language to learn for Nigerians. While the Church Missionary Society, the Protestant Mission, had been prepared to teach the Christian message in Yoruba and Igbo,the Catholic Mission came into the South-eastern part of Nigeria and insisted on English as a means of gaining an immediate advantage. The following is how Bishop Shanahan put the case for English:

> Why was the European D.O. [District Officer] in charge of tens of thousands of Ibos? Was it because he had more money or more wives or more influence? No, the answer was that he was more educated. Why was the interpreter so contemptuous of local

views and so insistent on heavy bribes before he would explain a
case properly? Because he knew English which he had learnt at
school, and because no local knew enough English to follow what
he was saying. And look at the Court Clerk and the Court
Messengers, the most influential and the most feared men in the
district. Why were they chosen for their jobs? Simply because
they had been to school and understand English. Why, they all
knew the Court Clerk could distort and recast every written word
while their titled men could not read a single line.[11]

The second development was the growing need for Africans
with basic English to work as clerks in colonial government
offices and with the commercial houses. Educated Africans from
Sierra Leone and the Gold Coast (now Ghana) had been brought
into the country to do these duties. Now, the colonial administration wanted local people to become the clerks and the petty
officers of the administration. They "even set up model schools
where the emphasis was placed on English".[12]

There was yet another development which made the acquisition of English part of the process of thwarting the plans of
some white supremacists within the missions. Sometime during
the second half of the nineteenth century quinine had been dis-
covered as a cure for malaria which until then had been deadly
for white people on the West African coast and had given the
region the epithet of 'the white man's grave'. This period
seemed to have coincided with the fall of Bishop Crowther, the
first African Bishop in West Africa.[13] With the possibility of
white people able to stay longer in West Africa, the white missionaries taught themselves the local languages. They also
insisted that Africans working with the church perform evange-
lization in local languages rather than in English to ensure that
white missionaries did not have competition from African clergymen able to use English.

The result of these developments was to make the acquisition
of English virtually mandatory for Nigerians. Given this situation, does it really make sense for Nigerians to say that imperialist colonial Britain imposed the English language on them?

Even if it was possible to make this accusation during the
period of colonial rule, does such an accusation against Britain
remain valid after the winning/granting of independence? If
African countries such as Namibia, newly independent in the
last decade of the twentieth century, decide to adopt English as
their national language, what has this got to do with the British
colonial government of a quarter of a century ago?

As mentioned earlier, Chinua Achebe has experimented with traditional Igbo poetry and spoke about the possibility of doing some theatre work using Igbo.[14] But given the fact that he has to live outside of Nigeria at the present time, it is not likely that this plan will materialise.

As for Wole Soyinka, the language situation seems to be in his favour. Akinwunmi Isola has translated *Ake The Years of Childhood* as well as *Death and the King's Horseman* into Yoruba. This development gives a completely different dimension to the debate about the use of whichever language for creative writing in Africa. For one thing, the issue has been taken out of the realm of rhetoric to the plane of practical possibilities.

The Example of Ireland

On the basis that Chinua Achebe and Wole Soyinka are writing from behind the masks of their ethnic origins, and that some of their writings – at least in the case of Wole Soyinka – are being translated into Yoruba, these two writers bring African literature to the same situation that Irish writers have pushed what has become known as Anglo-Irish literature. For centuries Irish writers have written about Irish culture in the English language, providing a little acknowledged precedence for African writers using European languages.

Ireland was the first colony of England. The way and manner in which Ireland was treated pointed to the way the English colonies of the future were to be maltreated. One of the major effects of colonisation on Ireland is the complete replacement of the Irish language, Gaelic, with English to the extent that by the end of the eighteenth century English had virtually replaced Gaelic in Ireland.

Recent writings on the history, culture and literature of Ireland have had recourse to the analysis made of colonial and post-colonial Africa in order to understand the present situation of Ireland. Using the cultural history of Ireland to buttress points about African cultural situation is only natural.[15]

Just as Caliban's speech in Shakespeare's *The Tempest* (Act I Scene 2)

> You taught me language; and my profit on't
> Is, I know how to curse:

is often quoted in writings by Africans and people of the African diaspora, on the language issue in African literatures,[16] the speech of Captain MacMorris in Shakespeare's *Henry V* (Act III, Scene 2) is usually quoted in writings about nationality in Irish culture and literature. In a military camp discussion, an English soldier says to Captain MacMorris:

> FLUELLEN: Captain Macmorris, I think, look you, under your correction, there is not many of your nation–
>
> MACMORRIS: Of my nation! What ish my nation?... What ish my nation? Who talks of my nation?

The question which Captain Macmorris asks as an English Irishman fighting for the English crown is pertinent to the situation of the African writer. When Ngugi wa Thiong'o insists on writing in Gikuyu in modern day Kenya, what is Ngugi's nationality? When Chinua Achebe says that he is an Igbo writer and Wole Soyinka says he is a Yoruba writer and both of them write in English, what is their nationality?

It is necessary to bring the issue of language close to that of nationality if critics are to put to rest finally the literary and linguistic problems raised by the use of the language of former colonisers in the expression of the identity and culture of the colonised.

The most critical political revolutions of the last two hundred years have not emphasised the right of every human being to his or her own language. The French Revolution worked hard to destroy the minority languages of France with little protest. The Bolshevik Revolution recognised the rights of different languages in the newly put together Union of Soviet Socialists Republics, but it still saw expressions of individual languages and cultures as nationalistic and so dangerous to the overall interest of the larger state. At the end of the twentieth century, the right to speak one's language seems finally to have made it to the tablet of human rights.

The struggle for Ireland had begun with the effort to re-suscitate the Gaelic language and the language struggle formed part of the ambitions of those who fought to free Ireland from centuries of English colonisation. The details of the Irish experience of English imperialism and colonialism differ from those of Africa. All the same, being a settler type of colonialism, the general implications remain the same for all colonized, Irish or African. In this particular instance, it is the issue of language which is relevant to the present study.

Over a period of five centuries Ireland was occupied and colonized by the English. Deliberate policies were pursued to erase
the Gaelic language and culture of the Irish.

By the end of the 19th century the linguistic balance had shifted radically in favour of English, there being $2\frac{1}{2}$ million English
speakers to roughly $\frac{1}{2}$ million Irish speakers.[17]

Thus, an almost total language change took place in Ireland.
Against such a language loss, cultural retention and efforts at
language retrieval, the writings of Oscar Wilde, George Bernard
Shaw, W.B. Yeats, John Millinton Synge, James Joyce and
Samuel Beckett, to name a few of the well-known Irish writers,
the works of these writers demanded an added refining term
where Irish and English join to become Anglo-Irish – something
more than Irish and English. What is the implication of this dual
composition that expresses Irish culture in the English language,
a language imposed far more forcefully on the Irish than on
Africans?

The Irish accept rather grudgingly that

> in adopting the English tongue the Irish, though losing some-
> thing of their national heritage, have gained in many respects...
> with the English tongue comes too the English literature, more
> rich and varied than that of any modern European nation... [18]

This grudging acknowledgement is made in the context of a
freedom of action and/or inaction which the Anglo-Irish writer
has which an English (-in-England) writer does not possess. This
freedom is what the Argentine writer Jorgé Luis Borges
(d. 1986)suggested that,

> like the Jews in world culture, the Irish have been outstanding in
> English because they act within that culture and at the same time
> do not feel tied to it by any special devotion.[19]

The implication for Anglo-Irish literature then of expressing
Gaelic culture in English language was that critics had to
endeavour

> to throw up a body of criticism which might explain their limita-
> tions and point the way ahead [20]

In order to attempt such a criticism, it would be necessary to
accept that

> a total understanding of Anglo-Irish literature certainly depends
> on an accurate and sensitive knowledge of that Gaelic Irish litera-
> ture which has increasingly affected and conditioned it.[21]

In summary, what the Anglo-Irish experience tells African writers and critics is that it is possible and it is acceptable that one culture can express itself in the language of another culture. This is a position which Chinua Achebe has maintained all the time. Ernest Emenyonu, through his book, *The Rise of the Igbo Novel*, has also maintained this position but without the intellectual rigour that would permit extending the same arguments to other African languages which have provided the background to African literature in European languages.

Another fact emanating from the Anglo-Irish experience is that political convenience has been a major deciding factor in the making of language choices for creative writing by ex-colonial subjects who wanted to write. Both Chinua Achebe and Wole Soyinka have maintained the practicality of this option. Wole Soyinka has also pointed out the fact that nobody seems to question the fact that every African coup-maker has always found it necessary to address his nation in English, or any other European language, in setting out the reasons for the drastic military action taken. The basic supporting argument for this practical position is of course the validity of the modern nation-state which, in the case of Ireland as well as many African and Asian countries, had to be built and sustained in English, or any other of the European languages of colonisation. Should the nation-state lose its validity and be rejected as a platform for the collective action of the multi-ethnic, multi-lingual and multi-cultural populations of these nation-states, perhaps then there would be no longer any use for the European languages of colonisation.

Perhaps the most important lesson which the Irish experience provides for the African writer and critic is that the literature which results from writing African culture in a European language is more than the sum total of both the African culture expressed and the European language utilised.

As Flann O'Brien observed in a letter to Sean O'Casey, every Irish writer who uses the English language with resource and imagination owes an indirect debt to his native language, whether he has learned to speak it or not:

> 'I agree absolutely with you when you say that the Irish language is essential, particularly for any sort of literary worker. It supplies that unknown quantity in us that enables us to transform the English language – and this seems to hold good for people who know little or no Irish, like Joyce. It seems to be an inbred thing.'[22]

The current process of the re-integration of many African countries after civil wars or unrest calls for the use of one language rather than many, and European languages are still the instruments of such re-integration. If this is the situation, then the continued use of European languages for literary expression is guaranteed. What the critic needs to recognise is that to judge a work of Anglo-Yoruba expression with English aesthetics alone or Yoruba aesthetics alone is to produce an incomplete judgement. To do the same with Anglo-Igbo literature results in the same incompleteness. This is well-expressed in the first sentence of Declan Kiberd's book *Synge and the Irish Language*:

> In August 1970 at a symposium at Trinity College, Dublin, a professor remarked, to the outrage of many colleagues, that he 'would take no student of Anglo-Irish literature seriously unless that student were bilingual'. In a subsequent essay on Anglo-Irish poetry, another critic confirmed this judgement when he argued that 'a total understanding of Anglo-Irish literature certainly depends on an accurate and sensitive knowledge of that Gaelic Irish literature which has increasingly affected and conditioned it.'[23]

The ideal critic of African literature would be someone who knows the European language in which the writing has been done and the African language from which the writing situates its inspiration.

Notes

1. Obiajunwa Wali, "The Dead End of African Literature" in *Transition*, no. 10, pp. 13–18.

2. Wole Soyinka, "Declaration of African Writers" in *Research in African Literatures*, vol. 6, no. 1, 1975, pp. 58–9; and "The Scholar in African Society" in *Festac Colloquium and Black World Development*, pp. 125–134. These pages discuss in detail the ideas expressed in the paper.

3. Ime Ikiddeh's foreword to *Homecoming*, by Ngugi wa Thiong'o, p. xi, and Ngugi wa Thiong'o, *Decolonising the Mind: The Politics of Language in African Literature*, London: James Currey, 1986.

4. Peter Benson, *Black Orpheus, Transition and Modern Cultural Awakening in Africa*, p. 134.

5. *Transition*, no. 11, p. 9.

6. *Transition*, no. 18, pp. 27–30 and in *Morning Yet on Creation Day*, pp. 55–62.

7. *Research in African Literatures*, vol. 6, no. 1, p. 59.

8. *Festac Colloquium and Black World Development*, p. 128.

9. ibid. p. 209.

10. *Artrage,* interview with Nuruddin Farah, no. 14, 1986, pp. 4–5, p. 8.

11. Quoted by E.A. Afigbo in "The Place of the Igbo Language in our Schools: A Historical Explanation" from *Short Life of Bishop Shanahan* (Holy Ghost Fathers, Onitsha Diocese) in *Igbo Language and Culture* pp. 78–9.

12. ibid. p. 79.

13. ibid. p. 78.

14. interview with Ossie Enekwe in *Okike*, no. 30, November 1990, pp. 129–133.

15. interview with Declan Kiberd in *Graph* 13 (Irish Literary Review), Winter '92/Spring '93. pp. 5–8.

16. Both J.P. Clark of Nigeria and George Lamming of Barbados have commented on Caliban as a role model in the politics of language between the coloniser and the colonised.

17. *Reconsiderations of Irish History and Culture*, p. 48.

18. ibid. p. 85.

19. ibid. p. 110.

20. ibid. p.104.

21. *Synge and the Irish Language* (second edition), Dublin: Gill & Macmillan Ltd. 1979, 1993. p. 1

22. ibid. pp. 15–16.

23. ibid. p. 1.

XI

Achebe and Soyinka:
Critics and Craftsmen

No matter what the African has done to tame the European language to respond positively to the yearning of the African, such a European language still manages to retain a cluster of historical ideas inimical to the self-image of the African.

In wishing to eliminate such aspects of the European language the African risks rejection by the European owners of the language. The European would call the attention of the African to what he or she shares with Europe – a humanistic education for instance – rather than acknowledging the African's traditional ways. Michael J.C. Echeruo puts it clearly[1] when he points out that the European novelist of Africa presents two images of Africa and the African: there is the permanently primitive human and then there is the educated African – the transitional person who unfortunately is not on the move to a renaissance but rather petrified into an unchanging imitation of the white man.[2] Both the permanent primitive and the educated imitation of Europe are not capable of changing themselves and their continent.

If the African writer was motivated to write fiction to correct what he or she considered superficial fiction about Africa by the imperial persons, should it not be asked if the writer is attempting to fill a gap in the imperial literature, the voice of the native etc, or attempting to focus the attention of his or her own people on issues important to the interpretation of their lives and cultures? If after writing 'deep' fiction about Africa and the imperial person still does not give the necessary recognition commensurate with the contribution of Africa and the African, should the African writer go on to write 'deep' criticism to correct the 'superficial' criticism which makes the withholding of such recognition possible? If Janus-like, the African writer faces the literary heritage of the colonising power as well as the totality of his oral traditions, who can best understand and interpret what he writes except someone who takes on these two aspects of the writer's heritage? Literary critics who are, say English-speaking and are interested in say, Russian literature, would read everything they can find about the circumstances of the production of that particular literature. They might also see the mastering of the relevant language as the ultimate achievement which admits them to a fuller involvement in the literature of their interest. This situation, normal in other places, would seem not to be normal when applied to Africa and African writers. Because the African writer pampered the European and North American reader, explaining everything, simplifying everything, the European and North American readers of African writing have come to feel that they do not have to make any effort towards understanding the literary expressions of a complex and complicated human experience.

None of the European and North American critics who have written on the works of Chinua Achebe have anything to say about the Igbo language and its influence on Achebe's writing beyond the fact that Ibo people use proverbs as if proverbs are not used in all known human languages. A quick check in the index of any of the publications on Achebe's works show that there are no references at all to the Igbo language.[3] The same statement can be made about those who write about Wole Soyinka's work. They have nothing to say about the power of the Yoruba language in its influence on Soyinka's English. And this goes for critics of African origin as well.[4] Although the subtitle of Simon Gikandi's book is 'Language & Ideology in Fiction' the book, *Reading Chinua Achebe,* has nothing to say about the major language which has determined the nature of Achebe's writing – the Igbo language.

So, a knowledge of the African language of the writer is a prerequisite for any critic of African writing and African writers.

Achebe and Soyinka as Critics

In the case of Chinua Achebe and Wole Soyinka, we have two writers who have also had formal training in western literary criticism, who are extensively well read in western literature and western philosophy. There is no way that they could not have been influenced by their reading of western literature. Wole Soyinka insists that an existing tradition anywhere in the world is fodder for his creativeness. Both writers represent the Africans who have so much power packed in their double culture: that of their African origin and that of western Europe. The critical writings of African writers sometimes pretend that the western European influence does not exist and that only the African one should be given validity. On the other hand, the critical writings of European, North American and even African critics on African writing pretend that the African linguistic and literary influence does not exist.

Chinua Achebe writes his literary criticism from the point of view that his writing is definitely different from western writing. In the first place western literary interpretations have denigrated both Africa and the African. In order to correct the negative image of Africa and the African which western writers have propagated, Chinua Achebe needs to write differently. In the second place western literature glorifies the individual, and holds up the individual against the claims of the collective or the community. Chinua Achebe, on the other hand, writes from the supreme right of the community over its individuals. A part cannot be greater than a whole in the same way that "No man however great can win judgement against all the people."[5]

Achebe might make this point in his critical statements; his authorial comments, especially at the end of *Arrow of God*, as pointed out in chapter two, do not seem to approve of the victory of the people over their chief priest, an individual who stands for an individual point of view.

The experience of the West in its development and its philosophy is the opposite of this position. Whatever material achievement the West has gained has been made through the efforts of individuals who took leave of whatever was going on in their community and dared to go beyond its limits. Dr. Faustus, Coriolanus, Galileo, Addison, Newton, Martin Luther – the list of individuals who challenged the ideas current in their communities and were later proved right is endless.

Can one uphold the claims of the community using a literary tradition which defers to individuals? Or would the case have been better made in Igbo and left to be translated into English or any other languages for that matter, when and if it mattered? Wole Soyinka takes the view that what he is doing is not really different from what the western writer or critic does. What is important is that he is extending the possibilities of the western writer and critic. He takes the position that it is right to recognise what Aristotle has to say about tragedy, but Aristotle is not the last word when the issue of tragedy, is to be discussed and the western writer and critic had better listen.

These two different positions of the two writers have been arrived at through their ethnic cultural heritage. C.L. Innes says: "In these essays Achebe questions the assumption that African literature must follow the patterns established by European writers and that the same aesthetic criteria should apply to both."[6]

However much one wishes that African literature should not follow the patterns established by western writers, and that the same aesthetic criteria should not apply, the use of a European language in writing African literature implies that the language and literary tradition of that language would influence the African context. Why should the western critic be concerned about African criteria for judging English literature? Why is it important that the western critic must acknowledge the possibility of these new criteria? Why does an English critic have to learn something about *mbari* in order to pronounce on a novel or poem or play written in English? Would the case not have been better made if the writing had been in Igbo in the first place?

In essays such as "The Writer and his Community",[7] "The Igbo World and its Art"[8] and "*Chi* in Igbo Cosmology"[9] Chinua Achebe uses the mbari as the central reference of his work.

> *Mbari* is an artistic 'spectacular' demanded of the community by one or other of its primary divinities, usually the Earth goddess. To execute this 'command performance' the community is represented by a small group of its members selected and secluded for months or even years for the sole purpose of erecting a befitting 'home of images' filled to overflowing with sculptures and paintings in homage to the presiding god or goddess.[10]

Achebe clarifies further the relationship between the art produced by these individuals and the community for which the art is produced:

> But once made, art emerges from privacy into the public domain. There are no private collections among the Igbo beyond personal ritual objects like the *ikenga*.[11]

In spite of the above, the individual has his or her place in the Igbo world: "Without an understanding of the nature of *chi* one could not begin to make sense of the Igbo world-view;"[12]

According to Modupe Oduyoye, writing in *Nigeria Magazine* (no. 119, 1976) in his article "What is Mbari?" the word 'mbari' may have a distant Afro-Asian origin meaning 'to begin', 'to devise', 'to shape', 'to invent'.[13] Jeanne N. Dingome who quotes Oduyoye in her article "Soyinka's Role in Mbari" (meaning the

Writers' and Artists' Club which existed in Ibadan from March 1961,)[14] when the first committee was set up, and virtually ended with the return of Ibos to the Eastern Region after July 1966, provides the following information on mbari art criticism:

> But more importantly for our purpose, on the vanishing-day the public turned into critics; they made comments on the aesthetic achievement of the communal proxies, using as criteria for excellence the artists' ability to show confident daring in their ideas and to innovate on old forms.[15]

This statement leads naturally to the need of identifying the guardian traditional Igbo god of art and the artist. As if taking a leaf from Soyinka's adoption of Ogun , Achebe, in *Anthills of the Savannah*, presents Agwu thus:

> Agwu does not call a meeting to choose his seers and diviners and artists: Agwu, the god of healers; Agwu, the brother to Madness! But though born from the same womb he and Madness were not created by the same chi. Agwu is the right hand a man extends to his fellows; Madness, the forbidden hand. Madness unleashes and rides his man roughly into the wild savannah. Agwu possesses his own just as securely but has him corralled to serve the compound. Agwu picks his disciple, rings his eye with white chalk and dips his tongue willing or not, in the brew of prophecy; and right away the man will speak and put head and tail back in the severed trunk of our tale.[16]

In other essays such as "Language and the Destiny of Man",[17] "The African Writer and the English Language",[18] "In Defence of English?"[19] and "Thoughts on the African Novel"[20] Chinua Achebe insists on the primacy of language; the relevance of the English language to African writers as long as the writers temper English with their own understanding of their mother tongue; chastises a Nigerian social critic who suggests that Nigeria should adopt Hausa as the national language; and attempts to define what is African about the African novel.

Sometimes the arguments in these essays sound like special pleading, because they do not wish to replace or add to the critical criteria of the western world, but merely to plead understanding of Africa and things African by those western critics who concern themselves with Africa.

Wole Soyinka's audacious agenda is expressed in the difficult essay "The Fourth Stage"[21] and the more accessible ones such as "Drama and the Revolutionary Ideal",[22] later published as "Drama and the Idioms of Liberation: Proletarian Illusions"[23] and "Theatre in African Traditional Cultures: Survival

Patterns".[24] Of all these essays, the most important is "The Fourth Stage" subtitled "Through the Mysteries of Ogun to the Origins of Yoruba Tragedy". Yoruba theatre tradition and practice constitute the basis of Soyinka's critical standards and demands.

As Al Imfeld wrote about Soyinka in the Deutsche Welle collection of interviews *African Writers on the Air*, Soyinka wants nothing to do with any black/white painting.

> There have always been losers and heroes; cruelty and tenderness have always been close neighbours. Ogun, a symbol of reality, has a double face. Permanent complaining does not help. Grief can and must turn to joy, now. Hell and paradise not only border on one another, they are also superimposed on one another.[25]

Both Chinua Achebe and Wole Soyinka come to the same conclusion about white critics who refuse to see eye to eye with them:

> Now to tell a man that he is incapable of assuming responsibility for himself and his actions is of course the utmost insult, to avoid which some Africans will go to any length, will throw anything at the deal; they will agree, for instance, to ignore the presence and role of racism in African history or pretend that somehow it was all the black man's fault. Which is complete and utter nonsense. For whatever crimes he committed (and they were, and are, legion) he did not bring racism into the world. And no matter how emancipated a man may wish to appear or how anxious to please by his largeness of heart he cannot make history simply go away. Not even a brilliant writer could hope to do that. And as for those who applaud him for trying, who acclaim his bold originality in 'restoring historical initiative' to people when in reality all he does is pander to their racist and colonialist attitudes, they are no more than unscrupulous interrogators taking advantage of an ingratiating defendant's weakness and trust to egg him on to irretrievable self- incrimination.[26]

In an interview entitled "Post Mortem For A 'Death...',", Soyinka speaks of the unacceptable reviews of his play *Death and the King's Horseman* in the USA:

> There is definitely more than an overtone of racism in some of the language used. The very idea that somebody from Africa, from the ex-colonial jungle should (1) come and challenge their theatrical ideas in such a demanding way and, (2) even propose the idea of an African tragedy in which whites supply the comic relief: that is very clearly there. You only have to read the sort of reluctant write-up which John Gross did as a follow-up, where he tried to show himself more intelligent, and was indeed more

intelligent, but in which he too refuses to come to full terms with this play. For instance, he writes, 'Oh the tragedy would have been more powerful if it had not in effect diverged into politics. If it had stayed entirely within its parameter of the tragedy', and note by the way, he refuses to call it a tragedy – he says it's a 'ritual', thereby suggesting almost a kind of unformed... almost preliterate. This is his own very subtle denigration of this play. It is interesting that he suggests that it would have been a fuller play if there had not been the political aspect. Now, if he were writing about Chekhov then he would remember that one of the strengths of Chekhov's plays is the way he combines – what is described as characteristic of Russian drama – the way in which tragedy is combined with the most hilarious fun. But no,that is a privilege reserved only for Europeans or Russians. No, we Africans, no, no, no.[27]

As shown by these two examples of reactions to western critics the problem is that the African writer and critic writes his or her criticism of African literature from the point of view of an African emphasising the African elements in the work of art. The western critic, on the other hand, responds only to the elements of the work of art which speak to him through the language and literary tradition. On the basis of these two items, the work of art could appear inferior to its western antecedents. It is merely churlish for African writers to object to this almost natural response to any work of art: we all react to works of art from our initial cultural antecedents. Our more sophisticated response come later, after due training and practice to see the roots of African writing in western literature and African oral narratives.

Achebe and Soyinka as Craftsmen

A general survey of existing critical work on African literatures divides into three main types: the universal dimension, the national dimension and the ethnic dimension.

The universal dimension, which is the commonest form of criticism applied to African literatures, deals with the so-called universal elements of African ideas expressed in African literatures. Here, pan-African ideals such as liberation, freedom from oppression and enjoyment of human rights by all, are given pride of place whatever the literary merit of the work. Political correctness, if it did not begin with African literary criticism, has definitely matured under its umbrella.

In the case of criticism emphasising the national dimension, the critic deals with the writings produced by writers of a particular nation-state in terms of its history and social and political development. Such critical studies are few as far as African literatures are concerned. A good example which is unique to the genre is Richard Bjornson's *The African Quest for Freedom and Identity: Cameroonian Writing and the National Experience.*[28] There is also Carol Sicherman's *Ngugi wa Thiong'o: The Making of a Rebel: A Source Book in Kenyan Literature and Resistance.*[29] There is no doubt that more national studies of African literatures are needed to stamp on the face of critical writing the particularities of different African communities and countries.

Finally, there is the critical study emphasising the ethnic dimension of the writer and the writing. Again, this type of critical study is not as common as it should be. Robert Wren's *Achebe's World: The Historical and Cultural Context of the Novels of Chinua Achebe* is one. Various studies of the beginnings of prose writing in Sotho or Tswana or Zulu are also contributions to these types of literary criticism.

Most critical comments on African literatures have been on the subject matter of the writings rather than on their crafting process, their technical competence. Perhaps it needs to be stated that criticism written about peculiar uses of language, the deployment of proverbs and wise sayings, and the general feel of difference from English-English was to be taken for that kind of criticism. Such deployment of particular stylistics was never seen as existing for its own sake but rather in the service of the particular special pleading that the writer is engaged in.

Perhaps Nadine Gordimer was not convinced that this aspect of African writing had been given sufficient attention, and she attempts to make a theory out of this neglect, a theory that does not and cannot get off the ground:

> African writers have their stories to tell... For most of them, the straightforward narrative suffices to carry it, and the form of the conventional novel, story, biography, or essay to contain it.[30]

African writers, it would seem, had no interest in purely experimental writing; all they cared about was the telling of their story. This statement was made at a time when novels such as Gabriel Okara's *The Voice* had appeared (1964) and Amos Tutuola's novels had been accepted in the West as experiments rather than the limits of the English language capabilities of the author.[31] So, even when the African writers were experimenting with form, few western critics recognised that writers were experimenting.

It needs to be pointed out that while literary movements in Europe and North America have come about as a result of a previous movement inspiring a next one, usually opposed to it, and in formal matters, literary movements in Africa have followed purely political movements. Negritude and the Pan-African Movement, independence and the period of disillusionment, military rule and the re-assertion of the possibilities of the African peoples, these are some of the possible movements in recent African literatures. The difference in the origins of literary movements in Western countries and in African countries needs to be stressed. At the same time it is true that in the earlier periods of the western literatures political issues influenced literary movements.

All the same, comments on the craft of African writing which insist that African writing has been satisfied with simply employing the conventional forms of the European novel or short story, play or poem is rash and in need of serious re-consideration. In the same vein as Nadine Gordimer's comments is that of Eustace Palmer:

> In fact, most African novelists have been quite content to use the established forms of the English, American and continental novel. From the point of view of form, there isn't much to choose between Achebe and Hardy, Ngugi and Conrad, Camara Laye and Kafka.[32]

Instinctively, one recoils from this type of generalization. Stated briefly, the conventional form of the European novel is just one of the three main components of the African novel, the other two being (1) the language and literary tradition of the particular European language in use, and (2) the form of African oral narratives.[33] Each African novel can be said to be made up of these three components to a lesser or a larger degree.

In the specific cases of Chinua Achebe and Wole Soyinka, critical comments on their craft have been few. They themselves have not been too forthcoming about the processes which made their works what they are. They have also been reticent in commenting on each others work. This makes the few comments available extremely important and instructive. Chinua Achebe refers to Wole Soyinka's style as "irrepressible"[34] while Wole Soyinka has called Achebe's technique "unrelieved competence".[35]

During a question and answer session at the University of
Washington, Chinua Achebe made the following comments on
Wole Soyinka's plays:

> Well, I think he makes a cult of obscurity, especially in his later
> work, which to my mind is unnecessary and unfortunate. It's got
> to a point, I think, when he's almost embarrassed if you talk
> about his earlier, or not earlier necessarily but simple plays, like
> *The Trials of Brother Jero*, which people like. I think he will prefer
> to be remembered by *The Road*, which is interesting if you are
> ready to work at it. But the thing with him is that he has a gift for
> words which gets him out of trouble so that even if you don't
> know what is going on, you suspect that something is being
> said...[36]

Chinua Achebe highlights the problem of language and com-
pares the problem of language in the theatre with the problem
of language in the novel:

> I think, for instance, that one of the problems with modern
> Nigerian theatre is the language – the English language. You are
> likely to produce theatre for the West rather than theatre for
> Nigeria, if you didn't stop to think about the language problem.
> Now you might say: well, isn't that the same with the novel; isn't
> it the same with poetry? No, I don't think it is. Art is a conven-
> tion. Then there are various forms, various conventions which are
> applied. Probably you could say no convention. There are various
> forms, various conventions. But once you choose the convention I
> think you are *bound* by the rules of the convention. Now, the the-
> atre, being a very direct, almost participatory form, does require a
> different convention from the novel. You go to watch a play, you
> see actual people moving, and talking on stage. If you are reading
> a novel, you don't see anybody. You are using your imagination.
> So what I'm saying is that it's a different convention.[37]

The conclusion which Achebe reaches here is that he would
work in Igbo when and if he worked in the theatre since there
would be a greater artistic credibility in using the language of
his characters rather than English, which might not be the language of the characters he wishes to depict. One comment can
be made here: if English is the language of the Nigerian nation-
state, the language of nation-building and the language that cuts
across the cultures and mores of the multi-ethnic nation, the language in which the history, the recent collective past of the
many peoples of the country and the hoped for future of the
nation are expressed, then it would not help towards creating a
new community of sensibilities not to use English on the
Nigerian stage.

It is instructive to set against Achebe's comments on language in the theatre the comments by John Arden, British playwright, on Wole Soyinka and the Third World theatre:

> I suspect that in Wole Soyinka we may be seeing a kind of inde-terminate prodigy. His work is not exactly rootless – but it has an awkward double root – one half in Europe and one half in Nigeria. It may be that one half root is set in dry sand and the other in fertile soil. Western official culture – as taught in our uni-versities and at the Royal Court Theatre – has nothing of lasting benefit to say to Africans or Indians or anyone else in the Third World.[38]

What is important here is the fact that many African intellectu-als, including many writers and critics, keep on pretending that African literatures can deny the dual nature of their roots. Achebe's comments must be applicable to both the theatre and the novel. While the theatre might be a physical object in front of the audience, the reader of the novel is also having to enact in his or her mind the drama that is being described in the novel. If the reader can accept an Igbo character speaking English on the pages of the novel, why would the reader demur in accepting the same character speaking English on the stage?

Soyinka's natural milieu is the theatre. He usually has recourse to other genres such as the novel when there is a lull in his playwriting or when he does not have a theatre group with which to work.[39]

One of the major contrasts between Achebe and Soyinka is that while Achebe is a writer bound by the conventions of his chosen genre, Soyinka refuses to be bound by any convention in any genre. At the level of style Achebe's novels make their points, using the conventional forms of the European novel of the nineteenth century and a measure of the forms of oral narra-tive, while Soyinka's novels attempt to break away from those very conventions. Soyinka's fiction and autobiographies carry the imprint of the adventurous language and literary tradition of the English novel. His rejection of convention is even more drastic when we come to his natural genre – the theatre.

When he came back to Nigeria in 1960 he founded two theatre companies – the 1960 Masks and Orisun Theatre. The first was made up of people he knew were already involved in theatre, but the kind of theatre he had come to demolish, the English language "drawing room plays, Galsworthy, Bernard Shaw, Shakespeare of course, the repertory of secondary school, from the kind of middle class young professional amateur theatre

companies usually presided over by some enthusiastic expatri-
ate."[40]

The second company was made up of younger men and
women and he trained them to be able to perform in both the
traditions of the English and the Yoruba theatres. They could
take on Shakespeare if they had to, or they could pick up the
talking drum in Yoruba plays if they had to use them. While
these two sources constitute the basics of Soyinka's theatre, he
has never restricted himself to these two traditions. Rather, he
sees all existing conventions as choices that he has and is free to
use. Asked about his attitude to the dual theatrical culture in a
situation where the Yoruba language theatre has had a huge
impact on the theatre-conscious public, Soyinka responds:

> Well, it's not just dual. There is Ibo theatrical culture, Hausa the-
> atrical culture, especially contemporary one, the puppet theatre
> which is very active in the Tiv region. I have come across a num-
> ber of these and for me they are all part and parcel of what I call
> the seam of theatrical tradition which is constantly acquiring new
> fabric all the time, bringing it into our contemporary experience
> and the European foreign language theatre culture. [41]

> ...what you should learn is to enrich a particular style by a depar-
> ture from an aspect of expectation and you stay within the same
> tradition. So adherence, puritanism as far as style is concerned,
> for me is very limiting to the fullness of theatrical creation,... [42]

Two issues are crucial to Soyinka's theatre practice: the
absolute necessity for him to have an acting company to work
with and the primacy of the text of the play.

If there is less acrimony today on the issue that Ngugi wa
Thiong'o calls the "politics of language in African Literature" it
is because both old and new writers have settled into positions
most comfortable for them to work in and to defend. Ngugi
himself has turned to writing in Gikuyu. Achebe, while continuing to write in English, has written poetry in Igbo; and Soyinka
continues to write mainly in English, Pidgin and Yoruba where
and when the need arises.

There is an area of language which must be seen as unique to
Wole Soyinka and his writing. This is the issue of the accidental
concurrence either in sound or in meaning of Yoruba words and
sentences with words and sentences in English and other
European languages. First of all, Soyinka records this phenome-
non. Secondly, he uses it to further indulge in the celebration of
his involvement with the dual language and dual cultural background of his writing. This form of engagement between two

languages is not to be mistaken for regional varieties of the same language or the development of particular variants or nuances of meaning. Rather, we have here a situation where the Yoruba language takes over words or expressions from English and any other language and, having made it a Yoruba word or expression, gives it a new meaning within the context of Yoruba culture.

The heading of the first chapter of Soyinka's *Isara* is entitled 'ex-ile'. The word 'exile' here is a good example of the encounter mentioned above. The young men from Isara, going to different parts of the country in search of education or employment are exiles. They are, in the combination of these two words 'ex' (from) Latin/English and 'ile' (home) Yoruba they are away from home. These young men and women were, in both English and Yoruba, away from home, they were exiles. They were also, those of them who were at the Teacher Training College in Ilesa, ex-students of Ilesa and so ex-iles.

Another example can be seen in Sipe Efuape, in pursuit of his trade relations with Europe. He picks up catalogues from Italy. Italian names in this catalogue provide another occasion for the Yoruba indulgence in this language engagement:

> Morigi? Do I see a tree? No, I see no tree, only profit. Benito? As one who can do it, so does one proceed. Milano? Indeed it is I, Sipe, who blazes the path.43

One of the funniest incidents in *Isara* is that in which Soditan turns the tables against his pupils who were playing this language game with the morning march song:

> Boys wanted, boys wanted
> Boys won ntedi, tedi
> Boys, they bend their buttocks!44

Other examples of this language-play are scattered over Soyinka's various writings. The impassioned speech of the Old Man in *Madmen and Specialists* is a gem of this system of language engagement, where the logic of one language is fed into another language to provide entertainment of a sophisticated mental nature:

> ...the dog in dogma, the tick of heretic, the tick in politics, the mock of democracy, the mar of marxism, a tic of the fanatic, the boo in buddhism, the ham in Mohammed...45

This type of language engagement speaks volumes for the argument that critics of African literatures would benefit from a knowledge of the language, or even languages, of the particular African writer on whose work they might be pronouncing.

Faction

In the recent past, "Faction, the art of juxtaposing facts, real and identifiable, with fiction is the latest trend in the Nigerian novel."[46] Continuing on the same page, Ernest Emenyonu says:

> It is evident in the works of established as well as emerging writers but much more so in the latter. It is evident in Wole Soyinka's *Isara* (1989). There are traces of it, if one reads with a fine lens, in Chinua Achebe's *Anthills of the Savannah* (1988)[47]

The critical problem with this genre is the issue of the proportions of the mixture of facts with fiction, "the degree and manner of the infusion of the real into the unreal".[48] Emenyonu permits himself to address the relevance of faction at this period of Nigerian history suggesting that it "may stem from a more urgent need to satirize more directly and lucidly, in order to reform more effectively".[49]

For me, as a writer, the validity of faction – factual material written as fiction along with feeling and atmosphere – in the present situation of Nigeria is to make the history of the country immediately accessible to all Nigerian citizens instead of disguising it with fiction. Wole Soyinka does not acknowledge the use of faction in *Isara*. Not until the publication of *Ibadan: The Penkelemes Years* do we read about his attitude to faction:

> *Ibadan* does not pretend to be anything but faction, that much abused genre which attempts to fictionalise facts and events, the proportion of fact to fiction being totally at the discretion of the author. My adoption of the genre stops short at the actual *invention* of facts or events, however, or the deliberate distortion of the history or character of any known figure.[50]

Although the word 'faction' does not occur in the author's note in *Isara*, Soyinka states the following in that note:

> I have not only taken liberties with chronology, I have deliberately ruptured it.[51]

Faction has definitely become an important factor in the literature of Nigeria. Nigerian writings and the writings of both Achebe and Soyinka have become more and more documentary if only to shock their readers into a greater awareness of the situation in the country. Here, then, is one of the first examples of a material finding its own peculiar genre.

Notes

1. Michael J.C. Echeruo, *Joyce Cary and the Novel of Africa*, especially the first chapter 'The Novel of Africa' pp. 1–27. See Bibliography for Echeruo's publications.

2. ibid. p. 23.

3. See for instance (1) David Carroll, *Chinua Achebe Novelist, Poet, Critic*, published in 1980, 1990; (2) C.L. Innes, *Chinua Achebe*, published 1990; (3) Robert M.Wren, *Achebe's World: The Historical and Cultural Context of the Novels of Chinua Achebe.*

4. See Simon Gikandi, *Reading Chinua Achebe: Language and Ideology in Fiction*, 1991.

5. Chinua Achebe, *Morning Yet on Creation Day*, p. 99.

6. C.L. Innes, Chinua Achebe, p. 103.

7. Chinua Achebe, *Hopes and Impediments*, pp. 32–41.

8. ibid. pp. 42–5.

9. Chinua Achebe, *Morning Yet on Creation Day*, pp. 93–103.

10. Chinua Achebe, "The Writer and His Community" in *Hopes and Impediments* pp. 32–3.

11. Chinua Achebe, "The Igbo World and Its Art" in *Hopes and Impediments*, p. 43.

12. Chinua Achebe, "*Chi* in Igbo Cosmology" in *Morning Yet on Creation Day*, p. 93.

13. Modupe Oduyoye is basically interested in etymology in relation to African traditional religions and religious rituals. One of his publications is *The Vocabulary of Yoruba Religious Discourse*, Ibadan: Daystar Press, 1971.

14. The Club was proposed to the Congress for Cultural Freedom in November 1960, when the Congress expressed a willingness to make funds available for a project in Nigeria, as a contribution to Nigeria's independence. The contract with the owners of the house where the Club was to be located was signed in March 1961. The first management committee was made up of the following writers: Wole Soyinka, Christopher Okigbo, J.P. Clark, Chinua Achebe, Ezekiel Mphahlele. Amos Tutuola and D.O. Fagunwa were brought in at Soyinka's insistence. Ezekiel Mphahlele became the first president, a position he held until he left Nigeria for Kenya in August 1963. Ulli Beier took over as president of the Club. Begum Hendrickse – a fellow South African as Ezekiel Mphahlele – was the first Secretary. Demas Nwoko and Uche Okeke were also prominent members of the Club. This information comes from Donald Denoon's unpublished *A Biography of Ulli Beier*, pp. 125–128.

15. Jeanne N. Dingome, "Soyinka's Role in Mbari", in *African Theatre Review*, vol. 1, no. 3, April 1987 – Special Edition on Wole Soyinka. pp. 9–10.

16. Chinua Achebe, *Anthills of the Savannah*, p. 125.

17. Chinua Achebe, *Hopes and Impediments*, pp. 87–94.

18. Chinua Achebe, *Morning Yet on Creation Day*, pp. 55–62.

19. ibid. pp. 87–9.

20. ibid. pp. 49–54.

21. Wole Soyinka, *Art, Dialogue and Outrage*, pp. 21–34.

22. Karen L. Morell, (ed.) *In Person: Achebe, Awoonor and Soyinka at the University of Washington*, pp. 61– 88.

23. *Wole Soyinka, Art, Dialogue and Outrage*, pp.42–60.

24. ibid. pp. 190–203.

25. *African Writers on the Air*, pp. 5–6.

26. Chinua Achebe, *Hopes and Impediments*, pp.53–54.

27. Wole Soyinka, *Art, Dialogue and Outrage*, pp. 331–332.

28. See Bibliography for details.

29. See Bibliography for details.

30. Nadine Gordimer in *Kenyon Review*, No.128, p.16.

31. There were critics such as Adrian Roscoe who supported artistic experiments such as happens in *The Voice*; see his *Mother is Gold*.

32. Eustace Palmer, *An Introduction to the African Novel*, p. x.

33. Kole Omotoso, *The Form of the African Novel*, p vi.

34. *Morning Yet on Creation Day*, p. 82.

35. Reported by Chinua Achebe in the preface to the second edition of *Girls at War*, 1977.

36. *In Person: Achebe, Awoonor, and Soyinka at the Univeristy of Washington*, pp. 50–51.

37. Interview with Onuora Ossie Enekwe published in *Okike*, no. 30, November, 1990, p.132.

38. in *New Theatre Magazine*, Third World Theatre Issue, vol. xii, no. 2, 1967.

39. in interview with Chuck Mike published in *Soyinka as Director*, publication of the Department of Literature in English, University of Ife, 1986.

40. ibid. p.2.

41. ibid. pp. 5–6.

42. ibid. p. 17.

43. Wole Soyinka, *Isara*, (Fountain Publications, Ibadan), p. 52.

44. ibid. p. 99.

45. Wole Soyinka, *Madmen and Specialists*, (University Press Ltd, Ibadan), p.76.

46. Ernest Emenyonu, *Studies on the Nigerian Novel*, p. 133. The last chapter of this book, is entitled "Faction: An Emerging Trend in the Nigerian Novel – Kole Omotoso's Just Before Dawn".

47. ibid. p. 133.

48. ibid. p. 134.

49. ibid. p. 133.

50. Wole Soyinka, *Ibadan: The Penkelemes Years*, Foreword, p. ix.

51. Wole Soyinka, *Isara: A Voyage Around Essay*, Author's note, p. vii.

XII

Conclusion: Something for Us and Something for Me

Neither Achebe nor Soyinka has found the right formula for linking the ethnic to the national in order to bring about the successful establishment of a Nigerian nation-state. In fact, no African writer has been able to resolve this basic political problem of Africa and the African in the twentieth century. African politicians have not been able to resolve the issue either. The unresolved political problem is that the relationship between ethnic identity, which goes back to pre-colonial times, and national identity, has come into being as a result of the colonial experience of Africa.

The struggle against colonialism was organised under the pan-African umbrella. Pan-Africanism recognised the nation-states demarcated by European colonial powers of Africa, while denying ethnicity a role in the forging of the new identities. As far as Nigeria was concerned this meant that the identity that was paramount was the Nigerian identity. Whatever else you were before January 1, 1914 – the date on which Nigeria came into existence through the amalgamation of the Northern and Southern Provinces – forget it and become a Nigerian. In fact to claim that you were anything else thereafter was seen as a crime against the Nigerian nation-state for whom there must be unity to be expressed in the existence of one language, one religion and one ruler. This was what the nineteenth century model of the European nation-state dictated.

In fact Chinua Achebe elevates ethnicity to the level of the "trouble with Nigeria" and by extension the trouble with other African countries.[1] The ideal, according to Chinua Achebe, is the pan-Nigerian dream of a country with no ethnic feelings, only Nigerian sentiments.

> You could always find idealistic people from every part of Nigeria who were prepared to do battle if anyone (especially European or American) should ask them: *What is your tribe?* 'I am

a Nigerian' they would say haughtily, drawing themselves to
their fullest height.[2]

This 'idealism' persisted in spite of warnings and alternative
concepts from Chief Obafemi Awolowo in his first published
book *Path to Nigerian Freedom* which had a foreword by Margery
Perham.[3]

> But as long as every person in Nigeria is made to feel that he is a
> Nigerian first and a Yoruba or Ibo, or Hausa next, each will be
> justified to poke his nose into the domestic issues of the others.
> The only thing of common interest to all Nigerians as such, and
> in which the voice of one must be as acceptable as that of any
> other, is the constitution of the central or federal government of
> Nigeria. The constitution of each national group is the sole con-
> cern of the members of that group.[4]

Margery Perham, in her foreword to the book seemed to agree
with Awolowo's position:

> If Mr. Awolowo is right, as I believe he is, that in face of the deep
> divisions of race, culture and religion in Nigeria, political
> advance through natural groups and regions is the only way to a
> wider unity, then Britain may for long be required to provide the
> framework which holds these groups together until they are able
> to fuse into unity or federation.[5]

It is thus understandable for Chinua Achebe to dub Awolowo as
a tribal leader and as the politician who introduced the crime of
tribalism into the vocabulary of the country.[6]

Chinua Achebe began his writing career, as is now widely
known and as I have set out in earlier chapters, to do battle with
European writers, especially Joseph Conrad and Joyce Cary,
who had mis-represented Africa and Africans in their novels of
Africa. Achebe seemed satisfied to simply present to his readers
the dignity of Igbo traditional society and dare these European
and North American readers to call it primitive. This objective
fitted the agenda of the pan-African political movement. Igbo
traditional society, as presented by Achebe in his novels, could
be given a pan-African role. The problem was to give Igbo traditional society a role in the building of the new nation-state of
Nigeria. As far as Achebe was concerned neither Ibo, nor
Yoruba nor Hausa nor any other traditional society should be
recognised in the building of the new nation-state of Nigeria. It
now seems to me clear that beyond the one single objective with
which Chinua Achebe set out to write his novels nothing else
was thought through:

Again, this is a subject on which I've made statements. I was born at a time when you simply had to make statements. Writing is not just something you might or might not do, it's a very serious life and death thing. So statements are made to supplement the artistic and the airy-fairy stuff... These statements need not stand for ever. If somebody comes up with a better idea, then let these statements be disconfirmed.[7]

According to Kolawole Ogungbesan, Chinua Achebe took three positions, one after the other, as a result of what was happening in the world, what was happening in Nigeria and what was happening in Biafra.[8] First he wanted to "help my society regain its belief in itself and put away the complexes of the years of the denigration and self-abasement."[9] By 1964 when political violence was showing that the Nigerian ideal would not work, Chinua Achebe wrote *A Man of the People* and insisted that the African writer "should 'expose and attack injustice' all over the world, but particularly within his own society in Africa."[10] In 1966 the violence that was to lead to the civil war in Nigeria began and when the Republic of Biafra was declared Chinua Achebe supported the young republic. "Achebe has moved from criticizing his society to directly taking a hand in remoulding it."[11] At the end of the civil war and for a long time afterwards Chinua Achebe could not write. All along he had explored Igbo tradition and society for the furtherance of pan-Africanism while the nation-state whose passport he carried disintegrated. He had recorded some of the causes of that disintegration in *A Man of the People* and some of his short stories such as 'Sugar Baby' in *Girls at War*. Where was he to seek the positive that make the nation-state work and at the same time protect the Igbo ethnicity? For me, this question and the attempt to answer it makes *Anthills of the Savannah* such a crucial work in Achebe's writing. Taken along with the lecture "African Literature as Restoration of Celebration"[12] Chinua Achebe proffers to the world, both at home in Nigeria and abroad, not only the contributions that the Igbo society can bring to the larger Nigerian community but also what can be gained from moving away from the Igbo community to look at the other communities in the country. Along with this new position Chinua Achebe also makes a case for the teller of tales:

The trees had become hydra-headed bronze statues so ancient that only blunt residual features remained on their faces, like anthills surviving to tell the new grass of the savannah about last year's brush fires.[13]

Through various experiences Chinua Achebe had arrived, by
the time of his last novel was published in 1988, at the position
which Wole Soyinka started with right at the beginning of his
career as a writer – offering his ethnic national background as
equivalent to, and sometimes having far more to offer, than that
of the Europeans and North Americans who thought it their natural role to rule Africans.

The position of both writers 'universalizes' their ethnic traditions without defining roles for these traditions within the
Nigerian nation-state. It is all well and good to find parallels
between Yoruba Gods and Goddesses and Greek Gods and
Goddesses, but what do Yoruba Gods and Goddesses have to
say to Igbo Gods and Goddesses and in what language would
they say it? For me, this is the measure of the subject matter of
both writers as well as most African writers writing in European
languages. What should be the way out?

The issue of the relationship of the ethnic and the national
agendas in African countries cannot be adequately dealt with in
this conclusion. For one thing, it only marginally belongs here
and, secondly, there is no space to spell it out in detail. Only the
barest minimum of the arguments can be deployed here to make
the point that both Chinua Achebe and Wole Soyinka were
moving to a situation in which they had to put both the ethnic
and the national agendas on priority levels and work out the
relationship that should ensue.

For a nation-state such as Nigeria to succeed in the modern
world an economous state must be created as a matter of necessity. This term needs further explanation. The nation(s) must be
seperated from the state in the (hypenated) nation-state. The
nations are the ethnic/tribal/language communities while the
state is the modern structure of economy, thus an economous
state created by the nations which make up a country such as
Nigeria. The economous state becomes the central icon to which
the multiplicity of ethnicities, languages and religions must
relate. The economous state is the collective big pot to which the
multiple ethnicities bring the contents of their little pots. Having
poured their individual possibilities into the corporate pot, they
do not then smash their pots as pan-Africanism would wish
them to do. Rather, they keep for themselves those details of rituals peculiar to themselves which the economous state does not
need. The collective corporate identity exists and prospers
because the individual ethnic identities exist and prosper.

One of the implications of such a dual identity is the need for a dual system of education. There has to be one education which prepares all citizens living within the borders of the country to ensure active and meaningful participation in the vibrancy of the economous state. In Nigeria, the language of that corporate state would be English while it would be French in Senegal. Over time this situation might change. As for the language of education at the ethnic level, it would have to be in the language of the particular ethnic nationality. This proposal can be ended with an observation. What happened in South Africa as a result of the elections of April 27, 1994 has been described by many people as a miracle. This 'miracle' took place in the context of an already existing economous state to which all and every section and every segment of the South African society could relate. There is room enough, it would seem, for everybody, around the economous state of South Africa.

One point that arises among many others, is to ask if particular forms of roles in capitalist establishments no longer mould the daily rituals of the individuals involved. Does the market system not dictate a market morality or immorality? If this is so, would the ensuing rituals of the market not override the rituals contained in the languages of the ethnic nationalities? What seems to be clear is that capitalism has been far more inventive than it was ever given credit for and some of the assumptions of its earlier period are mere assumptions to be proved wrong.

If the above resolves the political issues raised by the works of Chinua Achebe and Wole Soyinka, what about the artistic problems of their writings?

The experience of Irish writers has been mentioned earlier. The artistic problem posed for writers with bi-lingual backgrounds who choose to write in the colonising language rather than the language of the colonized is posed by Synge thus:

> Has any bilingual person ever been great in style? crois pas?[14]

What inhibits the writer with the bilingual background who writes in the language of colonisation is what W.B. Yeats touches here:

> We who write in English have a more difficult task, for English is the language in which the Irish cause has been debated and we have to struggle against traditional points of view...[15]

Ngugi's rejection of English goes back to this "traditional points of view" of Africa and the African contained in English. Synge's solution rests on two points: that Ireland was, by the end of the nineteenth century English enough for the language to be the language of literary expression and that the English that would benefit ordinary English would have to be the English dialect of the Irish peasant. Transferred to the situation of our two writers, these points underline their practice of writing. The critics of their writings need to do more in order to elucidate the maximum from these writings.

There are two major aspects to African literatures: an African aspect in that Africans are the producers of the literatures, and a European aspect in that the literatures are being produced either in European languages or else under the genre influence of European literatures. The first major point to be made is that any critic of these literatures ignores the language and literary tradition of the language of the writing to the detriment of their critical work on these literatures. This includes the writers themselves. The second point which needs to be made is that critics of African literatures cannot avoid getting to know in some detail the history, sociology and the politics which have inspired these writings.

I do not share the opinion that only those who come from a particular cultural background can understand its cultural products. This opinion is based on the sane knowledge that anyone can by hard work and with serious self-application take in enough cultural consciousness of any community. Foreign critics, as well as African critics, have not acknowledged the need to equip themselves with the necessary knowledge and know-how with which to mediate and re-interpret African literatures.

The third point is that any critic, foreign or domestic, who takes himself or herself seriously and takes seriously the works they are analysing must acquire a working knowledge of the mother-tongue of the writer or writers that they examine.

Both Achebe and Soyinka have chalked up tremendous achievements both internationally and locally in their country of origin. Looking at their works from a particular point of view, in this case from the point of view of their contribution to a Nigerian community of sensibilities, is not to run down their work. Rather, it is necessary to realise that both writers, like many other writers from other parts of Africa, have made political issues in Africa the centre piece of their inspiration.

But there is another, perhaps more important motive. Younger writers often wonder what to write about. A critical look at the areas still uncovered by older writers might re-define the field for the young.

A final paradox: both Achebe and Soyinka believe that the problem of Nigeria is the problem of leadership. They look forward to the coming into being of a leader who will know everything and will do everything right. For writers coming from an Africa where we are told forever how communal they are and how much against the individual they are, this is a strange position to be in. Where is the collective work of the community? Where are the benefits of the communal nature of African societies? What should be the role of the followers in the new Nigeria?

According to Declan Kiberd,

> The problem faced by nineteenth-century Irish writers was the linguistic disorder resutling from rapid loss of Irish and the yet imperfect assimilation of English. That problem, in Synge's opinion, was solved by 1902, when he wrote that 'the linguistic atmosphere of Ireland has become definitely English enough, for the first time, to allow work to be done in English that is perfectly Irish in essence' (*Prose*, p. 385).[16]

Is it not possible to make the same statement about many parts of Africa today?

Notes

1. Chinua Achebe, *The Trouble with Nigeria*, chapter 2 entitled "Tribalism" pp.5–8.

2. ibid. p.6.

3. Awolowo, Obafemi, *Path to Nigerian Freedom*, London: Faber and Faber, 1947. See Bibliography for Awolowo's publications.

4. ibid. p.53.

5. ibid. p.14.

6. Chinua Achebe, op. cit. p.5.

7. interview in *Artrage* – Inter-Cultural Arts Magazine, Autumn Issue, No. 14, p.8.

8. Kolawole Ogungbesan, "Politics and the African Writer" in C.L. Innes and Bernth Lindfors, *Critical Perspectives on Chinua Achebe*, pp.37–46.

9. ibid. p.38.

10. ibid. p.39.

11. ibid. p.40.

12. in Kirsten Holst Petersen and Anna Rutherford (eds.) *Kunapipi* – Special Issue in Celebration of Chinua Achebe, vol. xii, no.2, 1990, pp.1–10.

13. Chinua Achebe, *Anthills of the Savannah*, p.31.

14. Declan Kiberd, *Synge and the Irish Language*, p. 199.

15. ibid. p. 197.

16. ibid. p. 201.

Bibliography

This bibliography is in five sections.

The first section covers books on Nigeria and the history of Nigeria as well as some comparative studies. Few books on Nigerian history have made any attempt to incorporate the history of parts of the country prior to British conquest into a single claim of historical chain for example the way Arab–Islamic historians have done with the history of islamized countries prior to Islam and Arab intervention. The singular exception is Elizabeth Isichei.

The second section is on pan-Africanism. This is a pretty thin area of scholarship for many reasons. Outside of the initial documents and studies of the fifties and sixties there has been little to add to this area of African scholarship.

The third section of the bibliography deals with the works of creative writers mentioned in the study. Achebe and Soyinka are representatives of these writers but it has also been necessary to make more than casual references to the works of other African writers confronted with the same issues as are discussed with reference to the two main authors.

The fourth and fifth sections cover primary and select secondary sources on Chinua Achebe and Wole Soyinka. Few studies have dealt with the two writers the way they have been treated in this study. While many of the issues raised about their work might have been raised before in various guises, the issue of their contribution to the creation of a Nigerian community of sensibilities has never been raised at such length. Nor has this been done for any other Nigerian or African writers for that matter. In one or two cases where both writers are treated together, such critics seem anxious to disclaim any comparison between the two. This book is a comparative study of the two writers.

Generally speaking, the problem of agreeing to a common history and a common body of knowledge about Nigeria is one that all new nations have to confront. This study and this bibliography must be seen as contributing towards such an acceptable body of knowledge about Nigeria.

Nigeria
(and comparative studies)

Abdulrahim, Al-Tayyib, *Nigeria in a Thousand Years*, (in Arabic, unfinished, unpublished) Bayero University Library, Kano, 1985.

Adamolekun, Ladipo, *The Fall of the Second Republic*, Ibadan: Spectrum Books, 1985.

Adamolekun, Ladipo and Alex Gboyega, *Leading Issues in the Nigerian Public Service*, Ile-Ife: University of Ife Press, 1979.

Adamolekun, Ladipo, *Public Administration: A Nigerian and Comparative Perspective*, Lagos: Longman Nigeria, 1983.

Ade-Ajayi, J.F. and Tekena N. Tamuno, (eds.) *The University of Ibadan 1948 – 1973 History of the First 25 Years*, Ibadan: Ibadan University Press, 1973.

Ade-Ajayi, J.F. *Christian Missions in Nigeria 1841 – 1891: The Making of a New Elite*, London: Longman, 1965.

Ade-Ajayi, J.F. and Smith, Robert, *Yoruba Warfare in the 19th Century*, Ibadan: Ibadan University Press, 1971.

Adebayo, Augustus, *White Man in Black Skin*, Ibadan: Spectrum Books, 1981.

Adebiyi, T.A., *The Beloved Bishop: a Biography of Bishop A.B. Akinyele*, Ibadan: Daystar Press, 1969.

Adebo, Simeon O, *Our Unforgettable Years*, Ibadan: Macmillan, 1984.

Adeleye, R.A., *Power and Diplomacy in Northern Nigeria 1804 – 1906 – The Sokoto Caliphate and its Enemies*, London: Longman, 1971.

Adeloye, Adelola, *Nigerian Pioneers of Modern Medicine*, Ibadan: Ibadan University Press, 1972.

Ademoyega, Adewale, *Why We Struck: The Story of the First Nigerian Coup*, Ibadan: Evans, 1981.

Aderibigbe, A.B., *Lagos: The Development of an African City*, Lagos: Longman Nigeria, 1975.

Afigbo, E.A., *The Warrant Chiefs: Indirect Rule in South Eastern Nigeria 1891 – 1929*, London: Longman, 1972?

Afigbo, Adiele, *Ropes of Sand: Studies in Igbo History and Culture*, Ibadan: University Press Ltd. 1981.

Ajaegbu, H.I., *Urban and Rural Development in Nigeria*, Ibadan: Heinemann Educational Books, 1976.

Ajibola, Chief J.O., *Administration of Justice in the Customary Courts of Yorubaland*, Ibadan: University Press Ltd., 1982.

Akeredolu-Ale, E.O., *The Underdevelopment of Indigenous Entrepreneurship in Nigeria*, Ibadan: Ibadan University Press, 1975.

Akinjogbin, I.A. and Osoba, S.O. (eds.) *Ife History Series: Topics on Nigerian Economic and Social History*, Ile-Ife: University of Ife Press, 1980.

Akintoye, S.A., *Revolution and Power in Yorubaland 1840 – 1893*, London: Longman, 1971.

Akpan, N.U., *The Struggle for Secession 1966 – 1970, a Personal Account of the Nigerian Civil War*, London: Frank Cass, 1971.

Allen, C., and Dwivedi, Sharada, *Lives of the Indian Princes*, London: Century Publishing, 1984.

Amadi, Elechi, *Sunset in Biafra*, Ibadan: Heinemann, 1973.

Amadi, Elechi, *Ethics in Nigerian Culture*. Ibadan and London: Heinemann, 1982.

Amobi, Isaac Okey, *A Biography: Alvan Ikoku*, Onitsha: Africana Educational, 1981.

Amoda, Moyibi, *Festac Colloquium and Black World Development*, Lagos: Nigeria Magazine, 1978.

Ananaba, Wogu, *The Trade Union Movement in Nigeria*, Benin: Ethiope Publishing Corporation, 1969.

Ashcroft, Bill; Griffiths, Gareth and Tiffin, Helen, *The Empire Writes Back: Theroy and Practice in Post-Colonial Literatures*, London: Routledge, 1989.

Ashiwaju, G., and Enem, U., (eds.) *Cities of the Savannah, a History of some Towns and Cities of the Nigerian Savannah*, Lagos: Nigeria Magazine, nd.

Atanda, T.A., (ed), *Travels and Exploration in Yorubaland by W.H. Clarke*, Ibadan: Ibadan University Press, 1972.

Atanda, J.A., *The New Oyo Empire: Indirect Rule and Change in Western Nigeria 1894 – 1934*, Lagos: Longman, 1973.

Awolowo, Obafemi, *My Early Life*, Lagos: John West, 1968.

Awolowo, Obafemi, *Path to Nigerian Freedom*, London: Faber and Faber, 1947.

Awolowo, Obafemi, *The Problems of Africa: the Need for Ideological Reappraisal*, London: Macmillan Education Ltd., 1977.

Awolowo, Obafemi, *Awo on the Nigerian Civil War*, Lagos: John West, 1981.

Awolowo, Obafemi, *Voice of Reason*, (selected speeches), Akure: Fagbamigbe Publishers, 1981.

Awolowo, Obafemi, *Voice of Courage*, (selected speeches), Akure: Fagbamigbe Publishers, 1981.

Awolowo, Obafemi, *Voice of Wisdom*, (selected speeches), Akure: Fagbamigbe Publishers, 1981.

Ayandele, E.A., *Holy Johnson: Pioneer of African Nationalism 1836 – 1917*, London: Frank Cass, 1970.

Ayandele, E.A., *The Educated Elite in the Nigerian Society*, Ibadan: Ibadan University Press, 1974.

Ayida, A.A. and Onitiri, H.M.A. (eds.) *Reconstruction and Development in Nigeria: Proceedings of a National Conference*, Ibadan: Oxford University Press Nigeria and NISER, 1971.

Azikiwe, Nnamdi, *My Odyssey: An Autobiography*, London: C. Hurst, 1970.

Azikiwe, Nnamdi, *Democracy with Military Vigilance*, Enugu: African Books Ltd. 1974.

Azilide, Mike, *Echoes of Biafra*, Enugu: Skola Publications, 1983.

Babalola, Chief E.A., *My Life Adventures: Autobiography*, Ibadan: Caxton Press, nd.

Balewa, Abubakar Tafawa, *Shaihu Umar*, London: Longmans, Green and Co., 1967.

Balogun, Ismail A.B., *The Life and Works of Uthman Dan Fodio*, Lagos: Islamic Publications, 1975.

Balogun, Kolawole, *Village Boy: My Own Story*, Onitsha: Africana Publishers, 1969.

Barrett, Lindsay, *Danjuma – The Making of a General*, Enugu: Fourth Dimension, 1979.

Beer, C.E.F., *The Politics of Peasant Groups in Western Nigeria*, Ibadan: Ibadan University Press, 1976.

Belasco, Bernard I., *The Entrepreneur as Culture Hero: Preadaptations in Nigerian Economic Development*, New York and London: Praeger, 1980.

Bello, Ahmadu, *My Life*, London: Cambridge University Press, 1962.

Berghe, Pierre van de, *Power and Privilege at an African University*, Rochester, VT: Schenkman Publishing Co., 1973.

Biobaku, S.O., (ed.) *Sources of Yoruba History*, Oxford: Clarendon Press, 1973.

Booth, J. *Writers and Politics in Nigeria*. London: Hodder and Stoughton, 1981.

Boro, Isaac, Adaka, Jasper, *The Twelve Day Revolution*, Benin: Delta Press, 1982.

Brown, Terence, *Ireland: A Social and Cultural History 1922–1985*, London: Fontana, 1981.

Cabral, Amilcar, *Unity and Struggle*, London: William Heinemann, 1980.

Cary, Joyce, *The Case for African Freedom*, London: Secker and Warburg, 1944.

Cary, Joyce, *Mister Johnson*, Harmondsworth: Penguin Books, 1962.

Carroll, John, *Humanism The Wreck of Western Culture*, London: Fontana, 1993.

Chamberlain, M.E., *The Scramble for Africa*, London: Longman, 1974.

Cervenka, Zdanek, *A History of the Nigerian War, 1967 – 1970*, Ibadan: Onibonoje Press, 1972.

Clough, Raymond Gore, *Oil Rivers Trader*, London: C. Hurst and Co., 1972.

Cohen, Abner, *Custom and Politics in Urban Africa: A study of Hausa migrants in Yoruba Towns*, London: Routledge and Kegan Paul, 1977.

Coleman, James S., *Nigeria: Background to Nationalism*, Berkeley: University of California Press, 1971.

Collins, Kevin, *The Cultural Conquest of Ireland*, Dublin: The Mercier Press Ltd. 1990.

Collins, Robert, *Nigeria in Conflict*, London: Secker and Warburg, 1970.

Conrad, Joseph, *Heart of Darkness*, London: Penguin Classics, 1985.

Crampton, E.P.T., *Christianity in Northern Nigeria*, London: Longmans, 1975.

Crocker, Walter R., *Nigeria: A Critique of British Colonial Administration*, Freeport, NY: Books for Libraries Press, 1936, reprinted 1971.

Crowder, Michael and Ikime, Obaro, (eds) *West African Chiefs: Their Changing Status under Colonial Rule and Independence*, Ile-Ife: University of Ife Press, 1970.

Crowder, Michael, *Revolt in Bussa: A Study of British Native Administration in Nigerian Borgu, 1902 – 1935*, London: Faber and Faber, 1973.

Crowder, Michael, *The Story of Nigeria*, London: Faber and Faber, 1973.

Davidson, Basil. *The Black Man's Burden: Africa and the Curse of the Nation State*, New York: Times Books, 1992.

Davies, H.O., *Nigeria, Prospects for Democracy*, London: Weidenfeld and Nicolson, 1961.

Denoon, Donald, *A Biography of Ulli Beier*, (unpublished), 1987.

Denyer, Susan, *African Traditional Architecture*, London: William Heinemann, 1978.

Dike, K.O. *Trade and Politics in the Niger Delta 1830 – 1885*. Oxford: Clarendon Press, 1956 and 1966.

Dike, K.O. *Origins of the Niger Mission 1841 – 1891*. Ibadan: Ibadan University Press, 1957.

Dudley, B.J., *Instability and Political Order: Politics and Crisis in Nigeria*, Ibadan: Ibadan University Press, 1973.

Dudley, B.J., *An Introduction to Nigerian Government and Politics*, Bloomington: Indiana University Press, 1982.

Echeruo, Michael, C.J., *Victorian Lagos – Aspects of 19th Century Lagos Life*, London: Macmillan, 1977.

Ekanem, I.I., *The 1963 Nigerian Census: A Critical Appraisal*, Benin: Ethiope Publishing Corporation, 1972.

Eleazu, Uma O, *Federalism and Nation Building: The Nigerian Experience 1954 – 1964*, Ilfracombe: Arthur H. Stockwell, 1977.

Elias, T.O., (ed.) *Nigerian Press Law*, Ibadan: Evans, 1969.

Ellis, H.J. and Johnson, James, *Documents of Nigerian Church History: Two Missionary Visits to Ijebu Country 1892*, Ibadan: Daystar Press, 1974.

Enahoro, Anthony, *Fugitive Offender: The Story of a Political Prisoner*, London: Cassell, 1965.

Falola, Toyin, *The Political Economy of a Pre-Colonial African State: Ibadan 1830 – 1900*, Ile-Ife: University of Ife Press, 1984.

Falola, Toyin, and Oguntomisin, S.D., *The Military in 19th Century Yoruba Politics*, Ile-Ife: University of Ife Press, 1984.

Feinstein, Alan, *African Revolutionary: The Life and Times of Nigeria's Aminu Kano*, London: Davison Publishing, 1973.

Ferguson, John, *Some Nigerian Church Founders*, Ibadan: Daystar Press, 1971.

Finer, S.E., *The Man on Horseback*, London: Pall Mall, 1962.

Forster, R.F., (ed.) *The Oxford History of Ireland*, Oxford: Oxford University Press, 1992.

Garba, Joseph, *Revolution in Nigeria: Another View*, London: Africa Journal, 1982.

Gibbon, Edward, *The Decline and Fall of the Roman Empire*, Dero A. Saunders,(ed.) Harmondsworth: Penguin Books, 1981.

Gbulie, Ben, *Nigeria's Five Majors: The Coup d'etat of 15th January 1966, First Inside Account*, Onitsha: Africana Educational Publisher, 1981.

Hindley, Reg, *The Death of the Irish Language* London and New York, Routledge, 1990.

Home, Robert, *City of Blood Revisited*, London: Rex Collings, 1982.

Hubbard, James Patrick, *History of Katsina College, 1921 – 1942*, unpublished doctoral thesis, University of Wisconsin, 1973.

Hydle, Lars Holman, *The Press and Politics in Nigeria*, unpublished doctoral thesis, Columbia University, 1972.

Ike, V. Chukwuemeka, *University Development in Africa – The Nigerian Experience*, London: Oxford University Press, 1976.

Ilogu, Edmund, *Christianity and Igbo Culture*, New York: Nok Publishers, 1974.

Isichei, Elizabeth, *A History of Nigeria*, London: Macmillan, 1983.

Johnson, Paul, *Intellectuals*, London: George Weidenfeld and Nicolson Ltd., 1988.

Johnson, Reverend Samuel, *The History of the Yorubas – From the Earliest Times to the Beginning of the British Protectorate*, London: Church Missionary Society, 1921.

Jalingo, A, *The Radical Tradition in Northern Nigeria*, unpublished doctoral thesis, University of Edinburgh, 1982.

Jemibewon, David M., *A Combatant in Government*, Ibadan: Heinemann, 1978.

Kennedy, Paul, *The Rise and Fall of the Great Powers: Economic Change and Military Conflict from 1500 – 2000*, Glasgow: Fontana, 1988.

Kiberd, Declan, *Synge and the Irish Language*, (2nd edition), Dublin: Gill & Macmillan, 1993.

Kiberd, Declan, Interview in *Graph 13*, (Irish Literary Review.) Winter'92/Spring'93, Dublin. pp.5–8.

Kirk-Green, A.H.M., *Crisis and Conflict in Nigeria*, (two volumes) London: Oxford University Press, 1976.

Kirk-Green, A.H.M., *A Biographical Dictionary of the British Colonial Service 1939 – 1966*, London: Hans Zell Publishers, 1991.

Kirpal, Viney, "The Structure of the Modern Nigerian Novel and the National Consciousness", *Modern Fiction Studies*, Spring 1988, vol. 34, no.1, pp. 45–54.

Kurfi, Amadu, *The Nigerian General Elections of 1959 –1979 and the Aftermath*, Ibadan: Macmillan Nigeria, 1983.

Langley, J. Ayo, *Ideologies of Liberation in Black Africa, 1856 – 1970. Documents on Modern African Political Thought from Colonial Times to the Present.* London: Rex Collings, 1979.

Luckham, Robin, *The Nigerian Military: A Sociological Analysis of Authority and Revolt 1960 – 1974*, London: Oxford University Press, 1967.

Mabongunje, Akin L., *Urbanization in Nigeria*, London, University of London Press, 1968.

Mabogunje, Akin and Adetoye Faniran, (eds.) *Regional Planning and National Development in Tropical Africa*, Ibadan: Ibadan University Press, 1977.

Mackintosh, J.P. (ed) *Nigerian Government and Politics*, London: Allen and Unwin, 1966.

Madiebo, Alexander A., *The Nigerian Revolution and the Biafran War*, Enugu: Fourth Dimension, 1980.

Madunagu, Edwin, *The Tragedy of the Nigerian Socialist Movement and Other Essays*, Calabar: Centaur Press, 1980.

McLuckie, C.W., *Nigerian Civil War Literature: Seeking an 'Imagined Community'*, Lewiston, NY: Edith Mellen Press, 1990, 163pp.

Maisara, A.M., *The Five Majors: Why They Struck*, Zaria: Hudahuda, 1982.

Mellanby, K. *The Birth of Nigeria's University*, Ibadan: Ibadan University Press.

Milne, June, (compiler) *Kwame Nkrumah – The Conakry Years: His Life and Letters*, London: PANAF (an imprint of Zed Press Ltd.), 1990

Mphahlele, Ezekiel, *The African Image*, London: Faber and Faber, 1962, 1974.

Murray, D.J., (ed.) *Studies in Nigerian Administration*, London: Hutchinson, 1970.

Muffett, D.J.M., *The Story of Sultan Attahiru I*, Lagos: African Universities Press, 1964.

Muffet, D.J.M., *Let Truth Be Told: The Coups d'etat of 1966*, Zaria: Hudahuda, 1982.

Nelson, R and Wolpe, H (eds.) *Nigeria: Modernization and the Politics of Communalism*, Ann Arbor: Michigan State University Press, 1971.

Niven, Sir Rex, *The War of Nigerian Unity 1967 – 1970*, London: Evans, 1970.

Niven, Sir Rex, *Nigerian Kaleidoscope: Memoirs of a Colonial Servant*, London: C. Hurst, 1982.

Nwabara, S.N., *Iboland: A Century of Contact with Britain 1860 – 1960*, London: Hodder and Stoughton, 1977.

Nwala, T. Uzodinma, *Igbo Philosophy*, Lagos: Literamed Publications, 1985.

Nwankwo, Arthur A, *Nigeria: The Challenge of Biafra*, Enugu: Fourth Dimension, 1980.

Nwankwo, Arthur A, *Can Nigeria Survive?*, Enugu: Fourth Dimension, 1981.

Nwankwo, Arthur A. *Corruption in Anambra State: The Jim Nwobodo Legacy*, Enugu: Frontline Publishers, 1983.

Odeh, Rosaline, *Muhammadu Buhari, Nigeria's 7th Head of State*, Lagos: Federal Department of Information, 1984.

Ofodile, Chris, *Dr. M.I. Okpara: A Biography*, Enugu: Fourth Dimension, 1980.

Offonry, H.K. *Portrait of a Leader: The Biography of Dr. Michael Okpara*, Owerri: New Africa, 1983.

Ojiako, James O., *13 Years of Military Rule*, Lagos: Daily Times Publications, 1979.

Ojigbo, Anthony Okian, *200 Days to Eternity, the Life and Death of Murtala Muhammad, Nigeria's Head of State from July 1976 to February 1977*, Lagos: Quest Publishers, 1979.

Ojukwu, C. Odumegwu, *Biafra: Random Thoughts of C. Odumegwu Ojukwu, General of the People's Army*, New York: Perenial Library, 1969.

Ojukwu, C. Odumegwu, *Biafra: Selected Speeches with Journals of Events*, New York: Perennial Library, 1969.

Ojukwu, C. Odumegwu, *Ahiara Declaration: The Principles of Biafran Revolution*, Enugu: Biafra Information Service, 1969.

Okafor, S.O. *Indirect Rule: The Development of Central Legislature in Nigeria*, Lagos: Nelson Africa, 1981.

Okonjo, Isaac M, *British Administration in Nigeria 1900 – 1950: A Nigerian View*, New York: Nok Publishers, 1974.

Okoye, Mokwugo, *Storms on the Niger*, Enugu: Eastern Nigeria Printing Corporation, 1964.

Okoye, Mokwugo, *A Letter to Dr. Nnamdi Azikiwe*, Enugu: Fourth Dimension, 1979.

Olayide, S.O., *Economic Survey of Nigeria 1960 – 1975*, Ilesha: Aromolaran Publishers, 1976.

Oluleye, Major-General James J., *Military Leadership in Nigeria 1966 – 1979*, Ibadan: University Press, 1985.

Olusanya, G.G., *The West African Students Union and the Politics of Decolonisation 1925 – 1958*, Ibadan: Daystar Press, 1982.

Omotoso, Kole, *Just Before Dawn*, Ibadan: Spectrum Books, 1988.

Omotoso, Kole, *Season of Migration to the South*, Cape Town: Tafelberg, 1994.

Omu, Fred I.A., *Press and Politics in Nigeria, 1880 – 1937*, Lagos: Longman, 1978.

Oni, Ola and Bade Onimode, *Economic Development of Nigeria: The Socialist Alternative*, Ibadan: Nigerian Academy of Arts, Sciences and Technology, 1975.

Onibonoje, G.O., Omotoso, Kole, Lawal, O.O., (eds.) *The Indigenous for National Development*, Ibadan: Onibonoje Press, 1976.

Orr, Sir Charles, *The Making of Northern Nigeria*, London: Frank Cass, 1965.

Osadebay, Dennis, C. *Building a Nation*, Ibadan: Macmillan Nigeria, 1978.

Osuntokun, Akinjide, *Nigeria in the First World War*, New York: Humanities Press, 1979.

Osuntokun, Akinjide, *Chief S. Ladoke Akintola: His Life and Times*, London: Frank Cass, 1984.

Oyediran, O, (ed.) *The Nigerian 1979 Elections*, Ibadan: Macmillan Nigeria, 1981.

Oyediran, O, (ed.) *Survey of Nigerian Affairs 1976 – 1977*, Ibadan: Macmillan Nigeria, 1981.

Oyejide, T.A., *Tariff Policy and Industrialization in Nigeria*, Ibadan: Ibadan University Press, 1975.

Oyewole, Fola, *Reluctant Rebel*, London, Rex Colligns, 1975.

Panter-Brick, S.K., (ed.) *Nigerian Politics and Military Rule: Prelude to the Civil War*, London: Athlone Press, 1970.

Pedraza, Howard J., *Borrioboolaha: The Story of Lokoja the First British Settlement in Nigeria*, London: Oxford University Press, 1960.

Perham, Margery, *West African Passage: A Journey through Nigeria, Chad and the Cameroons*, A.H.M. Kirk-Greene, (ed.) London: Peter Owen Publishers, 1983.

Rooney, David, *Kwame Nkrumah: The Political Kingdom in the Third World*, London: I.B. Tauris & Co. Ltd., 1988.

Sanneh, Lamin, *Translating the Message: The Missionary Impact on Culture*, Maryknoll, NY: Orbis Books, 1989.

Sanda, A.O. (ed.) *Ethnic Relations in Nigeria*, Ibadan: Sociology Department, University of Ibadan, 1976.

Saro-Wiwa, Ken, *On A Darkling Plain: An Account of the Nigerian Civil War*, Port Harcourt and London, Saros International Publishers, 1989.

Sklar, Richard L., *Nigerian Political Parties: Power in an Emergent African Nation*, New York: Nok Publishers, 1983.

St. Jorre, John de, *The Nigerian Civil War*, London: Hodder and Stoughton, 1973.

Usman, Y.B. *Studies in the History of the Sokoto Caliphate*, Zaria: Ahmadu Bello University Press, 1979.

Uwechue, Ralph, *Reflections on the Nigerian Civil War: Facing the Future*, New York: Africana Publishing Corporation, 1971.

Williams, Gavin, *State and Society in Nigeria*, Idanre: Afrografika, 1980.

Government Documents:

Firm, Just, Mature, Decision of the Supreme Military Council on the Future of ex-secessionist officers, Nigerian National Press, Malu Road, Apapa, Lagos: 1975.

Government of Eastern Nigeria, *The Verbatim Report of the Aburi Accord*, Enugu: 1967.

Government Information Office, *The North and Constitutional Developments in Nigeria*, vol. 5, Enugu: Government Printer, Enugu: 1966.

Government Information Office, *Nigerian Heroes*, Lagos: Federal Department of Information, 1982.

Proceedings of the Constituent Assembly, Federal Ministry of Information, Lagos: 1967.

Report of the Judicial Commission of Inquiry into the Shortage of Petroleum Products, Federal Ministry of Information, Lagos: 1976.

Report of the Panel of Inquiry into the Purchases of British Leyland Buses by the Secretariat of Festac, Federal Ministry of Information, Lagos: 1978.

Pan-Africanism

Adi, Hakim and Marika Sherwood, *The 1945 Manchester Pan-African Congress Revisited with Colonial and...Coloured Unity* (the report of the 5th Pan-African Congress) edited by George Padmore, London and Port of Spain: New Beacon Books, 1995

Appiah, Kwame Anthony, *In My Father's House Africa in the Philosophy of Culture*, London: Methuen, 1992.

Asante, S.K.B., *Pan-African Protest: West Africa and the Italo-Ethiopian Crisis, 1939 – 1941*, London: Longman, 1977.

Azevedo, M. "Obstacles to Pan-Africanism: Real and Imaginary", *Africa and the World*. vol. 1, no. 4. 1988. pp. 1–11.

Clarke, J.H. "Pan-Africanism: A Brief History of an Idea in the African World." *Présence Africaine*. no. 145, Paris, 1988, pp. 25–56.

Geiss, I., *The Pan-African Movement*, London: Methuen, 1974.

Kawada, Junzo, "Development and Culture – Is Japan A Model?" in *Development and Culture*: Discussions of the Inaugural Programme of the Africa Leadership Forum, Ota, Nigeria, Oct./Nov. 1988, pp. 25–61.

Langley, J.A., *Pan-Africanism and Nationalism in West Africa 1900 – 1945: A Study in Ideology and Social Classes*, Oxford: Clarendon Press, 1973.

Lohata, T.O. "L'idéologie panafricanisme" *Le Mois en Afrique* 22, nos. 253–254. 1987, pp.149–161.

Makonnen, R., *Pan-Africanism from Within*, Nairobi: Oxford University Press, 1973.

Okadigbo. C. "The Odyssey and Future of Pan-Africanism" *Africa and the World*. vol. 1, no. 1, 1987, pp.11–17.

Padmore, G., *Pan-Africanism or Communism?*, London: Dobson, 1956.

Toure, S. "A Call for Revolutionary Pan-Africanism." *Africa and the World*. vol. 1, no. 4, 1988, pp.39–44.

Writers and Literary Works

Akinlade, Kola, *Alosi Ologo*, Ibadan: Longman Nigeria, 1974.

Akinlade, Kola, *Tal'o pa Omooba*? Ibadan: Macmillan Nigeria, 1971.

Akinlade, Kola, *Owo Eje*, Ibadan: Paperback Publishers, 1986

Akinlade, Kola, *Sangba Of*, Ibadan: Paperback Publishers, 1984.

Alkali, Zaynab, *The Stillborn*, Lagos: Longman Nigeria, 1984.

Alkali, Zaynab, *The Virtuous Woman*, Lagos: Longman Nigeria, 1987.

Alkali, Zaynab, "*Saltless Ash*" (short story) in *The Heinemann Book of African Women's Writing*, Charlotte H. Bruner, (ed.), London: Heinemann Educational Books, 1993. pp.26–33.

Aluko, T.M., *One Man, One Wife*, Lagos: Nigerian Printing and Publishing Co., 1959.

Aluko, T.M., *One Man, One Matchet*, London: Heinemann Educational Books, 1965

Aluko, T.M., *Kinsman and Foreman*, London: Heinemann Educational Books, 1966.

Aluko, T.M., *Chief the Honourable Minister*, London: Heinemann Educational Books, 1970.

Aluko, T.M., *His Worshipful Majesty*, London: Heinemann Educational Books, 1973.

Aluko, T.M., *Conduct Unbecoming*, Ibadan: Heinemann Educational Books, 1993.

Amadi, Elechi, *The Concubine*, London: Heinemann Educational Books, 1966.

Amadi, Elechi, *The Great Ponds*, London: Heinemann Educational Books, 1969.

Amadi, Elechi, *Sunset in Biafra*, London: Heinemann Educational Books, 1973.

Amadi, Elechi, *Peppersoup and the Road to Ibadan*, Ibadan: Onibonoje Press, 1977.

Amadi, Elechi, *The Slave*, London: Heinemann Educational Books, 1978.

Amadi, Elechi, *Dancer of Johannesburg*, Ibadan: Onibonoje Press, 1978.

Amadi, Elechi, *Isiburu*, Ibadan: Heinemann Educational Books (Nigeria) Ltd., 1980.

Amadi, Elechi, *Ethics in Nigerian Culture*, Ibadan: Heinemann Educational Books (Nigeria) Ltd., 1982.

Armah, Ayi, Kwei, *The Beautyful Ones are not Yet Born*, Boston: Houghton Mifflin, 1968.

Armah, Ayi, Kwei, *Fragments*, Boston: Houghton Mifflin, 1970.

Armah, Ayi, Kwei, *Why are we so Blest?* New York: Doubleday, 1972.

Armah, Ayi, Kwei, *Two Thousand Seasons*, Nairobi: East African Publishing House, 1973.

Armah, Ayi, Kwei, *The Healers*, Nairobi: East African Publishing House, 1978.

Awoonor, Kofi, *Rediscovery and Other Poems*, Ibadan: Mbari, 1964.

Awoonor, Kofi, *Night of My Blood*, New York: Doubleday, 1971.

Awoonor, Kofi, *This Earth, My Brother...*, New York: Doubleday, 1971.

Awoonor, Kofi, *Ride Me, Memory*, Greenfield Center, NY, Greenfield Review Press, 1973.

Awoonor, Kofi, *The House by the Sea*, New York: Greenfield Center, NY, Greenfield Press, 1978.

Awoonor, Kofi, *Until the Morning After Collected Poems 1963 – 1985*, Accra: Woeli Publishers, 1987.

Balewa, Alhaji Sir Abubakar Tafawa, *Shaihu Umar*, trans. Mervin Hiskett) London: Longman, 1968.

Bamgbose, Ayo, *The Novels of D.O. Fagunwa*, Benin City: Ethiope Publishing Corporation, 1974.

Bamgbose, Ayo, (ed.) *Mother Tongue Education: The West African Experience*, London and Paris: Hodder and Stoughton and The UNESCO Press, 1976.

Bamgbose, Ayo, *Yoruba Orthography: A Linguistic Appraisal with Suggestions for Reform*, Ibadan: Ibadan University Press, 1976.

Beti, Mongo, (as Eza Boto) *Ville cruelle*, Paris: Présence Africaine, 1972

Beti, Mongo, *Le pauvre Christ de Bomba*, Paris: Laffont, 1956.

Beti, Mongo, *Mission terminée*, Paris: Corrêa, 1957.

Beti, Mongo, *Main basse sur le Cameroun: autopsie d'une decolonisation*, Paris: Francois Maspéro, 1972.

Beti, Mongo, *Perpetué ou l'habitude du malheur: roman* Paris: Buchet-Chastel, 1974.

Beti, Mongo, *Remember Ruben*, Paris: Union Général d'Editions, 1974.

Beti, Mongo, *La ruine presque cocasse d'un polichinelle*, Paris: Edition des Peuples Noirs, 1979.

Beti, Mongo, *Les deux mères de Guillaume Ismael Dzewatama Futur Camionneur: roman*, Paris: Buchet-Chastel, 1982.

Beti, Mongo, *La revanche de Guillaume Ismael Dzewatama: roman*, Paris: Buchet-Chastel, 1984.

Beti, Mongo, *Lettre ouverte aux Camerounais ou la deuxième mort de Ruben Umnyobe*, Paris: Edition des Peuples Noirs, 1986.

Cabral, Amilcar, *Unity and Struggle*, Speeches and Writings, trans. Michael Wolfers, London: Heinemann, 1980.

Césaire, Aimé, *Discourse on Colonialism*, trans. Joan Pinkham, New York and London: Monthly Review Press, 1972.

Césaire, Aimé, *Return to My Native Land*, Paris: Présence Africaine, 1939.

Césaire, Aimé, *Et les chiens se taisaient*, Présence Africaine, 1956.

Césaire, Aimé, *Une saison du Congo*, Présence Africaine, 1966.

Césaire, Aimé, *La tragedie du roi Christophe*, 1963.

Chinweizu, *The West and the Rest of Us: White Predators, Black Slavers and the African Elite*, New York: Random House, 1975. London and Lagos: Nok Publishers, 1978.

Chinweizu, with Onwuchekwa Jemie and Ihechukwu Madubuike *Towards the Decolonization of African Literature* vol.1 *African Fiction and Poetry and their Critics*, Enugu: Fourth Dimension, 1980. London: Routledge, 1985.

Chinweizu, *Voices From Twentieth-Century Africa: Griots and Towncriers*, London: Faber and Faber, 1988.

Clark, J.P. (Bekederemo) *Song of a Goat*, Ibadan: Mbari,1961.

Clark, J.P. (Bekederemo) *Poems*, Ibadan: Mbari, 1961.

Clark, J.P. (Bekederemo) *Three Plays*, London: Oxford University Press, 1964.

Clark, J.P. (Bekederemo), *America, their America*, London: Andre Deutsch, 1964.

Clark, J.P. (Bekederemo) *A Reed in the Tide*, London: Longman, 1965.

Clark, J.P. (Bekederemo) *Ozidi*, London: Oxford University Press, 1966.

Clark, J.P. (Bekederemo), *The Example of Shakespeare*, London: Longman, 1970.

Clark, J.P. (Bekederemo) *Casualties*, London: Longman, 1970.

Clark, J.P. (Bekederemo) *A Decade of Tongues*, London: Longman, 1981.

Delano, I.O., *L'Ojo Ojo 'Un*, Lagos, Thomas Nelson and Sons Ltd., 1963. The following titles also by I.O. Delano:
> *The Soul of Nigeria*
> *An African Looks at Marriage*
> *One Church for Nigeria*
> *Notes and Comments from Nigeria*
> *The Singing Minister of Nigeria*
> *Iran Orun*
> *Itan Ogun Adubi*
> *Atumo Ede Yoruba* (Yoruba Dictionary)
> *Agbeka Oro Yoruba* (Appropriate Words and Expressions in Yoruba)
> *Iranti Anfani*
> *Yoruba Conversations Simplified*

Dingome, Jeanne N., "Soyinka's Role in Mbari", *African Theatre Review*, vol. 1 No. 3, April 1987

Echeruo, Michael J.C., *Joyce Cary and the Novel of Africa*, London: Longman, 1973.

Echeruo, Michael J.C., *Joyce Cary and the Dimensions of Order*, Ibadan: Ibadan University Press, 1979.

Echeruo, Michael J.C., *Victorian Lagos*, London: Longman, 1975.

Echeruo, Michael J.C., *The Conditioned Imagination from Shakespeare to Conrad*, London: Longman, 1982.

Ekwensi, Cyprian, *When Love Whispers*, Lagos: Chuks, 1947.

Ekwensi, Cyprian, *People of the City*, London: Dakers, 1954.

Ekwensi, Cyprian, *Jagua Nana*, London: Hutchinson, 1961.

Ekwensi, Cyprian, *Burning Grass*, London: Heinemann Educational Books, 1962.

Ekwensi, Cyprian, *Yaba Roundabout Murder*, Lagos, self-published, 1962.

Ekwensi, Cyprian, *Beautiful Feathers*, London: Hutchinson, 1963.

Ekwensi, Cyprian, *Iska*, London: Hutchinson, 1966.

Ekwensi, Cyprian, *Lokotown and other stories*, London: Heinemann Educational Books, 1966.

Ekwensi, Cyprian, *Restless City and Christmas Gold*, London: Heinemann Educational Books, 1975.

Ekwensi, Cyprian, *Survive the Peace*, London: Heinemann Educational Books, 1976.

Ekwensi, Cyprian, *Divided We Stand*, Enugu: Fourth Dimension, 1980.

Ekwensi, Cyprian, *Jagua Nana's Daughter*, Ibadan: Spectrum Books Ltd., 1986

Children's titles:

Ekwensi, Cyprian, *Ikolo the Wrestler, and other Ibo tales*, London: Nelson, 1947.

Ekwensi, Cyprian, *The Leopard's Claw*, London: Longmans, 1950.

Ekwensi, Cyprian, *The Drummer Boy*, London and New York: Cambridge University Press, 1960.

Ekwensi, Cyprian, *The Passport of Malam Ilia*, London and New York: Cambridge University Press, 1960.

Ekwensi, Cyprian, *An African Night's Entertainment*, Lagos: African Universities Press, 1962.

Ekwensi, Cyprian, *The Rainmaker and Other Stories*, Lagos: African Universities Press, 1965.

Ekwensi, Cyprian, *The Great Elephant Bird*, (a re-issue of *Ikolo the Wrestler, and other Ibo tales*) London: Nelson, 1965.

Ekwensi, Cyprian, *The Boa Suitor*, London: Nelson, 1966.

Ekwensi, Cyprian, *Trouble in Form Six*, London and New York: Cambridge University Press, 1966.

Ekwensi, Cyprian, *Juju Rock*, Lagos: African Universities Press, 1966.

Ekwensi, Cyprian, *Coal Camp Boy*, Lagos: Longman Nigeria, 1973.

Ekwensi, Cyprian, *Samankwe in the Strange Forest*, Lagos: Longman Nigeria, 1975.

Ekwensi, Cyprian, *Samankwe and the Highway Robbers*, London: Evans, 1979.

Ekwensi, Cyprian, *The Rainbow-Tainted Scarf and Other Stories*, London: Evans, 1979.

Ekwensi, Cyprian, *Motherless Baby*, Enugu: Fourth Dimension, 1980.

Enekwe, Ossie Onuora, *Broken Pots*, New York: Greenfield Review Press, 1977.

Enekwe, Ossie Onuora, *Come Thunder*, Enugu: Fourth Dimension, 1981.

Fagunwa, D.O. *Ireke Onibudo*, Lagos: Thomas Nelson and Sons Ltd., 1949.

Fagunwa, D.O., *Igbo Olodumare*, Lagos: Thomas Nelson and Sons Ltd., 1949.

Fagunwa, D.O., *Ogboju Ode Ninu Igbo Irunmole*, Lagos: Thomas Nelson and Sons Ltd., 1950 trans. Wole Soyinka as *The Forest of a Thousand Daemons: A Hunter's Saga*, London: Nelson, 1968.

Fagunwa, D.O., *Irinkerindo Ninu Igbo Elegbeje*, Lagos: Thomas Nelson and Sons Ltd., 1954.

Fagunwa, D.O., *Adiitu Olodumare*, Lagos: Thomas Nelson and Sons Ltd., 1961.

Gbadamosi, Rasheed, *3 Plays: The Mansion, The Greener Grass and Sing the Old Song for Me*, Lagos: Kraft Books Ltd., 1991.

Ike, Chukuemeka, *Our Children Are Coming*, Ibadan: Spectrum Books, 1990.

Ike, Chukuemeka, *The Search*, Ibadan: Heinemann Educational Books, 1991.

Isola, Akinwunmi, *Ake ni igba ewe mi*, Ibadan: Fountain Publishers, 1992. (Yoruba translation of Wole Soyinka's *Ake – The Years of Childhood*.)

Isola, Akinwunmi, *Iku Olokun Esin*, Ibadan: Fountain Publishers, 1994. (Yoruba translation of Wole Soyinka's play *Death and the King's Horseman*.)

Isola, Akinwunmi, *Ogun Omode*, Ibadan: University Press, 1990.

Iyayi, Festus, *Violence*, London: Longman, 1979.

Iyayi, Festus, *The Contract*, London: Longman, 1982.

Iyayi, Festus, *Heroes*, London: Longman, 1986.

Jeyifo, Biodun, *The Truthful Lie, Essays in a Sociology of African Drama*, London: New Beacon Books, 1975.

Jeyifo, Biodun, *The Yoruba Popular Travelling Theatre of Nigeria*, Lagos: Nigeria Magazine Publications, 1986.

Jeyifo, Biodun, *Contemporary Nigerian Literature: a Retrospective and Prospective Exploration*, Lagos: Nigeria Magazine Publications, 1987.

Jones, Eldred D., with Clifford N. Fyle (compilers) *A Krio – English Dictionary*, London and Freetown: Oxford University Press and Sierra Leone University Press, 1980.

Kane, Cheikh Hamidou, *Ambiguous Adventure*, trans. Katherine Woods, London: Heinemann Educational Books, 1963.

Laye, Camara, *The African Child*, trans. James Kirkup, London: Collins, 1955.

Laye, Camara, *The Radiance of the King*, trans. James Kirkup, London: Collins, 1956.

Laye, Camara, *A Dream of Africa*, trans. James Kirkup, London: Collins, 1968.

Laye, Camara, *The Guardian of the Word*, trans. James Kirkup, Glasgow: Fontana/Collins, 1981.

Mphahlele, Ezekiel, *Man Must Live, and other Stories*, Cape Town: African Bookman, 1947.

Mphahlele, Ezekiel, *The Living and the Dead, and other stories*, Ibadan: Western Region Ministry of Education, 1961.

Mphahlele, Ezekiel, *Down Second Avenue*, London: Faber and Faber, 1959.

Mphahlele, Ezekiel, *In Corner B*, Nairobi: East African Publishing House, 1967.

Mphahlele, Ezekiel, *The Wanderers*, New York: Macmillan, 1970.

Mphahlele, Es'kia, *Chirundu*, Johannesburg: Ravan, 1979.

Mphahlele, Es'kia, *The Unbroken Song*, Johannesburg: Ravan, 1981.

Mphahlele, Es'kia, *Afrika My Music, An Autobiography 1957 – 1983*. Johannesburg: Ravan, 1984.

Mphahlele, Ezekiel, *The African Image*, London: Faber and Faber, 1962.

Mphahlele, Ezekiel, *Voices in the Whirlwind and Other Essays*, London: Macmillan, 1973.

Nkrumah, Kwame, *The Autobiography of Kwame Nkrumah*, London: Nelson, 1957.

Nkrumah, Kwame, *I Speak of Freedom*, London: Panaf, 1961.

Nkrumah, Kwame, *Towards Colonial Freedom*, London: Heinemann, 1962.

Nkrumah, Kwame, *Consciencism* , London: Heinemann, 1964.

Nkrumah, Kwame, *Africa Must Unite*, London: Panaf, 1964.

Nkrumah, Kwame, *Neo-Colonialism. The Last Stage of Imperialism*, London: Panaf, 1965.

Nkrumah, Kwame, *Dark Days in Ghana*, London: Panaf, 1968.

Nkrumah, Kwame, *Revolutionary Path*, London: Panaf, 1973.

Nkrumah, Kwame, *Rhodesia File*, London: Panaf, 1974.

Nwankwo, Nkem, *Danda*, London: Andre Deutsch, 1964.

Nwankwo, Nkem, *My Mercedes is Bigger than Yours*, London: Andre Deutsch, 1975.

Ogungbesan, Kolawole, (ed.) *New West African Literature*, London: Heinemann Educational Books, 1979.

Okara, Gabriel, *The Voice*, London: Andre Deutsch, 1964.

Okara, Gabriel, *The Fisherman's Invocation*, London: Heinemann, 1978.

Okara, Gabriel, "Towards the Evolution of an African language for African Literature" in Kirsten Holst Petersen and Anna Rutherford (eds.) *Kunapipi*, Special Issue in Celebration of Chinua Achebe, vol. XII, no. 2, 1990. pp. 11–30; also published in *Semper Aliquid Novi: Littérature Comparée et Littératures d'Afrique: Mélanges Albert Gérard*, ed. Janos Riesz and Alain Ricard, Tübingen: Gunter Narr Verlag, 1990. pp. 305–316.

Okpewho, Isidore, *Tides*, Harlow: Longman Group, 1993.

Okri, Ben, *Flowers and Shadows*, London: Longman, 1980.

Okri, Ben, *The Landscapes Within*, London: Longman, 1981.

Okri, Ben, *Incidents at the Shrine*, London: Flamingo, 1987.

Okri, Ben, *Stars of the New Curfew*, London: Secker & Warburg, 1989.

Okri, Ben, *The Famished Road*, London: Jonathan Cape, 1991.

Okri, Ben, *Songs of Enchantment*, London: Jonathan Cape, 1993.

Osofisan, Femi, *Kolera Kolej*, Ibadan: New Horn Press, 1975.

Osofisan, Femi, *A Restless Run of Locusts*, Ibadan: Onibonoje Press, 1975.

Osofisan, Femi, *The Chattering and the Song*, Ibadan: Ibadan University Press, 1977.

Osofisan, Femi, *Who's Afraid of Solarin?*, Calabar: Scholars Press, 1978.

Osofisan, Femi, *Morountodun and Other Plays*, Lagos: Longman, 1982.

Osofisan, Femi, *Midnight Hotel*, Ibadan: Evans Brothers (Nigeria Publishers) Ltd. 1985.

Osofisan, Femi, *Another Raft*, Lagos: Malthouse Press Ltd., 1988.

Osofisan, Femi, *Birthdays Are Not For Dying & Other Plays*, Lagos: Malthouse Press Ltd., 1990.

Osofisan, Femi, *Once Upon Four Robbers*, Ibadan: Heinemann Educational Books, 1991.

Osofisan, Femi, *Aringindin and the Nightwatchmen*, Ibadan: Heinemann Educational Books, 1991.

Osofisan, Femi, *Esu and the Vagabond Minstrels*, Ibadan: New Horn Press, 1991.

Osofisan, Femi, *Yungba Yungba and the Dance Contest. A Parable for our Times*, Ibadan: Heinemann Educational Books, 1993.

Osofisan, Femi, *The Album of the Midnight Blackout*, Ibadan: University Press plc., 1994.

Osofisan, Femi, (as Okinba Launko) *Minted Coins*, Ibadan: Heinemann Educational Books, 1987.

Osofisan, Femi, (as Okinba Launko) *Cordelia*, Lagos: Malthouse Press Ltd., 1989

Osundare, Niyi, *Songs of the Marketplace*, Ibadan: New Horn Press, 1983.

Osundare, Niyi, *Village Voices*, Ibadan: Evans Brothers, 1984.

Osundare, Niyi, *The Eye of the Earth*, Ibadan: Heinemann Educational Books (Nigeria) Ltd., 1986.

Osundare, Niyi, *Moonsongs*, Ibadan: Spectrum Books, 1988.

Osundare, Niyi, *Waiting Laughters*, Lagos: Malthouse Press, 1990.

Osundare, Niyi, *Songs of the Season*, Ibadan: Heinemann Educational Books, 1990.

Osundare, Niyi, *Midlife*, Ibadan: Heinemann Educational Books, 1993.

Ousmane, Sembene, *God's Bits of Wood*, trans. Francis Price, Garden City, NY: Doubleday, 1962.

Ousmane, Sembene, *Tribal Scars and Other Stories*, trans. Len Ortzen, London: Heinemann, 1973.

Ousmane, Sembene, *The Money Order with White Genesis*, trans. Clive Wake, London: Heinemann, 1971.

Ousmane, Sembene, *Xala*, trans. Clive Wake London: Heinemann, 1976.

Ousmane, Sembene, *The Last of the Empire, A Senegalese Novel*, trans. Adrian Adams London: Heinemann, 1983.

Saro-Wiwa, Ken, *The Ogoni Nationality Today and Tomorrow*, Port Harcourt: self-published, 1968.

Saro-Wiwa, Ken, *Letter to Ogoni Youth*, Port Harcourt: self-published, 1983.

Saro-Wiwa, Ken, *Sozaboy. A Novel in Rotten English*, Port Harcourt: Saros International Publishers, 1985.

Saro-Wiwa, Ken, *A Forest of Flowers*, Port Harcourt: Saros International Publishers, 1986.

Saro-Wiwa, Ken, *Adaku and Other Stories*, Port Harcourt: Saros International Publishers, 1989.

Saro-Wiwa, Ken, *On A Darkling Plain: An Account of the Nigerian Civil War*, Port Harcourt: Saros International Publishers, 1990.

Saro-Wiwa, Ken, *Ogoni Bill of Rights* presented to the Government and Peoples of Nigeria, 1990.

Saro-Wiwa, Ken, *Prisoners of Jebs*, Port Harcourt: Saros International Publishers, 1990.

Saro-Wiwa, Ken, *Nigeria: On the Brink of Disaster*, Port Harcourt: Saros International Publishers, 1991.

Saro-Wiwa, Ken, *Similia. Essays on Anomic Nigeria*, Port Harcourt: Saros International Publishers, 1991.

Saro-Wiwa, Ken, *Pita Dumbrok's Prison*, Port Harcourt: Saros International Publishers, 1991.

Saro-Wiwa, Ken, *The Singing Anthill* Ogoni Folk Tales, Port Harcourt: Saros International Publishers, 1991.

Senghor, Léopold Sedar, *Selected Poems*, trans. John Reed and Clive Wake, London: Oxford University Press, 1964.

Senghor, Léopold Sedar, *Prose and Poetry*, trans. John Reed and Clive Wake) London: Oxford University Press, 1965.

Tahir, Ibrahim, *The Last Imam*, London: Hodder and Stoughton, 1984.

Tutuola, Amos, *The Palm-wine Drinkard, and his Dead Palm–wine Tapster in the Dead's Town*, London: Faber and Faber, 1952.

Tutuola, Amos, *My Life in the Bush of Ghosts*, London: Faber and Faber, 1954.

Tutuola, Amos, *Simbi and the Satyr of the Dark Jungle*, London: Faber and Faber, 1955.

Tutuola,Amos, *The Brave African Huntress*, London: Faber and Faber, 1958.

Tutuola, Amos, *Feather Woman of the Jungle*, London: Faber and Faber, 1962.

Tutuola, Amos, *Ajaiyi and his Inherited Poverty*, London: Faber and Faber, 1967.

Tutuola, Amos, *The Witch Herbalist of the Remote Town*, London: Faber and Faber, 1981.

Tutuola, Amos, *Yoruba Folktales*, Ibadan: Ibadan University Press, 1987.

U Tam'si, Tchicaya, *Brush Fire*, trans. Sangodare Akanji, (Ulli Beier) Ibadan: Mbari, 1964.

U Tam'si, Tchicaya, *Poems*, trans. Gerald Moore, London: Heinemann, 1970.

U Tam'si, Tchicaya, *The Glorious Destiny of Marshal Nnikon Nniku*, trans. Timothy Johns, Paris: Ubu Repertory Theater Publications, 1985.

Chinua Achebe

Novels
Things Fall Apart, London: Heinemann, 1958.
No Longer at Ease, London: Heinemann, 1960.
Arrow of God, London: Heinemann, 1964.
A Man of the People, London: Heinemann, 1966.
Anthills of the Savannah, London: Heinemann, 1987.
The African Trilogy: Things Fall Apart, No Longer at Ease, Arrow of God, London: Picador in association with Heinemann, 1988.

Short Stories
The Sacrificial Egg and Other Stories, Onitsha: Etudo, 1962.
Girls at War and Other Stories, London: Heinemann, 1972.

Children's Books
Chike and the River, Cambridge: Cambridge University Press, 1966.
How the Leopard Got His Claws, (with John Iroaganachi), Enugu: Nwamife, 1972.
The Drum, Enugu: Fourth Dimension, 1977.
The Flute, Enugu: Fourth Dimension, 1977.

Poetry
Beware Soul Brother and Other Poems, Enugu: Nwankwo-Ifejika, 1971.

Actuality
The Trouble with Nigeria, Enugu: Fourth Dimension, 1983.

Criticism
Morning Yet on Creation Day, London: Heinemann, 1975.
Hopes and Impediments: Selected Essays, 1965 – 1987, London: Heinemann, 1988.
Nigerian Essays, Ibadan: Heinemann, 1988.

Edited Collections
Don't Let Him Die: An Anthology of Memorial Poems for Christopher Okigbo, (with Dubem Okafor), Enugu: Fourth Dimension, 1978.
Aka Weta: Egwu Aguluagu, Egwu Edeluede, (with Obiora Udechukwu) Nsukka: Okike Magazine, 1982.

African Short Stories, (with C.L. Innes), London: Heinemann, 1985.

Bibliographic Resources

Alvarez–Pereyre, J., "Contribution à la bibliographie sur Chinua Achebe." *Echoes du Commonwealth*, 5, 1979 – 80, p. 196.

Anafulu, Joseph C. "Chinua Achebe: a Preliminary Checklist." *Nsukka Library Notes* vol. 3, nos. 1, 2 and 3, 1978, 51p. Special issue.

Evalds, Victoria K., "Chinua Achebe: Bio-bibliography and Recent Criticism, 1970 – 75." *Current Bibliography on African Affairs*,10, 1977/78, pp. 67–87.

Evalds, Victoria K., "Chinua Achebe: Bio-bibliography and Selected Criticism, 1970–1975". *Africana Journal* vol. 8 1977, pp. 101–30.

Hann, S.J., "Bibliography." *Studies in Black Literature* vol. 2, no. 1, 1971, pp. 20–21.

Lindfors, Bernth, "A Checklist of Works by and about Chinua Achebe." *Obsidian: Black Literature in Review*, vol. 4, no. 1, 1978, pp.103–17.

Lindfors, Bernth, "Recent Scholarship on Achebe." *Literary Half-yearly*, vol.21, 1980, pp.180–86.

McDaniel, Richard Bryan, "An Achebe Bibliography." *World Literature Written in English*, vol. 20, 1971, pp.15–24.

Okpu, B.M., *Chinua Achebe. A Bibliography*. Apapa, Lagos: Libriservice, 1984.

Saint-Andre-Utudjian, Eliane, "Chinua Achebe: A Bibliography." *Annales Univ. du Benin*, série Lettres 4, no. 1, 1977, pp.91–103.

Severec, Alain, "Chinua Achebe" *Annales Faculté des lettres et sciences humaines*, Univ. de Dakar,vol. 2, 1972, pp.60–66.

Silver, Helene, "Chinua Achebe: A Select Bibliography." *Africana Library Journal*, vol. 1, 1970, pp.20–22.

Some general studies (see also Note on p. 182)

Awoonor, Kofi, *The Breast of the Earth*, New York: Anchor Press, 1975.

Bhabha, Homi K. (ed.) *Nation and Narration*, London: Routledge, 1990.

Bjornson, Richard. *The African Quest for Freedom and Identity: Cameroonian Writing and the National Experience*, Bloomington: Indiana University Press, 1991.

Cairns, David and Shaun Richards, *Writing Ireland: Colonialism, Nationalism and Culture*, Manchester: Manchester University Press, 1988.

Carroll, David, *Chinua Achebe*, London: Macmillan, 1980.

Cartey, Wilfred G.O., *Whispers from a Continent: Writings from Contemporary Black Africa*, New York: Random House, 1969.

Cook, David, *African Literature: A Critical View*, London: Longman. 1977.

Darah, G.G., and Wole Ogundele, *Reading Achebe's Politics in A Man of the People: Two Contrastive Views*, Ile-Ife:Ife Monographs on Literature and Criticism, 1985.

Dathorne, O.R., *The Black Mind: A History of African Literature*, Minneapolis: University of Minnesota Press, 1974.

Diamond, L. "Fiction as Political Thought." [review article of *Anthills of the Savannah* by Chinua Achebe.] *African Affairs*, vol. 88, no. 352, 1989, pp.435–445.

Duerden, Dennis, *The Invisible Present: African Art and Literature*, New York: Harper and Row. 1975.

Echeruo, M.J.C. and E.N. Obiechina, (eds.) *Igbo Traditional Life, Culture and Literature*. Owerri: Conch Magazine, 1971.

Egudu, Romanus and Donatus Nwoga, *Igbo Traditional Verse*. London: Heinemann, 1973.

Emenyonu, Ernest, *The Rise of the Igbo Novel*, Ibadan: Oxford University Press Nigeria, 1978.

Gakwandi, Shatto Arthur, *The Novel and Contemporary Experience in Africa*, London: Heinemann, 1977.

Gikandi, Simon, *Reading Chinua Achebe, Language and Ideology in Fiction*, London: James Currey, 1991.

Gleason, Judith S.I., *This Africa: Novels by West Africans in English and French*, Evanston: Northwestern University Press, 1965.

Glenn, Ian, *Achebe and the Dilemma of the Nigerian Intellectual*, Cape Town: Centre of African Studies, University of Cape Town, 1983.

Gordimer, Nadine, *The Black Interpreters*, Johannesburg: Ravan, 1973.

Griffiths, G. "Chinua Achebe: When Did you Last See your Father?" *World Literature Written in English*, vol. 27, no. 1, 1987, pp.18–27.

Innes, C.L., *Chinua Achebe*, Cambridge: Cambridge University Press, 1990.

Innes, C.L. and Bernth Lindfors, (eds.) *Critical Perspectives on Chinua Achebe*, Washington D.C.: Three Continents Press, 1978.

Isichei, Elizabeth, *Igbo Worlds*, London: Macmillan, 1977.

Killam, G.D. *The Writings of Chinua Achebe*, London: Heinemann, 1977.

King, Bruce, and Kolawole Ogungbesan, (eds.) *A Celebration of Black and African Writing*, Zaria: Ahmadu Bello University Press, 1975.

Klima, V. *Modern Nigerian Novels*. Prague: Academia, 1969.

Larson, Charles R., *The Emergence of African Fiction*, Bloomington: Indiana University Press, 1972.

Laurence, Margret, *Long Drums and Cannons: Nigerian Dramatists and Novelists, 1952 – 1966*, London: Macmillan, 1968.

Lindfors, Bernth, *Early Nigerian Literature*. New York and London: Africana Publishing Corporation, 1982.

Lindfors, Bernth, *Nigeria's First Novelists*. *Power Above Power*, Mysore, India: Centre for Commonwealth Literature and Research, University of Mysore, 1986.

Lindfors, Bernth, *Critical Perspectives on Nigerian Literature*, Washington D.C.: Three Continents Press, 1975.

Mahood, M.M., *The Colonial Encounter*, London: Rex Collings, 1976.

McDougall, R. "Okonkwo's Walk: the Choreography of *Things Fall Apart*" *World Literature Written in English*, vol. 26, no. 1, 1986. pp.24–33.

McDougall, R. "The 'Problem of Locomotion' in *No Longer at Ease*", *World Literature Written in English*, vol. 29, no. 1, 1989, pp.19–25.

Moore, G., *Seven African Writers*, London: Oxford University Press, 1962.

Moore, G., (ed.) *African Literature and the Universities*, Ibadan: Ibadan University Press, 1965.

Moore, G., *Twelve African Writers*, London: Hutchinson, 1980.

Nnolim, S.A., *The History of Umuchu*, (edited and prepared for publication by Charles E. Nnolim), Enugu: Ochumba Press, 1952.

Mphahlele, Ezekiel, *The African Image*, London: Faber and Faber, 1962, 1974.

Obiechina, Emmanuel, *Culture, Tradition and Society in the West African Novel*, London: Cambridge University Press, 1975.

Odinamadu, Benedict Obidinma, *Politics and the Igbo Elite*, Ibadan: Sketch Publishing Company, 1979.

Ogbaa, Kalu, *Gods, Oracles and Divination: Folkways in Chinua Achebe's Novels*, Trenton NY: Africa World Press, 1992.

Ogungbesan, Kolawole, "Politics and the African Writer" in C.L. Innes and Bernth Lindfors, (eds.) *Critical Perspectives on Chinua Achebe*, Washington, D.C.: Three Continents Press, 1978. pp. 37–46.

Ojinmah, Umelo, *Chinua Achebe: New Perspectives*, Ibadan: Spectrum Books, 1991.

Okeke-Ezigbo, E. "The Impossibility of Becoming a Gentleman in Nigeria: a Neglected Theme of Chinua Achebe's *No Longer at Ease.*" *Journal of African Studies*, vol. 12, no. 2, 1985, pp.93–97.

Okeke-Ezigbo, E.J. "Synge and Gabriel Okara: the Heideggerian Search for a Quintessential Language", *Comparative Literature Studies*, vol. 26, no. 4, 1989, pp.324–340.

Olney, James, *Tell Me Africa: An Approach to African Literature*, Princeton: Princeton University Press, 1973.

Opata, D. "The Sudden End of Alienation: a Reconsideration of Okonkwo's Suicide in Chinua Achebe's *Things Fall Apart.*" *Africana Marburgensia*, vol.22, no.2, 1989, pp.24–32.

Owomoyela, O. "Chinua Achebe on the Individual in Society", *Journal of African Studies*, vol. 12, no. 2, 1985, pp.53–65.

Palmer, Eustace Taiwo, *An Introduction to the African Novel*, London: Heinemann, 1972.

Petersen, Kirsten Holst and Anna Rutherford, (eds.), *Chinua Achebe: A Celebration*, Oxford: Heinemann, 1990.

Sharma, V. "'Leisure' in a Traditional West African Society as seen Through a Work of Fiction [i.e. *Things Fall Apart.*], *Africa Quarterly.* vol. 28, no.1–2, 1988, pp.67–74.

Ugah, Ada, *In the Beginning... Chinua Achebe at Work*, Ibadan: Heinemann Educational Books (Nig.) Ltd., 1990.

Walder, Dennis, (ed.) *Literature in the Modern World*: *Critical Essays and Documents*, Oxford: Oxford University Press, 1990.

Wren, Robert, *Achebe's World: The Historical and Cultural Context of the Novels of Chinua Achebe*, Harlow: Longman, 1981.

Interviews

Agetua, John, *Critics on Chinua Achebe*, (interview and book reviews), Benin City: John Agetua, 1977.

Duerden, Dennis and Cosmo Pieterse, (eds.), *African Writers Talking: A Collection of Radio Interviews*, London: Heinemann, 1972, pp.3–17.

Beier, Ulli, "The World is a Dancing Masquerade..." *A Conversation between Chinua Achebe and Ulli Beier*, Bayreuth:

Iwalewa Haus, 1991. This conversation took place on July 1st, 1989 in IWALEWA Haus, Bayreuth, Germany.

Farah, Nuruddin, "Just Talking: Chinua Achebe and Nuruddin Farah at the ICA 25.6.86." *Artrage* no.14, 1986 pp. 4–5, p. 8.

Lindfors, Bernth, Munro, Ian; Priebe, Richard; and Sander, Reinhard, (eds.), *Palaver – Interviews with Five African Writers in Texas*, Austin: African and Afro-American Research Institute, University of Texas at Austin, 1972, pp. 5–12.

Morrell, Karen, L., (ed.), *In Person: Achebe, Awoonor,and Soyinka at the University of Washington*, Seattle: African Studies Program, Institute for Comparative and Foreign Area Studies, University of Washington, 1975, pp.24–32.

Rowell, C.H. "An Interview with Chinua Achebe." *Callaloo*, vol. 13, no.1, 1990, pp.86–101.

Wilkinson, Jane, (ed.), *Talking with African Writers, Interviews with African Poets, Playwrights and Novelists*, London: James Currey, 1990 and 1992, pp.46–57.

Wole Soyinka

Novels
The Interpreters, London: Andre Deutsch, 1965.
Season of Anomy, London: Rex Collings, 1973.

Plays
Before the Blackout, Ibadan: Orisun Publications, 1965.
Collected Plays 1: A Dance of the Forests; The Swamp Dwellers; The Strong Breed; The Road; The Bacchae of Euripedes, London: Oxford University Press, 1973.
Collected Plays 2: The Lion and the Jewel; Kongi's Harvest; The Trials of Brother Jero; Jero's Metamorphosis; Madmen and Specialists, London: Oxford University Press, 1974.
Before the Blowout, Ibadan: Orisun Publications, 1983.
Six Plays: The Trials of Brother Jero; Jero's Metamorphosis; Camwood on the Leaves; Death and the King's Horseman; Madmen and Specialists; Opera Wonyosi; London: Methuen, 1984.
A Play of Giants, London: Methuen, 1984.
Requiem for a Futurologist, London: Rex Collings, 1985.
Childe Internationale, Ibadan: Fountain Publishers, 1987.
From Zia, with Love, and A Scourge of Hyacinths, Ibadan: Fountain Publications, 1992.

Short Story
The Search, Ibadan: Fountain Publications, 1989.

Poetry
Idanre and Other Poems, London: Methuen, 1967.
A Shuttle in the Crypt, London: Rex Collings and Methuen, 1972.
Ogun Abibiman, Ibadan: Opon Ifa, 1976.
Mandela's Earth, London: Andre Deutsch, 1989.

Autobiography/Biography
The Man Died: Prison Notes, London: Rex Collings, 1972.
Ake: The Years of Childhood, London: Rex Collings, 1981.
Isara: A Voyage Around 'Essay', Ibadan: Fountain Publications, 1989.
Ibadan: The Penkelemes Years: A Memoir: 1946 – 1965 London: Methuen; New York: Wiley, 1994.
Memories of a Nigerian Childhood, London: Mandarin, 1994

Criticism
Myth, Literature and the African World, Cambridge: Cambridge University Press, 1976.
Art, Dialogue and Outrage: Essays on Literature and Culture, Ibadan: New Horn Press, 1988. London: Methuen, 1994.

Translations
The Forest of a Thousand Daemons, (from the Yoruba novel *Ogboju Ode Ninu Igbo Irunmole*, by D.O. Fagunwa), London: Thomas Nelson, 1968.

Edited Collections
Poems of Black Africa, London: Secker and Warburg, 1975.

Lectures
Soyinka, Wole, "Twice Bitten: The Fate of Africa's Culture Producers" in *Development and Culture: Discussions of the Inaugural Programme of the Africa Leadership Forum*, Ota, Nigeria, Oct./Nov. 1988. pp.1–24.
Soyinka, Wole, "Ethics, Ideology and the Critic", in Petersen, Kirsten Holst (ed.) *Criticism and Ideology*: Second African Writers' Conference, Stockholm 1986, Uppsala: Nordiska Afrikainstitutet, 1988, pp.26–51.
The Credo of Being and Nothingness, *Yoruba Religious Discourse*, a lecture, Olufosoye Annual Lectures on Religions, delivered at the University of Ibadan on 25 January, 1991, Ibadan: Spectrum Books Limited, 1991.
Soyinka, Wole, "Culture, Memory and Development" in Ismail Serageldin and June Taboroff, (eds.) *Culture and Development in Africa*, Washington, D.C.: The World Bank, 1992.

Discography
Unlimited Liability Company, Ile-Ife: Ewuro Productions, 1983.

Films
Culture in Transition, 1963.
Kongi's Harvest, 1970.
Blues for a Prodigal, 1983.

Bibliographic Resources
Avery-Coger, Greta M. "Index of Subjects, Themes, and Proverbs in the Plays of Wole Soyinka," New York: Greenwood Press, 1988. 311p.

Carpenter, Charles A. "Studies of Wole Soyinka's Drama: An International bibliography." *Modern Drama* vol. 24, no. 1, 1981, pp.96–101.

Gibbs, James M. "Wole Soyinka: a Selected Bibliography," *Journal of Commonwealth Literature* vol. 10, no. 3, 1976, pp.33–45.

Gibbs, James; Katrak, Ketu H.; and Henry Louis Gates, Jr. *Wole Soyinka: A Bibliography of Primary and Secondary Sources*, Westport, Conn. and London: Greenwood Press, 1986.

Okpu, B.M. *Wole Soyinka: A Bibliography*. Lagos: Libriservice, 1984.

Page, Malcolm, *Wole Soyinka: Bibliography, Biography, Playography*. London: TQ Publications, 1979.

Some general studies (see also Note on p. 182)

Adejare, Oluwole, *Language and Style in Soyinka: a Systemic Textlinguistic Study of a Literary Idiolect*, Ibadan: Heinemann Educational Books (Nigeria) Ltd., 1993.

Adelugba, Dapo, (ed.), *Before Our Very Eyes: Tribute to Wole Soyinka*, Ibadan: Spectrum Books Limited, 1987.

Afolayan, Adebisi, *Yoruba Language and Literature*. Ile-Ife and Ibadan: University of Ife Press and University Press Ltd., 1985.

Appiah, Kwame, Anthony, "Myth, Literature and the African World", in Adewale Maja-Pearce (ed.) *Wole Soyinka: An Appraisal*, Oxford, Portsmouth, NH, and Ibadan: Heinemann Educational Books, 1994.

Babalola, S.A. *The Content and Form of Yoruba Ijala*, Oxford: Clarendon Press, 1966.

Banham, Martin with Clive Wake, *African Theatre Today*, London: Pitman, 1976.

Banham, Martin, "Initiates and Outsiders: The Theatre of Africa in the Theatre of Europe" *University of Leeds Review*, vol. 33, 1990/91, pp. 25–50.

Banham, Martin, "Wole Soyinka at Leeds" (edited and with additional commentary by Amanda Price and Martin Banham), *University of Leeds Review*, vol. 33, pp. 51–57, 1990/91.

Beier, Ulli, (ed.) *Yoruba Poetry: An Anthology of Traditional Poems*. Cambridge: Cambridge University Press, 1970.

Beier, Ulli, *The Story of Sacred Wood Carvings from One Small Yoruba Town*, Lagos: Nigeria Magazine, 1957.

Beier, Ulli, *A Year of Sacred Festivals in One Yoruba Town*, Lagos: Nigeria Magazine, 1959.

Beier, Ulli, *Yoruba Beaded Crowns: Sacred Regalia of the Olokuku of Okuku*, London: Ethnographica (in association with the National Museum, Lagos), 1982.

Benson, Peter, *Black Orpheus. Transition and Modern Cultural Awakening in Africa*, Berkeley: University of California Press, 1986.

Clark, Ebun, *Hubert Ogunde, The Making of Nigerian Theatre*, Ibadan: Oxford University Press, 1979.

Dingome, Jeanne N., "Soyinka's Role in Mbari." *African Theatre Journal*, Special Issue on Wole Soyinka, 1987, vol.1, no.3, pp.8–14.

Enem, Uche, *The National Theatre and Makers of Modern Nigerian Art*. Lagos: Nigeria Magazine FESTAC publication, 1977.

Etherton, Michael, *The Development of African Drama*, London: Hutchinson, 1982.

Feuser, W.F. "Wole Soyinka: the Problem of Authenticity." *Literary Half-yearly*, vol. 28, no. 2, 1987, pp.202–227.

Fioupou, Christiane, "Wole Soyinka/Jean Genet: Images et Reflèts du Pouvoir: 'Une Dance des Géants ou les Metamorphoses des Triples' in *Cahiers du C.E.R.L.E.S.H.*, no.1, Université de Ouagadougou, 1986; it has also appeared in *Nouvelles du Sud*, no. 5, Paris, Silex,1987.

Fioupou, Christiane, *La Route: Realité et Representation dans l'oeuvre de Wole Soyinka*, Amsterdam –Atlanta, GA: Editions Rodopi B.V., 1994.

Gates, Henry Louis,Jr., (Guest ed.), *Black American Literature Forum*, vol. 22, no. 3, 1988. Bloomington: Indiana University Press, 1988.

Gibbs, James, (ed.), *Critical Perspectives on Wole Soyinka*, London: Heinemann, 1981.

Gibbs, James, and Bernth Lindfors, (eds.), *Research on Wole Soyinka*, Trenton, NJ: Africa World Press, 1993.

Gibbs, J. "Soyinka in Zimbabwe: a Question and Answer session". *Literary Half-yearly*, vol. 28, no. 2, 1987, pp.50-110.

Gibbs, J. "Biography into Autobiography: Wole Soyinka and the Relatives who Inhabit 'Ake'. *Journal of Modern African Studies*, vol. 26, no. 3, 1988, pp. 517–548.

Gotrick, Kacke, *Apidan Theatre and Modern Drama: A Study in Traditional Yoruba Theatre and its Influence on Modern Drama by Yoruba Playwrights*, Göteborg: Almquist and Wiksell International, 1984.

Gotrick, K. "Why did Wole Soyinka Have to Wait so Long for Nobel Prize?" *Literary Half-yearly*. vol. 28, no. 2, 1987, pp.17–32.

Gugelberger, George, M. (ed.) *Marxism and African Literature*, London: James Currey, 1985.

Idowu, Bolaji, *Olodumare: God in Yoruba Belief*, London: Longman, 1962.

Jeyifo, Biodun, *The Yoruba Popular Travelling Theatre of Nigeria*, Lagos: Nigeria Magazine, 1984.

Jeyifo, Biodun, *The Yoruba Professional Itinerant Theatre: Oral Documentation*, Lagos: Nigeria Magazine, 1981.

Jeyifo, B. "What is the Will of Ogun?: Reflections on Soyinka's Nobel Prize and the African Literary Tradition." *Literary Half-yearly*, vol. 28, no. 2, 1987, pp.142–160.

Jeyifo, Biodun, and Ropo Sekoni, *Ideological and Semiotic Interpretations of Soyinka's* The Road: *Two Views*, Ile-Ife: Ife Monographs on Literature and Criticism, 1984.

Jones, Eldred Durosimi, *The Writing of Wole Soyinka*, London: Heinemann, 1973. 3rd ed. London: James Currey, 1988.

Jones, E.D. "Father of Man". [on Wole Soyinka] *Literary Half-yearly*, vol. 28, no. 2, 1987, pp.111–118.

Kacou-Kone, Denise, *Shakespeare et Soyinka: le théâtre du monde*, Abidjan: Les Nouvelles Editions Africaines – C.I., 1988.

Katrak, K.H. "Theory and Social Responsibility: Soyinka's Essays." *Black American Literature Forum*, vol. 22, no. 3, 1988, pp.489–501.

King, Bruce, (ed.) *Introduction to Nigerian Literature*, New York: Africana, 1972.

Maduakor, O. "Autobiography as Literature: the Case of Wole Soyinka's Childhood Memories, *Ake*." *Présence Africaine*, Nos.137/138, 1986, pp. 227–240.

Maja-Pearce, Adewale, *Who's Afraid of Wole Soyinka? Essays on Censorship*, London: Heinemann, 1991.

Maja-Pearce, Adewale, (ed.) *Wole Soyinka: An Appraisal*, Oxford, Portsmouth, NH and Ibadan: Heinemann Educational Books, 1994.

Marechera, D. "Soyinka, Dostoevsky: the Writer on Trial for his Time". *Zambezia*, vol. 14, no. 2, 1987, pp. 106–112.

McLuckie, C.W. "Soyinka's two 'Godspeak' Texts: Comedy as an Instrument of Social Development". *Black American Literature Forum*, vol. 22, no. 4, 1988, pp. 695–704.

Moore, Gerald, *Wole Soyinka*, London: Evans, 1981.

Morrison, K. "The Second Self as Vision of Horror in Wole Soyinka's *The Interpreters.*" *Black American Literature Forum*, vol. 22, no. 4, 1988, pp. 753–765.

Nkosi, L. "Wole Soyinka: Memory of a Trip with the Nobel Prize Winner." *Literary Half-yearly*, vol. 28, no. 2, 1987, pp. 46–49.

Ogunba, Oyin, *The Movement of Transition: A Study of the Plays of Wole Soyinka*, Ibadan: Ibadan University Press, 1975.

Ogunba, Oyin, and Abiola Irele, (eds.) *Theatre in Africa*, Ibadan: Ibadan University Press, 1978.

Ogunbiyi, Yemi, (ed.), *Drama and Theatre in Nigeria: A Critical Source Book*, Lagos: Nigeria Magazine, 1981.

Ogunbiyi, Yemi, (ed.) *Perspectives on Nigerian Literature* (in two volumes) Lagos: Guardian Books Nigeria Limited, 1988.

Ogungbesan, Kolawole, "Wole Soyinka: The Past and the Visionary Writer" in Bruce King and Kolawole Ogungbesan, *A Celebration of Black and African Writing*, Zaria: Ahmadu Bello Press, 1975. pp. 175–188.

Ojaide, Tanure, *The Poetry of Wole Soyinka*, Lagos: Malthouse Press, 1984.

Osofisan, Femi, "Wole Soyinka and a Living Dramatist: A Playwright's Encounter with Soyinka's Drama", in Adewale Maja-Pearce (ed.) *Wole Soyinka: An Appraisal*, Oxford, Portsmouth, NH, and Ibadan: Heinemann Educational Books, 1994, pp.43–60.

Osundare, Niyi, "Words of Iron, Sentences of Thunder: Soyinka's Prose Style" in Eldred Durosimi Jones (ed.) *African Literature Today* no. 13, London: Heinemann Educational Books, 1983.

Osundare, Niyi, "Wole Soyinka and the Atunda Ideal: a Reading of Soyinka's Poetry" in Adewale Maja-Pearce (ed.) *Wole Soyinka: An Appraisal*, Oxford, Portsmouth, NH and Ibadan: Heinemann Educational Books, 1994, pp. 81–97.

Ojo, J. Afolabi, *Yoruba Culture*, London: Oxford University Press, 1966.

Phillips, K.J. "Exorcising Faustus from Africa: Wole Soyinka's *The Road.*" *Comparative Literature Studies*, vol. 27, no. 2, 1990. pp. 140–157.

Ready, R.M. "Through the Intricacies of 'The Fourth Stage' to an Apprehension of *Death and the King's horseman.*" *Black American Literature Forum*, vol. 22, no. 4, 1988, pp. 711–721.

Ricard, Alain, *Livre et communication au Nigéria*, Paris: Présence Africaine, 1976.

Ricard, Alain, *Theatre and Nationalism*, (translated from the French by Femi Osofisan), Ile-Ife: University of Ife Press, 1983.

Ricard, Alain, *Wole Soyinka ou L'ambition démocratique*, Paris: Editions Silex/N.E.A., 1988.

Sabor, P. "Wole Soyinka and the Scriblerians." *World Literature Written in English*, vol. 29, no.1, 1989, pp. 43–52.

Sethuraman, R. "The Role of Women in the Plays of Wole Soyinka." *World Literature Written in English*, vol. 25, no. 2, 1985, pp. 222–227.

Sotto, W. "Comets and Walking Corpses: A Reading of Wole Soyinka's Play *Requiem for a Futurologist*." *Black American Literature Forum*, vol. 22, no. 4, 1988, pp.683–693.

Thorpe, M. "Soyinka's Clay Foot". *World Literature Today*, vol. 63, no.1, 1989, pp. 39–41.

Winestein, M. "The Biblical dimension of *Kongi's Harvest*." *World Literature Written in English*, vol. 29, no. 2, 1989, pp.126–129.

Interviews

Agetua, John, *When the Man Died: Views, Reviews and Interview on Wole Soyinka's Controversial Book*, Benin City: Bendel Newspapers Corporation, 1975.

Jeyifo, Biodun, in *Six Plays*, London: Methuen, 1984.

Mike, Chuck, *Soyinka as Director*, Ile-Ife: Department of Literature in English, University of Ife, 1986.

Wilkinson, Jane, *Talking with African Writers*, London: James Currey, 1990 and 1992.

Note:

For comprehensive bibliographic coverage of critical writings, interviews, etc. on both Chinua Achebe and Wole Soyinka the reader is referred to the four substantial bibliographic resources compiled by Bernth Lindfors:

Black African Literature in English: A Guide to Information Sources (Detroit: Gale Research Company, 1979; covering 1936–1976);

Supplement to Black African Literature in English, 1977–1981 (New York: Africana Publishing Co., 1985);

Black African Literature in English, 1982–1986 (London: Hans Zell Publishers, 1989); and,

Black African Literature in English, 1987–1991 (London: Hans Zell Publishers, 1995.)

Index